Names for the Sea

Strangers in Iceland

SARAH MOSS

COUNTERPOINT

BERKELEY

Library of Congress Cataloging-in-Publication data is available
ISBN 978-1-61902-122-8

Cover design by Emma Cofod
Typeset by M Rules

COUNTERPOINT
1919 Fifth Street
Berkeley, CA 94710
www.counterpointpress.com

Printed in the United States of America
Distributed by Publishers Group West

10 9 8 7 6 5 4 3 2 1

For all our friends in Iceland

Contents

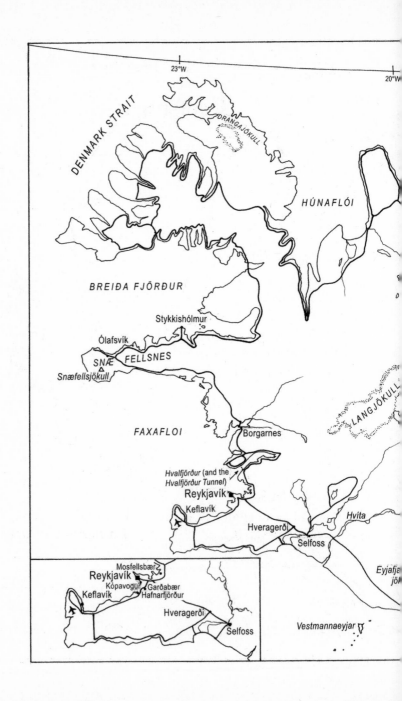

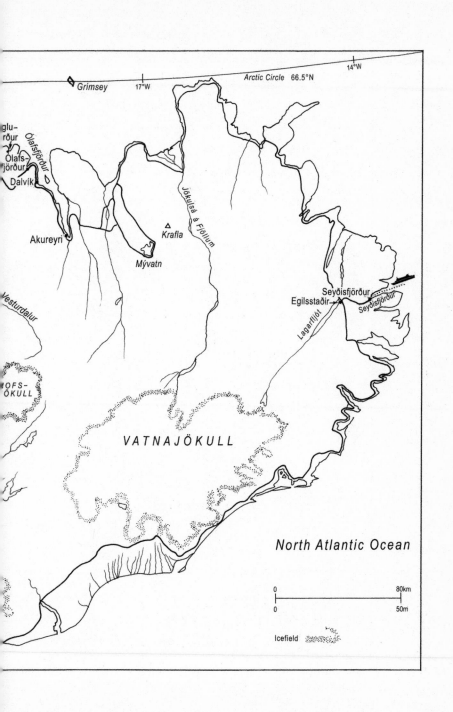

Grimsey

17°W

Arctic Circle 66.5°N

14°W

glu-
röur

Ólafsfjörður

Ólafs-
fjöður

Dalvík

Akureyri

Krafla

Mývatn

Vesturdalur

OFS-
ÖKULL

Jökulsá á Fjöllum

Seyðisfjörður

Egilsstaðir

Seyðisfjörður

Lagarfljót

VATNAJÖKULL

North Atlantic Ocean

0   80km
0   50m

Icefield

Prologue

The steam rising from the pool glows with reflected light. To passengers on the plane coming in overhead, the typography of the city's night, the snaking headlights and pin-prick street lights, must look like a jeweller's setting for the eleven turquoise pools. Garðabær, Kópavogur out on the headland, Álftanes with a slide, Seltjarnarnes filled with salt water, Laugardalur so big you can't see across it for steam on a cold day. At home I navigate by food shops and booksellers. There are perhaps half a dozen independent food shops left in Reykjavík, and only chain bookshops, but every pool is distinctive. I'm at the deep end in Garðabær now, and the water's colder. There is a faint smell of sulphur. I'm swimming slowly, more concerned to keep as much of my body as possible under water and out of the cold air than to reach the end of the lane any time soon. The branches of the pine trees around the pool are pressed against their trunks by the wind, black against a sky brown with light-pollution reflecting off snow. There's no-one else swimming at the moment, only groups of adults congregated like hippopotamuses or perhaps Roman senators in the shallow pool, chatting and drifting in the warmer water. I keep going; I'd feel like Banquo's ghost there, a lone foreigner, wearing glasses and the wrong kind of swimming costume, barely able to follow a conversation. I pause instead at the deep end, bring my feet down through the warm layers of water to the cold at the bottom, turn and stretch out my arms. And there, with my face below ground level, I see the light in the north, where the sky is veiled by the arc lights on the basketball court behind me and by the headlights of the SUVs I can hear ploughing through slush on the freeway over the wall. The northern sky, dark over the sea, is mottled with green that spreads like spilt paint, disappears and spreads again. I turn my head, wisps of wet hair chill as seaweed on my neck, to see a paler light flickering out like a flapped sheet in the north-west. The green and the white reach towards each other and then lunge away like opposing magnets forced together. I tread water, and watch.

Aurora borealis. Reykjavík, November 2009.

1

Iceland First Seen

I cannot remember the beginning of my longing for northerly islands. It may be hereditary; the childhood holidays that weren't spent driving across Eastern Europe took place in Orkney and the Hebrides. My grandfather, growing up in Leeds in the 1920s, found his way onto an Iceland-bound fishing trawler at the age of sixteen, not because he had any interest in fishing but because he'd always wanted to go North. My grandmother went camping with her friends on Mull in the 1930s, and returned there in the 1950s with my mother and in the 1980s with me. It's not the real, white Arctic, the scene of centuries of bearded latitude competitions, that sets me dreaming, but the grey archipelago of Atlantic stepping-stones. Scilly, Aran, Harris, Lewis, Orkney, Fair Isle, Shetland, Faroe. Iceland, southern Greenland, the Canadian Maritimes; a sea-road linking ancient settlements, travelled for centuries. The Arctic is just over the horizon, the six months' darkness always at the back of the mind, the summer-long day impossible to believe in winter and impossible to doubt when it comes. Here, just below the Earth's summit, there are towns and villages, a tangle of human lives, in the shadow of Arctic eschatology. I keep going back to the North Atlantic, working my way north and west as the Celts and Vikings did, as if I'm heading for the Vikings' westernmost point at L'Anse aux Meadows in Newfoundland. When we finish our A-levels, a friend and I rent a cottage on Rousay in Orkney, and spend two weeks walking the rocky shore and the moorland, climbing down the ladders into Neolithic tombs, and trying not to think about our pending – pendant – adult lives. As students, another friend and I embark on an ill-advised cycling trip around Shetland, where we have to pedal downhill into the wind but see a wilder, stranger landscape than the roundedness of Orkney. I make it to the Faroes, where some of the islands are no more than cliffs rising from the sea, and the Norse who once ruled Orkney and Shetland too are still, more or less, there. At university, I take an Old Norse class, expecting to be fascinated by the sagas, and plan to spend the summer of my first year in Iceland. I win an award given to undergraduates for 'the advancement of knowledge relating to the beauty of scenery', and buy a bus ticket that takes me once around Route 1, the one road circling the country. My friend Kathy, fellow lover of northern islands, agrees to come too.

There is a tradition of English travellers to Iceland, mostly nineteenth-century, mostly on the trail of the medieval sagas. I read W. G. Collingwood, who left a trail of watercolours in Iceland's museums of local history, and William Morris, who went to Iceland in 1871 and again in 1873, and wrote a series of rambling poems inflected by Old Norse, as if thinking of undoing the Norman Conquest's contribution to the English language:

Iceland First Seen

Lo from our loitering ship a new land at last to be seen;

Toothed rocks down the side of the firth on the east
guard a weary wide lea,

And black slope the hillsides above, striped adown with
their desolate green:

And a peak rises up on the west from the meeting of
cloud and of sea,

Foursquare from base unto point like the building of
Gods that have been,

The last of that waste of the mountains all cloud-
wreathed and snow-flecked and grey,

And bright with the dawn that began just now at the
ending of day.

Ah! What came we forth for to see that our hearts are so
hot with desire?

Is it enough for our rest, the sight of this desolate strand,

And the mountain-waste voiceless as death but for winds
that may sleep not nor tire?

Why do we long to wend forth through the length and
breadth of a land,

Dreadful with grinding of ice, and record of scarce-
hidden fire,

But that there mid the grey grassy dales sore scarred by
the ruining streams

Lives the tale of the Northland of old and the undying
glory of dreams?

(William Morris, 'Iceland First Seen', 1891)

Firth, strand, dale; there's a self-consciousness about this linguistic re-making that bothers me. It is not necessary, certainly not honest, to pretend that we're all Vikings really. I am going to Iceland, but not because I have a secret desire to wear a horned helmet or drink mead out of a skull, nor even to wear twisted silver brooches and speak in runes. I dislike Tolkien, another Oxonian Old Norse obsessive, with his war games and made-up languages in a world without women. Whatever I'm looking for in Iceland, it's not in the tradition of English writing about the place.

In July 1995, Kathy and I board the MS Norröna, the passenger ship linking Scotland with the Faroe Islands and Iceland, following the Viking route at five times Viking speed. We stand on the deck, watching sailors cast off cables, and then watching the coast of Aberdeenshire slipping over the horizon. Other people go inside, but other people have cabins and can afford to eat in the restaurant. As the sky dims, north of Scotland in midsummer, the ship begins to lurch. The last people go inside. We stay on deck, shivering and watching the foam streak dark waves, until I'm so cold and sea-sick that lying on a plastic berth in a communal cabin seems better than retching over the railings. Kathy stays on deck, hood up, stoical.

I wake up hours later. I'm still sick. It's so dark that opening and closing my eyes makes no difference. Nothing makes any difference. Men lodged in the bunks around me are snoring, and there's a smell of vomit and sweat. I can't swallow. I bury my nose in the pink-flowered down sleeping bag I had as a child for camping holidays, which smells of old dust and feels dry as paper against my skin. I want to die. (This thought has been reappearing in my mind like a goldfish coming back round the bowl every few minutes since I left the deck.) The engine throbs and my bunk sways, up and down, up and down. I know I'm not going to be sick again, not really, because there's nothing left, and I stopped trying to sip water around the same time as I stopped trying to sit up. Up and down – and down – and down. I hope we do sink. I want to die. The cabin is far down inside the hull. There is water up above my head, and if we started to sink the water would come into the cabin and rise and rise and even if I tried to find the door it's heavy and metal and there'd be a weight of water on the other side, and anyway I've seen where the iron doors in the corridors would lock, stabilising the ship but trapping people who can't afford proper cabins in cold sea that would come up and up, waists and shoulders and – not that it matters, because I want to die.

There is a rip in the darkness. It makes my eyes hurt.

'Sarah?' whispers Kathy. 'Sarah, come outside. You can see it. Iceland. And the sun's coming up.'

I turn away. I don't care.

'Come on,' she says. 'You'll feel better on deck. It's enough to make anyone sick down here. I'm going back out.'

I don't believe her. I'm beyond fresh air.

'The sun's rising,' she says. 'And it's shining on a glacier. It looks like one of those Japanese mountains. I'm going to paint it.'

So I sit up, and it is worse. But I can, just about, imagine that there might be a future in which I would regret not having seen sunrise on a glacier from the sea. I stand up and grab her, and Kathy helps me up the bucking stairs, spattered with vomit, over the metal ledge and out. And she's right. (Kathy is usually right.) There's a neon pink sunrise behind us, and a triangular snow-covered mountain coming up over the horizon to the north-west. The sea is still black, the waves foaming white in the new light. I sit down and Kathy wraps my shawl around me and finds a piece of Kendal mint cake for me to contemplate. 'It'd taste about the same on the way up as down,' she observes, pulling a small artist's block, her water-colours and a screw-top bottle of water out of her cagoule pocket. Later, I start trying to write a paragraph or a poem for every painting, but for now I'm content to sit there licking my Kendal mint cake and watching as a little mountain appears on either side of the big one. As the sun comes up, the spaces between the triangles fill up with green fjords. Soon the fjords have a scattering of white houses with red roofs and then sheep safely grazing and cars rushing around like ants, even though it's about four o'clock in the morning. Maybe I don't want to be dead.

We were nineteen – we celebrated Kathy's nineteenth birth-day with an afternoon in a jacuzzi on a mountainside in Akureyri and a cake covered with a simulacrum of marzipan – and we spent six weeks making our way around Iceland, camping rough because we couldn't afford campsites and living on an increasingly sparse and eccentric diet because we couldn't, really, afford food either. In 1995 students didn't have mobile phones and the internet was for geeks, some of whom checked their e-mail several times a week. (Why not just talk to people, we wondered. Or write a nice letter.) We were out of touch, gone, for the whole six weeks. It was towards the end of the years in which Radio Four would occa-sionally broadcast requests for Mr and Mrs Framlington of Ely, presently on holiday in the Ardèche, to contact their son

Henry, but we had no radio and wouldn't have been able to get Radio Four anyway. We wrote letters but stamps had to wait until we were back home and could spare money for postage. We each had a bus ticket taking us all the way round the island and back to Egilsstaðir for the ferry home. We had a tent and a Primus stove, a paperback Complete Shakespeare, root ginger, garlic and a few herbs. The Kendal mint cake went in the first two days, and after that we prowled the mini-marts trying to maximise calories per króna without actually drinking vegetable oil (though subsidised butter would have been nicer, and scarcely more expensive). I found a discounted jar of American peanut butter once, but after that we settled on Icelandic cream cheese with peculiar flavourings and the occasional bag of crisps. The bus stopped at petrol stations — roughly every thirty miles — but apart from that you just shouted to the driver when you wanted to get off. Sometimes we planned it, but more often we saw a likely spot and sang out. We camped foolishly on a cliff top and almost blew over in the night, ran out of meths for the stove and discovered that we were too young to buy it legally in Iceland. (Older German backpackers came to the rescue, but not until we'd been without cooked food or hot water for a couple of days.) We walked through a lunar landscape, where cracked black rock interspersed with white flowers spread to the horizon, and through orange and pink mud that boiled under our feet, and around a volcanic crater from which we could see to the Arctic sea. We saw puffins falling off cliffs onto the black sand beneath, and miniature turquoise icebergs calving off a glacier. It was light all the time, a summer day that lasted six weeks, and I woke and slept at whim like a baby, my lifelong insomnia for once seeming natural. I could piece together bits of modern

Icelandic, enough to read signs and the odd headline, but we didn't try to talk to anyone. Why should they want to talk to us? The local teenage girls — who had access to bathrooms and washing machines and clothes intended for indoor use — were more glamorous and confident than we were. And anyway, we weren't there for the people. There were plenty of people, too many people, at home. We'd come for the landscape, for the pale nights and dark shores, rain sweeping over birch scrub, the whole circle of a flat world empty but for ourselves.

I always meant to go back to Iceland. Kathy and I finished our degrees, and took some more degrees, and married and found jobs. I had two sons, she moved to the Netherlands. We met often, talked regularly, and, late at night, over the end of the bottle or after our husbands had come past for the fourth time muttering about international phone calls, we remembered Iceland. The time I ran out naked in heavy rain to tighten the guy-lines (because I didn't want to get my pyjamas wet). The time Kathy, out painting, found some blueberry bushes warm and heavy in the sun, and then there was a whole mountainside of blueberries which we grazed like famished sheep, having had no fruit or vegetables since we left home. The time an Icelandic child on the bus delivered the whole of the Dead Parrot Sketch, in English and with precisely copied intonation. It was the landscape of our coming of age that we were remembering, not the people who lived there.

I envied Kathy's new life in the Netherlands, her gradual mastery of a new language, her appreciation of a new place and discoveries in a new culture. My husband and I had always meant to live 'abroad', as if abroad were a place, defined only by not-Englishness. Scotland might have done, France would have been better, Denmark or especially Sweden, headquarters of Nordic social democracy, would have been ideal, but meanwhile I kept an eye on academic jobs in the US, Canada and Australia. We settled in Kent, less than ten miles from where Anthony had grown up. We owned a house. The children started school. We had interesting jobs at comfortable salaries. It was all perfectly nice, and there was no reason why it shouldn't continue to be perfectly nice for the next thirty years. Then Anthony lost his job. Max was unhappy at school. Iceland, sang a newspaper feature read late one night while the children slept, was the happiest country in the world, a Nordic paradise of gender equality, fine schooling and public art. It wasn't landscape that pulled us this time – or not only landscape – but the idea of a better society. According to the website of the National University which I chanced to encounter at work the next day, Iceland needed an expert in nineteenth-century British literature.

2

Leave of Absence

Six months later, I stand in Iceland's National Museum, under the flat-screen television showing rolling news at the end of the exhibition of twentieth-century Icelandic material culture, when the International Monetary Fund steps in to save Iceland from sovereign default. It's November 2008, and I've just finished my interview and verbally accepted the job. Over lunch, my future colleagues were talking about arranging new courses around texts available on Project Gutenberg, because they were expecting the import of books to halt. The headmistress of the international school is frank about her concern that all the foreign families are about to leave the country. The value of my proposed salary drops by a third during the week. Well, we reason, Icelanders aren't going to starve, so there's no reason why we would. I don't know why the collapse of the Icelandic economy, the *kreppa*, doesn't put us off; I think it seems important not to fear poverty. I think it seems likely to be interesting.

Our boxes leave a week before we do, in the middle of July. The Icelandic school year starts in late August, so we're allowing ourselves a month for the children to accept a new house, a new language, new food and – maybe – new friends before we present them with a new school and playgroup. We're taking as little as possible, partly because shipping is expensive and partly because we are beginning to realise that we can escape all the stuff that clutters our house, just walk off and leave it like people fleeing a plague. I pack everything I think the four of us will need for the year into seven cardboard cartons. One is full of toys, just the favourites and nothing large. The dolls' house goes to spend the year with our friends round the corner, the wooden garage on loan to the little boy down the road who has always coveted it, the toy cooker – after a spell in the attic to make sure no-one misses it – to Oxfam. We take winter clothes, Tobias's a size beyond his two-year-old summer self. Another box is almost all food, because we spent ten days in Reykjavík in May, house-hunting, and have some idea of the limits of Icelandic supermarkets. We have five litres of olive oil, a dozen tins of anchovies and a dozen jars of capers, miso paste, pomegranate syrup, cocoa nibs, seeds for growing coriander, basil and mint. Smoked chillies, sumac, allspice, dried dill, cumin. Preserved lemons, three kinds of paprika, dried lime leaves. Victorian Arctic expeditions took engraved silver cutlery, napkin rings and embroidered bedroom slippers, the objects that upheld explorers' sense of who they were even though these things didn't justify their presence on any other grounds, and were found scattered across the snow with their owners' bones a few years later. At least the manifestations of English metropolitan middle-class identity are edible. Three of the boxes are full of books, which are the hardest things to choose. How can I predict in July what I'll want to read in

February? Which of the thousands of volumes in the house can I not live without? I'm teaching a course on nineteenth-century fiction, which takes most of a box on its own, and another on Romantic poetry. I'll need my favourite cook-books (you can get recipes online, protests Kim, who is going to rent our house, and moves lightly around the country with all her possessions in the boot of her car, but it's not the same), and the novels I like to re-read. My book-buying becomes more extravagant as I try to anticipate a year's pur-chases, for myself and also for Max, who has a two-a-day fiction habit. Which books will fit him when he's rising eight? How big should Tobias's snow boots be?

I fold down the last box and wander around, browsing for last-minute additions. I have removed everything I think we'll need for a year and the house doesn't look different in any way. The playroom is still full of toys, the kitchen of plates and pans and cake tins and the wok and the ice-cream maker and the toaster (which we've decided we can do without – after all, nobody had toasters for most of history without apparent ill effect) and the teapot and the paella pan and the good knives. The bookshelves are still crammed, the books that won't fit lying on top of their serried companions. The hall is still full of shoes and blocked by the pushchair. Upstairs, there are still clothes bulging out of my chest-of-drawers, and the ones that won't fit in there are sliding off one of our herd of Victorian armchairs. We still can't squash all the towels into their allocated chest so there's a pile on its mahogany top, but-tressed by toys and post too boring to open but too important to throw away. The children's rooms are still full of more toys, and more books, and more drawings, mostly on the floor because the cupboards are full of Anthony's antique map

14

collection and my knitting wool and the crystal wine glasses
that are too good to use and my great-grandmother's tea-set
and the disintegrating woollen hangings that came with our
four-poster bed. It is clear to me that 'de-cluttering' is a kind
of capitalist bulimia, but I wonder for the first time whether,
like other forms of economic dysfunction, it might not also be
rather nice.

July is a good time to arrive in Iceland. The lava field beside
the road from the airport has wildflowers and rowan bushes
growing out of its fissures, and the mountains are sharp against
a blue sky. The city lies in a pool of sunlight, the red corrugated iron houses and white roofs small as Lego against the
dark northern sea. People sit outside cafés in the city centre
where we stay in a hotel for the first few days, and there's a
flow of tourists, of other people who also need a map and
someone who speaks English, around the craft shops and
museums of Reykjavík. We take the children out and show
them the place to which we have committed them. Look, we
say, a ship coming into harbour! Look, a playground! Look at
the light on the mountains! Aren't you glad to be here? We
take the foot ferry to Viðey, an island in the bay, and the children fly high on the swings, to the top of the mountain behind
them and up into the blue sky. We look around the Maritime
Museum and Max joins other little boys from other countries
yearning over the one gun on Iceland's coastguard ship. There
is no navy here, nor army nor air force. We walk up and down
the main street, Laugavegur, rationing our café breaks and
admiring the rows of prams in which babies await their parents' return.

We're waiting for the builders to finish our apartment,

which we haven't yet seen. It was organised for us by Hulda
Kristín, one of the PhD students in my new department. Hulda
Kristín is half-Lebanese, half-Icelandic, but grew up in London.
She married an Icelander and came here to live when her two
sons, born like mine four years apart, were pre-schoolers. We
met her when we came to Reykjavík in May to find an apartment, a school and a nursery, and had more trouble with the
apartment than we were expecting. Icelanders, by and large,
don't rent; ninety per cent of housing is owner-occupied and
renting is a sign of youth or indigence. We needed to be in
Garðabær, Iceland's wealthiest suburb, for the International
School, and, despite the newly built and empty blocks of flats
crowding the shore, there was nothing to rent. Hulda Kristín
heard me complaining to Pétur, my new head of department.
Let me make some calls, she said. I can probably sort something
out. Her husband is in charge of buildings safety inspections
across Iceland and knows most of the builders. She did indeed
sort something out, and we see our new home for the first
time through the tinted windows of her lumbering SUV.

The other apartments in our block are shells. The building
is on the corner of a development that was half-built when the
banks collapsed and the money ran out, and it's still half-built,
as if the builders had downed tools and walked away one day
in the winter of 2008. Our northward sea view will be
blocked if the luxury flats across the road are ever finished. For
now, we see the waves between the bars of metal rods that
grow out of concrete foundations. Looking the other way,
towards the city, a yellow crane towers over us, a line through
our view of Mount Esja. No-one else lives in our building.
The stairs are unfinished, raw concrete. The lift glides up and
down its glass tower just for us. The automatic doors in the

lobby sweep for us alone. The apartment comes with one of a catacomb of store-rooms, each labelled for one of the dwellings, and with a second store-room for skis and boats in the basement, opening off the heated underground garage where lights come on and doors open at our approach. The children, I suggest to Anthony, can play football down here in winter. Or we could cultivate mushrooms on an industrial scale.

The flat itself is full of light. When autumn comes, we will find that it is often somehow more light inside than out, but now, in July, light is the condition of Iceland, day and night, and it's magnified by our floor-to-ceiling windows and white walls. We have a laundry room, which I plan to commandeer as a study, and a walk-in wardrobe that would hold all the clothes we own in both countries and still leave space for my stash of smuggled chocolate. The lowest setting for the under-floor heating is twenty degrees. Anthony and I both grew up in old houses with draughts that came through the floorboards and continued up the chimneys, both remember lying in bed watching the curtains blowing around with the windows closed in winter, and we've bought a house with the same qualities in Canterbury. The new apartment has triple glazing, and no curtains. Now, on the hottest days of summer, it's almost as warm outside as in. We open all the windows, and hear children splashing on the beach at the end of the road. The boys rush out onto the balcony, which faces north and is shadowed by the unfinished block across the road.

Hulda Kristín drives me to IKEA to buy bedding, towels, a couple of pans, the least I think we can get away with. I choose four garden chairs – cheaper than dining chairs – and a table. Later, Pétur drives out from the other side of the city to bring us a set of flat-pack bookcases and an old table that can be my desk, and then, looking around, takes me off to the supermarket in the next town to stock up. Why not that one, I ask, as we pass the hypermarket nearest the apartment, the one to which we can walk so that we will be able to manage without a car. That's Hagkaup, he says. Far too expensive. It would be like buying your washing-up liquid from Harrods. When we get back, he comes in, guts and cleans the whole fish that I bought by accident and assembles the bookcases for us. I am childlike in my gratitude. At home, I would invite Pétur and Hulda Kristín to dinner, perhaps send flowers or give wine, take Hulda Kristín's children for the day or make a gluten-free cake for Pétur. But I have only four chairs, four plates, two pans. There is no florist in Garðabær. I need help to buy a light bulb, to register with a doctor, to connect the telephone, to buy bus tickets, which turn out to be sold at swimming pools. The instructions for configuring our internet connection are in Icelandic. There is no laundrette. We are helpless, the adults children again, with nothing to offer but our thanks, and our new friends are our parents, in whom we trust. Thank you, we say. Thank you.

And then they go away, Pétur to his summer house out in the west, Hulda Kristín accompanying her husband in a campervan on a holiday-cum-tour-of-public-buildings-in-outlying-towns, which must have their safety inspections in the summer when the roads are reliably clear. You need to start to feel you can manage this yourselves, says Pétur, making sure we have his mobile phone number. You'll be fine, says Hulda Kristín, checking again that I have the number for the out-of-hours medical service in case Tobias has another asthma attack. Our second childhood is over, and we must venture out.

Leave of Absence

We start at the beginning, with food. Hagkaup is fascinating in the way that foreign supermarkets are always fascinating, offering a glimpse into other assumptions. It is not international law to start with fruit and vegetables. Hagkaup begins with cosmetics, mostly French and mostly at twice French prices. Then there are two kinds of apple, called 'red' (big, mushy American ones) and 'green' (French Granny Smiths). There are Belgian strawberries, hard and sour, Chilean oranges and bananas. We left Kent in the middle of the cherry season, when the farmers send someone to every lay-by with a van full of cherries: small yellow-and-pink ones, big purple ones, the sort a child can't manage in one bite, and my favourite, slightly sour, deep reds. Our plum tree was fruiting and we could stand in the garden eating plums warm from the sun. The tomatoes were ripening, and Anthony, who grew up on a Kentish fruit farm, was beginning his yearly incantation of apples. James Grieve, St Edmund's Pippin, Maid of Kent, Worcester Pearmain. When we went for Sunday lunch with Anthony's parents, we picked pounds of red and white currants, courgettes fast threatening to become marrows, so many raspberries that I seriously considered making jam. There are few trees of any kind here, and the gardens past which we walk seem only deliberate arrangements of the open spaces between houses and roads: turf, rocks, dwarf birch and rowans no taller than me. Hagkaup has raspberries – Hagkaup has everything, including zebra steaks and Scottish pheasant, for a price – but they come resting on bubble wrap in a single layer with about a dozen in a packet costing the same as two pounds of fish. Well, we say, of course. We're on the edge of the Arctic Circle here. Who wants air-freighted fruit anyway? Icelanders must have lived for centuries without fruit. There's plenty of cabbage. There is plenty of cabbage, but it seems to have come a long way and got very tired. Even in Hagkaup, fruit is often squashy, courgettes wrinkled and sour, cabbage leaves floppy as damp towels. It's necessary to check the dates on dairy produce in the chiller because some of it will have expired. It's only the prices which make it like shopping at Harrods.

We go further afield. The bus service is cut back during the summer, on the assumption that the main users of public transport are high-school students. The buses used to run almost empty, Pétur tells us, except between seven-thirty and eight-thirty in the morning and two and three in the afternoon, when schools start and end. Adult Icelanders share Thatcher's view of bus travel. Car ownership, Pétur says, is higher than anywhere else in Europe. We are surrounded by houses with three or four cars on each drive, and the cars are newer than at home and larger, including monstrous SUVs that aren't imported to the rest of Europe. Icelanders adore America, Pétur says. Most people here won't be happy until we're beating the Americans on carbon emissions and pollution. Nobody walks anywhere; people think you're mad if you walk. Cycling? I ask, because there are what look to me like bicycle tracks running along the coast. No, he says. People say the weather's too bad, but it's not much worse than in Denmark, which has one of the highest rates of cycling in Europe. The Norwegians and Swedes drive less, walk more and have fewer and less damaging cars than Icelanders, though Scandinavian winters are in fact colder because Iceland is an island in the Gulf Stream and Norway and Sweden have continental climates. During the boom, says Pétur, sometimes Icelandic couples would each take their own Hummer to the same party. Yeah, and another one for the teenage son, adds his daughter. I think she is joking but I'm not sure.

At first, we think this car-dependence is reflected in the town planning. Walking in Garðabær, or anywhere in Reykjavík except the oldest parts of the city centre, feels like walking in American suburbia. There are no pavements. The only shops are in malls, which have no pedestrian access. We find ourselves pushing the pushchair across dual carriageways and up turf embankments. Going to the other supermarket, we have a choice between crossing the lava field and going along the freeway. Neither is easy with the pushchair, which we need for bringing the groceries back as well as getting Tobias there. (Later, we will find a network of paved off-road walking and cycle tracks, threading parks and gardens to make a pedestrian's web of the city quite separate from the drivers' map.) I raise my eyes to the hills, where the sun shines from the north-west onto pine woods, and flashes off streams. Behind the dual carriageway, the sea is too bright for my eyes, and across the inlet, the white church at Kópavogur stands like a lighthouse on the headland. Sea-birds glide about their lives on the Álftanes peninsula, calling to each other from rock to rock. The skies, the light and the water have a physical effect; every time I look up, there is more room for my lungs and my sense of inadequacy lightens on my shoulders. I am fascinated by this place, but I do not understand it, and all I think I have learnt so far is that understanding it won't be easy.

A couple of weeks after Pétur's and Hulda Kristín's departures, Matthew phones. Matthew took his doctorate at the same university a few years ahead of me, and we established in May that we know people who know each other. He fell in love with an Icelander and moved to Reykjavík as soon as he finished his DPhil, and has been working at Háskóli Íslands, the University of Iceland, for the last fourteen years. Even more than Hulda Kristín, he knows where I'm coming from. What can I do? he says. Tell me what you need. Someone to talk to, I say. Someone to talk about. And a washing machine, and a high chair because Tobias is too small for the garden chairs, and a rubbish bin, which is not sold anywhere within walking distance. And a fridge. But we are short of money. Where are the second-hand shops? Oh, he says. Ah. That's something about Iceland. There isn't a second-hand market. People just don't buy used goods. I'll come and see you.

Matthew takes us to the Zoo and Family Park. The sunshine is hot, and there are brides posing under the trees in the Botanic Gardens. Mount Esja basks across the water, and the children look at seals in a pool and horses in a paddock and ride on a merry-go-round. So, says Matthew, how's the culture shock? Do you want to go home yet? I take a breath. Most of the friends I made in my first year at university were international students who liked to spend their evenings complaining about England. Just the usual: plumbing, food, weather. Aged eighteen, I believed their dissatisfaction to be a sign of their cosmopolitan sophistication, but towards the end of the year found myself muttering that they should go home if they didn't like it here. I determined before we came to Iceland that I would not be a whingeing expat. Anthony and I have not complained to each other, but somehow, while Anthony takes the children on a pedalo in a lake where white-legged blonde children are paddling, it all comes out to Matthew. I am doing the laundry by hand in the bath, and drying it on an airer which we managed to bring from Hafnarfjörður on the bus. In dry weather and with twenty-two hours of sunlight, each load is not quite dry when I bring the next one dripping to the balcony. We are keeping food in a coolbox on the balcony. We are putting rubbish in plastic bags hanging off one of the array of empty cupboards in our granite and oak kitchen. I want to see Iceland, but it takes hours to get anywhere walking with a two-year-old, the buses are infrequent and days are passing without us going further than the beach and the supermarket. We are in each other's unrelieved company all the time and *I need to read and write.*

Matthew takes me to the Icelandic version of B&Q to buy a bin, and to the National Library, where he verifies my unconvincing assertion that I am a member of staff at the university and gets me a card. The top floor of the library looks over the tops of the pine trees waving in the old graveyard to Esja. It's a close-up version of the view from my desk in the flat, and I soon learn to monitor the weather by looking at the mountain. If you can see all of Esja from Reykjavík, it's not going to rain, although it doesn't rain much anyway, during our first month. The sun goes round and round the sky. The light is always changing: the yellow of morning, gone by 7 a.m., the white of day, during which the city's shadows are a sun-dial, edging round the buildings like wine in a swirled glass, and then the old-gold and pink of a sunset that goes on for hours. When I look up from my book, I can tell from the colour of the light on Esja when it's time to go home. I colonise a desk by the window and begin to feel like myself again, ensconced in a maze of bookshelves, high above the university. Some of the books I expect to find in anyone's National or University Library aren't there, including the Complete Sigmund Freud and a proper edition of Wordsworth, and a flicker of concern for the autumn's teaching crosses my mind, but for now I have found a refuge. I take a few days to work on my book, and between times, Matthew and Hulda Kristín get together and, over a week, produce a second-hand washing machine, a fridge and a Danish beech high chair. But I thought there was no second-hand market, I say. There isn't, they reply. Foreigners never understand this. The fridge comes from Hulda Kristín's step-father's garage. The washing machine is from her neighbour's cousin, who was buying a new one and is happy, though surprised, to take some money for the old one. The high chair was in Hulda Kristín's attic, waiting for a relative to need it. There are very few shops where you can buy second-hand goods, but the same network that produced the right apartment in the right place will, given time and patience, produce white goods. Thank you, I say again. Thank you.

I am grateful, but I am also uncomfortable with my gratitude. People we have not known long have given us a great deal of time and effort as well as material objects, and I have no way of reciprocating. Don't worry, says Matthew, as we pace the sculpture garden near his flat, following the children who are hiding in bushes. You'll have a chance sometime. That's how it works here: you tell people you're looking for a car and someone's uncle's girlfriend is moving to America so she sells it to you at a good price, and then maybe she needs someone who lives nearby to keep an eye on her apartment while she's gone. Or you help your second cousin move house and next year he gives your daughter a summer job. (Or a bank loan, I wonder, or a stake in the public utility he's just decided to sell off?) That's OK, I say, if you live here and it's your family, but none of you owes us anything. We've all moved here ourselves, he says. You're right, usually it's your extended family who looks after you, but Hulda Kristín and

Pétur and I all know what it's like when you land here and you're a foreigner and you haven't got anyone. You can't do anything here without a clan, not without spending insane amounts of money. So we'll help you and, don't worry, sometime you'll be able to do something for us.

Foreigner, I think. Foreigner, *útlendingur*. Ausländer. I have joined the Faculty of Foreign Languages. British people of my generation don't use that word, certainly not as casually as Icelanders. 'Foreigner' is a word I associate with the Daily Mail and the British National Party, a term used only by people who understand the world in binary terms of Us and Them. It jars every time I hear someone educated and intelligent say the word here, but people do it all the time. I won't, I think, however long we stay I won't inhabit that mindset, I won't define myself or anyone else as a foreigner. (It's not 'that mindset', Pétur says. 'That mindset' is English, imperial, colonial, nothing to do with Iceland. But it takes me months, blinded by my own foreign-ness and by my unexamined sense that the British own English, to understand what he's telling me: that although almost every Icelander speaks English, it's not the same language as my native tongue; that 'foreigner' may not always mean in Icelandic English what it would mean at home.) Matthew says that he has heard Icelanders refer to English as *útlenska*, 'foreignese', the language of foreigners. Hulda Kristín told me that the property developer required some reassurance about letting his apartment to foreigners. It's understandable, she adds, there were no drugs in Iceland until the immigrants started to come a few years ago, and you hear some terrible things.

So we begin to settle. The Icelandic school holiday lasts three months in the summer, long enough to go back to the farm and get the harvest in, and Reykjavík in July is like Paris in August: empty of locals, small businesses closed, only tourists moving slowly down the main streets. It's not time to start our real Icelandic lives yet – we're still tourists too – but we have a base now. I can take the bus to the city and work in the library when I need to, and meanwhile Anthony can walk with the children to our local pool, or to the swings on the headland along the coast path, or to the beach at the end of the road. We eat fish, which is much cheaper than at home and invariably, even from the cheapest supermarkets where the fruit and vegetables lie in mouldering heaps, perfectly fresh. Pétur tells me that when he first came to Iceland, many of his friends had a fisherman in the family and were supplied by obligation, not for cash. We learn that sticking to greenhouse-grown, Icelandic vegetables and salad is a guarantee of quality as well as being cheaper than imports (also a new situation, Matthew says; it was only during the boom, when wealthy Icelandic travellers started to demand rocket and red peppers instead of turnips and swedes, that Icelandic farmers began to grow salad leaves and greens). Icelandic lamb, we find, is a different beast from its small, fatty English cousin. The meat is like game, dense and with a flavour reminiscent of the turf growing in the sun outside. Icelandic potatoes descended from a particular strain in the nineteenth century, and are sweeter and firmer than English ones. I understand for the first time why the earliest English potato recipes are for custard tarts and puddings. So we eat simply, and notice the basics: fish and potatoes, or lamb and potatoes, with Icelandic salad, and barley flatbreads, *flatkökur*, with Icelandic cheese, most of which comes in yellow bricks labelled 'kase', 'cheese', and tastes like a very mild Gouda. Icelanders don't eat much fruit, says Hulda Kristín, but if you want it, buy frozen, and we find five kilogramme sacks of frozen Polish berries and bring them home stuffed under the pushchair. We try not to think about Kentish fruit, and it doesn't occur to us to think about what we'll do for fresh food in winter. Pétur, who has been here forty years, no longer notices what I consider to be the fruit and vegetable problem, even though his wife is vegetarian. I bought a book about Icelandic cuisine when we came in May, and then, hopefully, a book by a Norwegian chef which I thought might help me to do intelligent and authentic things with Icelandic ingredients. The Norwegian book has an excellent pancake recipe, but is otherwise full of bright suggestions for dishes involving freshly picked strawberries, crayfish caught in mountain streams, and a glut of salmon, none of which is available to me. The Icelandic book, Nanna Rögnvaldardóttir's *Icelandic Food and Cookery*, makes compelling reading. Rögnvaldardóttir begins by referring to the great change in Icelandic society after the Second World War brought sudden prosperity, Americanisation and, in 1944, full independence from Denmark:

> I grew up on a remote farm in northern Iceland in the 1960s. Icelandic society has changed so much since then that it sometimes seems to me this must have been the 1860s, not least in culinary matters. The food of my childhood was partly the old traditional Icelandic food – salted, smoked, whey-preserved, dried, and partly the Danish-influenced cuisine of the home academy my mother attended – heavy sauces, roasts, endless porridge, puddings, and soups.

*

I'll hear more about these 'home academies' from my students, many of whose grandmothers attended them in preparation for life as housewives, mostly on farms. Even after 1944, young women were taught to cook more or less adapted Danish food. It sounds like the half-hearted adaptation of English recipes for Indian ingredients and cooking methods under the Raj. The Danish influence on Icelandic food is still apparent in any bakery, where there are yeast-raised pastries and cinnamon biscuits, and in the staples of Icelandic home cooking: roast meat with 'brown sauce', layered cream cakes and scones. I want to know what came before that. I want authentic island cooking, even though I know that any cuisine is a miscegenation.

There is no written account of Icelandic food before the eighteenth century. Iceland was uninhabited until settlers arrived from Norway around AD 900. The settlers came up the western side of the British islands where they picked up Irish, Welsh and Scottish wives and servants. The Celts were largely excluded from the traditional narrative of Icelandic history, which is based on the sagas. The sagas are long narrative poems about the settlement years, which were first written down in the twelfth and thirteenth centuries, several hundred years after the events they describe. In the twentieth century, Icelandic historians questioned the status of the sagas as historical truth, and the poems are now widely seen as literary artefacts, but there is still something of the sacred text about them. Many Icelanders can quote the sagas in the way that seventeenth-century Puritans quoted the Bible. Every so often, a discussion in a faculty meeting will end with someone saying something in Icelandic alliterative verse. By the end of the year, I will be able to follow most of what happens in these meetings, but not the poetry. I'll hiss at Matthew to translate and he'll reply, with a straight face, something like 'The fair horse fares fast in frost.' What? I'll ask. What? But meanwhile everyone else will be nodding and agreeing, the issue somehow resolved, and I'll know the sagas have spoken again. They combine the functions of the Bible and the Domesday Book, but offer a narrative of heroic Viking exploration and conquest that skips over the presence of Celts.

In some respects, the foodways of the Hebridean islands from which the slaves came offered a better template for Icelandic subsistence than those of Norway. The Norwegian settlers were used to hunting deer, picking fruit and berries, and relying on nuts and acorns for extra protein. There was no shortage of firewood in Norway, which made it easy to harvest salt to preserve meat and fish, and also meant that it was possible to cook several times a day and to use fuel-intensive methods such as baking. In Iceland, as in the North Atlantic islands from which many of the settlers' wives and servants came, there were no native mammals except seals, no fruit, few berries, and no nuts. Although Iceland was forested when the settlers arrived, the woods were over-exploited from the beginning and the bare, treeless landscape familiar to Icelanders for most of the last millennium probably emerged in the early centuries of settlement, bringing with it fuel poverty alleviated by peat-cutting as practised in the Western Isles.

Given the length and harshness of Icelandic winters, food preservation was essential for survival. Fish was, and still is, wind-dried in sheds above the beach. Meat could be smoked in the chimney. But most things were preserved in whey. The settlers brought cows with them from Norway, and Icelanders have been heavily dependent on dairy produce from the beginning. There was, oddly, no tradition of cheese-making except the fresh curds called *skyr*, much like fromage frais and still eaten at least once a day by most Icelanders. The by-product of *skyr* is whey, which was often served as a drink but also used, in its fermented form, as a means of preservation akin to pickling. Everything went into barrels of fermented whey:

> Fish and cattle bones were sometimes kept in the fermented whey until they softened and then they were boiled and eaten ... Food that is to be preserved, for example blood puddings, liver sausages, fatty meat, sheep's head and headcheese, whale blubber, seal flippers, etc., is usually boiled and cooled, then placed in barrels and submerged in fermented whey. It will keep for many months in this manner and gradually acquire a more sour taste. It is sometimes said that all food will eventually taste the same if it is kept in whey for long enough and there is some truth in that.

It was never easy to grow grain in Iceland, and never possible to grow wheat. Ovens were unknown because of the shortage of fuel so, again as in the Western Isles, where grains were eaten they were either in porridge or in flatbreads and bannocks, but most people relied instead on dried fish, which was, and sometimes still is, spread with (unsalted) butter and eaten like bread as a side dish or snack. 'Iceland moss', which is a kind of lichen still used to make tea, and seaweed were used to stretch grains, and also seem to have been the only source of vitamin C.

I am not much encouraged. The barley flatbreads from the

Saturday market by the harbour are good, and remind me of the Staffordshire oatcakes that were a childhood treat with cheese or butter. The children like the wind-dried fish, but I can't get past the smell. We all eat *skyr*, but I can't face fermented whey, much less blood pudding or liver sausage. The recipes that make up most of *Icelandic Food and Cookery* involve covering everything from potatoes to smoked lamb in white sauce, sometimes diluted with ketchup or pineapple juice. Salads are made of cabbage or carrot and lots of mayonnaise. One recipe suggests that I simmer lambs' hearts in stock until they are tender, before thickening the stock with margarine and flour. How do you manage, I ask Pétur, what do you eat? Oh, he says vaguely, you get used to it all. But if I want to know about Nordic food, I should talk to Mæja's husband Mads. Mæja? I ask. Yes, Mæja, says Pétur. You know, Mæja. Mæja Garðarsdóttir. Everyone knows Mæja. I don't, but I soon will.

Mæja is a lecturer in linguistics with a special interest in second language acquisition. She grew up above and around her father's shop, just round the corner from the university, which makes her unusual in her generation because almost everyone else has childhood memories of life on the farm to which they return at every opportunity. Mæja may be unique among Icelanders in being seven generations off the land. She lives a couple of blocks from that shop with Mads, who is Danish, a trained chef who is now a lecturer in gastronomy at the Nordic House. The Nordic House is a pan-Scandinavian cultural centre, unofficially part of the university, housed in an Alvar Aalto building on the wetland reserve between my office building, Nýi Garður, and the domestic airport. Mads and I arrange to meet there so he can

31

tell me what I want to know about Iceland and new Nordic food.

It's a hot day, or at least would be a hot day if it weren't for the wind, which is the kind of thing people say as often in Iceland as northern England. I make my way across the car parks that spread like lakes across the spaces between buildings in this city, and up the shallow slate steps into the Nordic House. It's one of those buildings that seems to contain more sunlight than there is outside, and there are places to sit and things to read in English and all the Nordic languages. In the atrium there's an exhibition of knitted and felted hats in dragon shades of green and red, articulated like reptiles, and there's the menu for Dill, the New Nordic restaurant on site, which I read with envy. Like most of Reykjavík's restaurants, it's too expensive for anyone on a public sector salary, but I promise myself that when we find a babysitter and a reason to celebrate, Anthony and I will come at least once. Fish, herbs, berries, wild mushrooms, sorrel: I could learn from that.

Mads approaches, hand outstretched, smile shining from behind his beard and glasses. Welcome, he says. Welcome to the Nordic House; welcome to Iceland. Shall I show you around? We go along broad white corridors with wooden floors, the walls punctuated by framed pen-and-ink drawings. Everyone's office door is open, letting me peep into rooms full of light and honey-coloured furniture with bright rugs and cushions, where people are working on Nordic literature and art and design. The Nordic House has recently accepted gastronomy as one of the arts, Mads tells me, so all sorts of new projects are beginning now. We go down a flight of white stairs into the library, which is designed more as a workspace for readers and writers than as book storage, with big tables and low chairs. All the furniture, Mads says, was designed by Aalto for this building, even the door handles and light switches. It's an enviable place to work, I reply.

We come back to the atrium. Shall we go to the café? Mads suggests. I can show you our garden? We go out, across the turf where new goslings are practising walking and their mothers are watching out for intruders. There are vegetable beds, some currant bushes, and even a fruit tree behind what I take to be a greenhouse. This is one of my new projects, Mads tells me. People say you can't grow apples here, that the winters are too cold, but I think that probably now you can. Some varieties, anyway. The winters are so much shorter and milder than even a few years ago. And here is rhubarb, which is in most people's gardens. Rhubarb was about the only kind of jam in Iceland until recently. And currants, which you see are fruiting. And then we have Icelandic potatoes, which are genetically different from European ones, and cabbages and onions. Kale, sprouts, cauliflower. I want to grow everything possible. I want to show people how much we can grow in Iceland, even outdoors in the city. And of course, with the greenhouses, everything is possible. Shall we have coffee?

We go into the greenhouse, whose roof is reflecting a lighthouse beam back into the sun. It's a café as well as a greenhouse. The waitress opens the louvred panels, because it really is hot, and brings us coffee, and almond cakes which are the nicest thing I've eaten since we left the farmers' market in Canterbury. This is lovely, I tell Mads. Your garden, and the Nordic House, and the café. I nibble my cake, relax into the company of someone who understands how I think about food and why it matters so much to me, someone who, being an exile himself, understands emotionally as well as intellectually why it's hard to shrug off your own cuisine as you shrug off summer clothes and English newspapers. I thought this didn't exist in Iceland, I say. I thought nobody here was interested in where food comes from.

Mads smiles at me. Some people are, he says. At first it was just an upper-class trend, typical of people who travelled a lot and were much more interested in Italian artisanal food than anything Icelandic farmers could produce. But it's changing now, partly because of the financial crisis, the *kreppa*. The króna's collapse has made imported food much more expensive, and Iceland has been importing more and more of its food since trade restrictions were lifted in the 1970s. Almost all fruit and vegetables have always been imported, and while the economy was booming everyone could afford it and it was the Icelandic farmers who were struggling. Consumers' habits are shifting now. People are buying more local produce, meaning that farmers are able to invest in increasing the supply of local produce, and also buying the traditional foods again, switching back from chicken to lamb, picking up the blood puddings and liver sausage and sheep's heads again.

Is that, I ask, a patriotic response to the crisis, a willingness to support the local economy, or just because it's cheaper? There is no free-range chicken available in Iceland, free-range eggs are hard to find, and pork and beef are intensively farmed. There are organic vegetables and dry goods, but they are all American imports. It's rare to find anything labelled with its country of origin. There's little in the marketplace to suggest that this is a country that thinks much about where food comes from. From abroad, from *útlönd*, the foreign world.

Maybe some of each, Mads says. People say both, but of

course really they buy the cheapest thing. Icelanders have a higher consumption of ready meals than any other Nordic country. They are less critical of American models of consumption than other Europeans. But he is hopeful; he calculates that, with the right government policies, Iceland could be ninety per cent self-sufficient. There is no reason why fruit trees as well as salad leaves and tomatoes shouldn't grow in geothermally heated greenhouses. At the moment, farmers pay more for geothermal energy than Alcoa, the American company that runs the aluminium smelters and was highly favoured by the overthrown government, and a law forbidding farmers to sell their produce directly to the public has only recently been repealed. But things are changing, and Mads thinks there is a new willingness to develop shorter food chains. The gardens of Reykjavík won't foam with cherry blossom any time soon, but there will be Icelandic apples, new cheeses, winter cabbage, more than three kinds of fish (haddock, cod, salmon). In any case, he adds, most Icelanders still think of 'fish' as haddock. Cod is for when you can't get haddock and it's unusual to have a taste for salmon. But if we would like to come to dinner on Friday, he and Mæja would be delighted to show us some Nordic home cooking. We would love to, I say. Thank you.

We meet Mæja for a swim in their neighbourhood pool before dinner. We've swum a couple of times in our local pool in Garðabær, because the novelty of outdoor swimming in a heated pool is fun and because swimming is almost free and within walking distance of the flat and both children enjoy it, but I'm still learning the rituals of Icelandic swimming. Within the separate changing rooms for men and women, there are no cubicles, and no stalls for the showers. You remove your shoes in an ante-room and leave them on shelves, proceed to the main changing room where you strip naked and leave all your clothes in a locker. Then you walk through the changing room to leave your towel in the drying area, and then walk through to the showers, where signs in Icelandic, English, German and French instruct you to wash all over with soap and pay special attention to your underarms, genitals and feet. There are cartoon illustrations as back-up. Then you may put your swimming costume on – Icelandic women always do this under the shower – and go outside to the pool. The tradition of communal nakedness was one of the things I found liberating when I was nineteen. For the first time, I saw women's bodies that had not been airbrushed and arranged to present an ideal form, and for the first time I understood that the perfection I knew from magazines and films wasn't the norm. I even had the glimmer of a sense that my own active nineteen-year-old body was, comparatively, aesthetically acceptable. I am sure that it's important for the new generation of teenage girls to see bodies that have been stretched by child-bearing, scarred by surgery, over- or under-fed, shaped by exercise or by a life spent in the courtroom or the library or on the shop floor. I am less sure that I want to expose myself, my uncertain foreign self, to the gaze of Icelanders at home in their own pools, especially while Tobias likes to run off towards the water as soon as I've stepped out of my knickers.

Being with Mæja helps. She doesn't seem to notice that we're taking our clothes off as she tells me that the children will soon learn Icelandic, that I will enjoy my job, that she and Mads will take us around the city and show us the best food shops. She tells me about how Mads settled in here, that it took time, and of course sometimes he misses Copenhagen, but together they have found pleasures and discoveries they couldn't have anywhere else. Their summer project has been to learn to ride Icelandic horses. They spent the weekend picking blueberries out in the national park, which is barely ten minutes from our apartment in Garðabær. Mæja intercepts Tobias as he runs for the door, and smiles at me so that it feels like a hug. Let's swim, she says. Mads has been cooking all afternoon, we'll need our appetites.

The next week, we are able to reciprocate. I have begun to bake again. (I must be settling in.) We have an English afternoon tea party for Max's seventh birthday at the beginning of August, and Pétur and his wife Messíana bring bilingual grandchildren who play on the beach with Max and Tobias and Hulda Kristín's children while the grown-ups – admittedly sitting on cushions on the floor, and admittedly using mugs they brought themselves – drink Earl Grey and eat cucumber sandwiches and toast with Patum Peperium, which I brought for its Englishness even though we don't usually eat it at home. I find birthday candles in Hagkaup, and balloons, and we take two buses to get to a Toys R Us in a building like an aircraft hanger under a flyover, to buy a pogo stick on which Max can bounce on the coast path outside the flat. We have been here three weeks, and twelve people sing 'Happy Birthday' / *Til Hamingu* over my pirate ship cake.

Darkness doesn't fall. I stay up later and later, because there's no particular reason to go to bed, and because I want to see what happens. On the field on the peninsula across the inlet, people start to play football at 11 p.m., and are still playing two hours later. In May, I didn't believe the woman who told us that people go out to wash their cars at midnight in summer, but I find my own evenings stretching. The children go to bed late, around 9 p.m., and then I work on my book for a couple of hours, and then read for an hour or so, and then decide to go for a walk before bed. Icelandic children, out in unsupervised tribes as if it were the 1970s, swirl around the development and along the coast paths until midnight. Joggers come past in the early hours of the morning. We're south of the Arctic Circle here, and it's already July, a month past the solstice, so around 1 a.m. the light dims, the birds fall silent, the wind drops. It's not a sleep but a holding of breath, a sudden thought of death that gets longer each night.

Anthony and I each go for a walk every evening, taking it in turns to have the sunset slot, which is a few minutes earlier every day. The shore path from the city out to Hafnarfjörður passes our apartment, and I take the same walk every day, will continue to take the same walk every day as the nights lengthen and sunset slips along the horizon, further south and earlier day by day, and the warm breath on the air in July is replaced by a screaming wind that tears at my skin. I pass the blocks of half-finished and empty flats by which we are surrounded. Automatic doors glide open as I walk by, as if there are invisible New York doormen to go with the ghosts of wealthy Icelanders who never came into being and never bought these apartments, big enough to park a freight truck in the living room and with triple-glazed windows of a size to admit several. I glance in to see wires hanging out of the walls and hardwood kitchen units stacked on the (heated) floors. Ramps lead into heated basement garages, cavernous as mausoleums from which imperial bodies have been stolen. Obese SUVs jostle on Reykjavík's freeways, but here, in the cages built for them, there are none. The abandoned yellow crane reaches above the penthouses at the top, high as a holy statue set to watch over our folly. Reykjavík is ringed by these untenanted suburbs, whole townships built with imaginary money for people who never existed. There was a building boom but no housing shortage, a drive to cover the lava fields with more and more and more open-plan kitchens and steel-railed balconies and underground carports that reminds me of Max, aged about five, covering the floor with wooden train track that looped endlessly back on itself, going nowhere via flyover bridges and turntables and level crossings, a baroque engineering that was its own justification. I discover when autumn brings us darkness again that these Icelandic ghost towns blaze with light by night, even when the city council decides to turn the street lights on later and off earlier across Reykjavík to save money. They have to keep hot water running through the pipes, Pétur tells me, to stop the plumbing and sewage systems freezing in the winter. The doors open and close, like a museum diorama animated by the presence of an observer.

I go on, past the nursery beside the beach covered in imported pale sand. Icelandic sand is black, made by waves pounding cold lava, but some Icelanders – the non-existent rich Icelanders who were meant to buy these flats – want the pink sand they've seen abroad. Foreigners' sand. So they imported it in sacks and spread it along the edge of the Arctic Ocean, where the sea gradually pulls it away. Past the artificial beach, the real shoreline is rocky, with turf and reeds growing right down to the sea. There are more blocks of expensive apartments on my left, a few years older and therefore at least half occupied. Every balcony holds a gas barbecue the size of a bed. I play at fantasy apartment shopping. Even the most desirable places, the ones with cathedral ceilings and glass walls over the foreshore, have large china elephants, dancing shepherdesses and gilt vases along the window-sills. Inside, I can see stuffed foxes, reproduction late-Victorian furniture and embroidered tablecloths. Some of them have net curtains blocking their view of the sea. Not all Icelanders, I remind myself, live in the paradise of Nordic interior design about which I fantasise. Being Icelandic does not oblige people to bin their china figurines in order to conform to my stereotypes.

On my right, across the sea, there are mountains that are visible only at sunset and – I will learn in winter – sunrise, sharp, snow-covered mountains pink in the low light. They fade as the sun goes down. Nearer, there are filaments of cloud drifting in front of Esja, bright against a hillside matt as sugar paper. Curlews call across the water, and the Arctic terns flicker shrilling over my head, beaks and wings pencil-sharp in the soft sky. Geese are beginning to mass on the waves, their low conversation the bass line to the seagulls' fish-wife screaming on the headland. I'd like to walk on the headland, where there are paths leading to the President's official residence, which looks like a Danish farmhouse deposited in a lava field on the shores of the Arctic sea, but every time I try, the skuas come and mount guard, hanging low over my head and shouting at me to go away, and the seagulls land on the rocks by the faint path and swear as I approach. They've never attacked me, and a braver person would press on, but I am not a braver person and I don't. The sun rests on the horizon, and is already beginning to slip away. I try to memorise the light against a time when it will seem unimaginable, even though that time itself is at the moment unimaginable to me.

3

Vestmannaeyjar

If we want to travel, Pétur says, we should go now. Summer is passing. The geese are gathering for their winter migration and the blueberries are already over. Term starts at the end of August. Sometimes when I wake in the night there is darkness, and on late nights I need a bedside light for reading. We are beginning to stuff coats under the pushchair for days out, although most days it's still warm enough to find a hollow in the lava field and sit among the rowan bushes for a picnic of *flatkökur* and cheese. If you leave it much longer, Pétur warns, it will be too late. It's only weeks later that I understand what he's telling me. It's not that it's impossible to leave the city in autumn and winter, but you wouldn't do it without a good reason and a four-wheel drive car. The weather in the city tells you nothing about the weather over the mountains, and most roads beyond Reykjavík can be officially or practically closed at any time. Even if you set out on a clear day, blizzards can move across the skies faster than a car travels, and the roads outside the city aren't gritted. We don't understand yet that for several months the only way out of Reykjavík for us will be on a plane.

In any case, real travel will have to wait for next summer. We have recognised that we will need a car; bumping groceries over the lava field in the pushchair is all very well in summer, but we have already had a couple of days so windy that Tobias couldn't walk outside, and once there's snow on that wind we will not want to walk two miles for food. It's not only financial considerations that daunt us, nor alarm at the idea of trying to buy a second-hand car in Icelandic. Icelandic driving is terrifying. Nobody indicates. Even bus drivers accelerate towards junctions and then jump on the brakes at the last minute, sending passengers and shopping crashing to the floor. People swerve across lanes to leave the freeway from the inside. Icelanders have one of the highest rates of mobile phone ownership and usage in the world, and they don't stop when they're driving. Max and I, waiting for a bus, conduct an informal survey: at the junction outside Kringlan shopping mall, where two eight-lane highways intersect, one afternoon in mid-August, six in ten drivers are texting or talking on their phones, four in ten are eating – usually *skyr* with a spoon – and one has a laptop open on his lap. In one month we have seen four major accidents, the kind that write off cars, trigger airbags and leave glass and blood, and in one case a baby's car-seat, on the road. It's the only area of Icelandic life where I feel that I, a foreigner, can say with certainty that they are mad and I am sane. I am in no hurry to get my children on the roads of Reykjavík. But you can fly to the Westman Islands.

The Westman Islands are the tops of volcanoes sticking out of the sea, along the same fault as the volcanoes Eyjafjallajökull

and Katla. The largest island, Heimaey, has been inhabited
since Irish slaves took refuge there early in the settlement
period, and in the seventeenth century it was raided by
Algerian pirates who took most of the inhabitants back to
Algeria as slaves. (We heard the same story in Baltimore,
Cork, two years ago; like the Vikings, Arab sailors found the
North Atlantic sea-road, with its isolated farms scattered along
deep water, highly profitable.) One of the women kidnapped
made her way home overland from Algeria to Denmark, and
so back to Iceland where she married the poet Hallgrímur
Pétursson, after whom the church that dominates Reykjavík's
skyline is named.

One dark and stormy night in January 1973, the volcano on
Heimaey which had been sleeping for around five thousand
years woke up. There were just under five thousand people
sleeping in their houses on the island's lower slopes. There
had been some tremors during the evening of Monday 22nd
January, but the occasional rumble causes no-one in that part
of Iceland to pause. Storm-winds had confined the fishing fleet
to harbour, so all the island's men were home. Just before 2
a.m., someone called the town police to say that there was an
eruption of lava above the church farm, to the east of the town.
The police drove up to look, and found the mountainside
opening up, a fissure stretching down into the sea. Molten
lava had begun to pour down the hill. The police returned to
town, sounded the community's fire alarm and drove the
streets with their sirens sounding. Within half an hour, the first
boats were leaving, carrying children still in their pyjamas and
parents who had not waited to pack a case. By dawn, everyone
but emergency workers had left, ferried across forty miles of
rough sea to the harbour on the mainland at Þorlákshöfn.

I imagine a wall of flame sweeping through the town, a settlement left burnt-out and desolate. I imagine Pompeii, but what happened was more gradual, a partial apocalypse with wisps of good news. The boats returned the next day, and repeatedly over the following weeks, carrying men who worked through the abandoned houses, salvaging cars, refrigerators and sofas as well as toys and jewellery. There were teams of emergency workers on Heimaey throughout the eruption, spraying the lava with seawater, building a dam meant to hold it back above the town, trying to save the electricity station and the fish-processing factories, trying to keep the airport and the harbour open. Ash fell across the island, to a depth of several metres, so the men reinforced the roofs of schools and houses to bear the extra weight. Lava flowed over the dam and, inevitably, towards the houses on the eastern side of town, and then over them, and down towards the harbour. The harbour was vulnerable. Heimaey was, and remains, the base of southern Icelandic fishing. The island was so populous – five thousand people on an island four kilometres by seven – because it had a natural harbour sheltered from all winds and deep enough for the largest ships. But the harbour was so sheltered because it had a narrow entrance, and the lava was flowing towards the harbour mouth, layering new rock into the sea. Without the harbour, Heimaey would have no reason to exist. Even without the ash and smoking lava, there isn't enough land for more than half a dozen farms. The water supply has always been problematic, the mountainside being too steep and rocky to hold much of the abundance of rain, and access to the island, by air or sea, remains unreliable. Pétur's daughter, a vicar who regularly substitutes for her colleague on Heimaey, always arranges overnight care for her daughter before taking the twenty-minute flight, because the schedule depends on the weather in a particularly stormy corner of the Atlantic.

So the Westman Islanders increased their efforts as the lava approached the harbour. No-one had ever been able to stop or even direct molten lava, so vulcanologists and geologists from around the world peered over their shoulders as the men decided what to do. The US Army flew in pumps and hoses so that the islanders could pump seawater onto the lava as it edged across the mouth of the channel, having covered all the houses in its path. And it worked. (Or perhaps the volcano had always meant to stop there anyway). The entrance was left narrower but deeper than it had been, and angled so that when the sea outside is exploding white against the cliff-face and the waves are taller than boats and blowing back against the tide, the reflections of puffins' nests are unbroken in the channel. There was a reason to come back.

We fly from the little airport, the one by the university whose runway will distract me when I'm teaching. The planes to Greenland go from there. We arrive in good time, having taken the bus before the logical one in case of delay, and go to check in. There doesn't seem to be a queue, only a hall full of people milling and shoving, rucksacks bouncing into the people behind. Tobias gets knocked over and I pick him up, and then a rucksack hits his head so I put him down. A man stands on Max's foot and Max pushes him off. Icelanders are tall, especially the kind of Icelander who flies across the country with hiking gear and fishing rods, and I can't see over people's heads to the departures board. We sidle around the edge of the crowd, Anthony in front and me herding the children. We can't get to the check-in desk so we go to the outsize-baggage deposit. You're too early, barks the woman. Come back in an hour.

We struggle back out. Are we not going, asks Max, and Tobias starts to cry. A bus that would take us back to the flat goes by, and I can see the windows of my office across the marsh. Of course we're going, I say, but we're going to have a little walk before we get on the plane. No, says Max, I'm not going. We'll miss the flight. I go for a walk, says Tobias, setting off along the chain-link fence that separates the runway from the university. I follow him. We watch a cat flatten itself through a hole in the fence and scamper across the runway. We watch a plane land, count its six windows and wave to the twelve passengers, who don't wave back. We watch another plane take off and turn back to fly past the disused water towers of Perlan. Max joins us, brandishing a fistful of leaflets. He wants to go whale watching and ride in a helicopter and take a day trip to Greenland and is it safe to let people take guns on planes because he thought it said at Gatwick that you weren't allowed. What? He hands me the leaflet, Air Iceland offering friendly advice about what's 'Good to Know':

> You do not need to have a permit to carry firearms on domestic flights in Iceland. At check-in the firearm will be checked by an Air Iceland employee who will confirm that the firearm is not loaded. All ammunition must be separated from the firearm. The quantities of ammunition must not exceed 5 kilos.

I look up at Anthony. At Gatwick, I had to drink some of the water in Tobias's beaker to demonstrate that it wasn't whatever presumably toxic substance people have thought of using to blow up a plane (though surely anyone intent on blowing himself up wouldn't jib at a little poison). We had to take our shoes off and disassemble the pushchair so it would fit through the X-ray machine, and even then I set off the alarm and had to confirm that I was indeed wearing a bra with metal underwires. Five kilogrammes of ammunition? We discover when we return to the airport and, fifteen minutes before take-off, are allowed to check in, that you don't need to show a passport, or even a driving licence, to board a domestic flight with your gun and your explosives. Anyone could do it, anyone who had an interest in combining passenger aircraft with firearms. They don't, because this is Iceland and that's not the sort of thing that happens here.

After twenty minutes' flight, passing low over hills, farmland and a river carved deep into a plain, we land, and climb down the stairs onto the tarmac. It's a bright day, and the sun is warm on our faces and on the grass as we wander towards the terminal building, where we watch from the doorway as the pilot jumps down from the cabin and unloads the baggage onto a handcart, which he wheels inside so people can help themselves. The internet offered a timetable for a bus service into town. There's no bus stop. We wait. There are no taxis either. Beside the hill, the sea sparkles in the sun. There is birdsong, and the smell of warm grass. When's the bus coming, Mummy, asks Tobias. I go in and ask. No, there's no bus. Never has been. Taxis? Not here. It's not Reykjavík, you know. No, it's too far to walk into town. Especially with the children. Maybe two kilometres. Or three. I go back out and we set off. There are no pavements, which bothers the children, but there's little traffic and you can hear it a long way off.

The road leads down the mountainside, which is a brighter green than the open spaces in the city and smells quite different, of turf and sea and maybe heather, though I think the heather is imaginary, has wandered in from memories of Orkney where clear summer days can be just like this. And why not; it's part of the same archipelago, some more small islands a couple of hundred miles south, part of the same Norse empire for about half of the last millennium. The town appears below us, houses in Smartie colours huddled around the harbour and the fish-processing plant, scattered up the lower reaches of the volcano, which is still bare, black shale and red rock, with only a fuzz of green on its dark shoulders. We go down the hill. There's no-one else walking, even when we come to the main street. There's a shop selling children's clothes, a bakery and a branch of Bonus, the ubiquitous 'cheap' supermarket owned by one of the disgraced bankers. There are a couple of banks. But just as in Garðabær, everyone is somewhere else. I've booked us a hotel room, but when we find the hotel – the rucksack dragging on Anthony's shoulders now, Tobias beginning to pull on my arm – there's no-one there. The door is open, and we can go in and up the stairs, covered with the kind of kaleidoscopic carpet found in Blackpool hotels in the 1980s, and along halls that smell of air freshener and feet, and into a dining room with plastic flowers on the tables and something sticky on the floor, but there's no sign of life. We call, and our voices are absorbed by the carpet and the flock wallpaper and the silence. Mummy, what if they've died, whispers Max. Please can we go now? I hungry, says Tobias, for the tenth time.

We leave. We have to find somewhere to stay. I find myself suddenly, unreasonably, anxious, as if the rift in our plan to be tourists has turned us back into new immigrants, people with little power, jeopardised by inexperience. What if we can't find somewhere, what if there's nowhere vacant or nothing we can afford? Is there a flight back tonight? We took the children away from everything they knew and now we can't even provide a bed for the night and although it's August it's too cold to be out at night, too cold for the children, and probably even the airport closes after the last flight of the day. Calm down, says Anthony. Why don't we try the youth hostel? So we do, and they have a family room with bunk beds and there's a kitchen and a couple of more-or-less clean bathrooms and we could stay three nights for the cost of one in the hotel. Tobias asks which bed is his, climbs onto it and demands his toys. He doesn't want to leave. Not now, not later. No. He will stay here until we go back to the airport. No, he doesn't want to go to the bathroom, or the bakery, or to see the sea or the puffins or the boats. No, he doesn't want to look for the swings or – we are becoming desperate – have an ice cream. No. He takes his rainforest jigsaw out of the box and begins to reassemble it.

We carry him, first to the supermarket, where we buy the basis of the kind of student cooking I haven't done for fifteen years, and then down to the harbour. We can see the path going up the volcano from here, and another path leading across the hill to the other side of the island. The sky is still blue and the wind gentle. If we didn't have children, or at least if we didn't have Tobias, we could go up there, crunching over the lava to the empty heart of Eldfell, the fire mountain, and we could peer down into the crater and turn to see the sea crawling against the new coastline. Heimaey gained a third of its present landmass during the eruption. But we do have

Tobias, and so we join a boat trip around the island, acting like the tourists we are.

The guide is an off-duty fisherman who has a blonde beard flowing down his smock – I can't remember now if the smock was actual or metaphorical, but either way it was there – and speaks the idiomatic, placelessly American English of the Nordic countries. The boat slides out between the edge of the lava and the cliffs which make a steep wall on the other side of the channel. There are sheep strolling along the edge of the cliff, a hundred metres above the quiet water, and sea-birds patrolling the airspace on the way down. We begin to bounce on the waves outside the channel, and Tobias holds on to me, which is a relief because it means that falling off a boat must be one of the few dangers apparent to a two-year-old. We're looking up at the new lava, the guide tells us, seeing a mountainside that wasn't there when he was a boy. And here is the cliff where the coolest man in Iceland swam ashore. The coolest man in Iceland was one of four fisherman who survived when their boat sank offshore – he points out to sea, where clouds are gathering in the south-east and the waves are, I'm sure, bigger than they were ten minutes ago – in a winter storm. The men clung to their upturned hull, shouting encouragement to each other, for as long as they could, but the wind and waves strengthened until they were washed off the keel. The water temperature was six degrees and it was dark, but the coolest man knew his way and began to swim the six miles to land. (All the best stories have repeating numbers.) When he was close enough to hear the waves, the coolest man realised that he was coming in too far to the north, where the cliffs lean out sheer over the sea, so he swam back out and made a second approach, further south. He climbed out of the waves in the dark, and up those cliffs there, and made his way to the nearest house, there (not very near at all, really) and woke the inhabitants, but although he'd broken his leg climbing the cliff he refused to go to hospital until he was satisfied that a rescue operation was under way for his comrades. By the time he was ready to see the doctor, his blood temperature was less than twenty degrees, which is why they call him the coolest man in Iceland.

Anthony, who finds most swimming pools unpleasantly cold, looks rather despondent at this, and it's only later, when we find a signboard above the cliff confirming the story, that he finds that I didn't believe it and I find that he did. Any ordinary person, I assert, probably even most Icelandic men, would give up somewhere between the sinking bit and the getting washed off the keel bit and succumb regretfully to hypothermia, which is apparently not a bad way to go. It's not normal to take yourself that seriously.

We bob on, the Americans and Spanish taking shelter in the cabin while we and the Danes lift our faces to the wind and wrap our scarves around our heads. We go round the bottom of cliffs that are shrieking tenements of sea-birds, gannets and fulmars, and we hear stories about how people (men) used to climb down the rock-face to take the eggs. There are thousands of puffins, blundering and tipping in flight but sleek as seals when seen underwater from above. The islanders used to kill them in great number, and there are still puffin breasts on the menus in the main street. Now there is the annual puffling rescue, for which we are too late. Sometime in August, the fledgling puffins (which really are called pufflings; when I first read about this I thought it was one of the more beguiling examples of Icelandic English) notice the bright lights of town and fly off to investigate. The island's children collect them in cardboard boxes, take them down to the harbour and put them back in the sea, a moment which the tourist leaflet describes as 'full of joy and delight'. On, round the far end of Eldfell, where no lava flowed, the land is bright and green as if nothing had happened and a couple of old farms sit undisturbed where they have always been. We are hugging the cliffs here, in a way that would make me nervous if something about being a tourist hadn't made me suspend judgement. (Is this what happens to all those people who die doing foolhardy things in foreign places, is it something in the infantilising process of becoming a tourist and a stranger that makes you stop thinking like a grown-up, something that makes it OK to board a plane with people carrying ammunition and take a toddler round a North Atlantic island in a small boat?) There is a rock formation like a rose and one like an elephant, which disappoints Tobias who was expecting a real elephant, and then the guide turns off the engine and we glide into a cave, where the water lies black and still, and pale green stalagmites prod the surface. Drips fall, amplified, and then the fisherman takes out his clarinet and drops a few bars of slow jazz overboard, his body swaying with the boat while he plays. The boat is moving slowly towards the rock, but he finishes the melody before starting the engine. The echoes sing back, and back again.

The next morning, after a surprisingly refreshing night because the only way of getting the children to sleep is to lie in darkness ourselves, we go for a walk. Tobias sits, dressed, on his bed, playing with his puzzles, and doesn't want to go anywhere but the airport. We bully him into his shoes and coat and set off. Max capers ahead. He's been reading about Pompeii and is ready to be interested in a town drowned in lava.

The road ends in a wall of black rock. We follow the wall towards the sea, and find the end of a white house sticking out, its wooden wall buckled half-way down. There's a path at the side, taking us up onto the new part of Heimaey, so we follow it. It's colder than it was yesterday and the sky is full of grey cloud. There are outbreaks of white flowers in the lava, and a few rowan trees along the track. Birds sing. Every few metres, there are signs giving the names and sometimes floor-plans of the houses entombed below our feet. At first we are walking over the remains of wooden houses from the early twentieth century. A few like this survive in Reykjavík, painted Danish red and Swedish blue with white wooden lace under the eaves, and we've been inside the collection of old houses at Árbæjarsafn, the outdoor museum. Because these houses are recognisably part of Northern European heritage and pretty, I feel a proper sadness for their destruction. It's harder to know how to respond to the 1970s pebble-dash poking out of the rock further up the hill; these were people's homes, and yet I'm not acculturated to grieve for the loss of such buildings. There's a grid system here, part of it laid out on the hillside, part drowned under black rock. In the surviving streets cars smaller than in Reykjavík are parked on crazy-paved drives, and there are net curtains in the windows and basketball hoops on the garages. Then, cutting across suburbia, there's a river of stone, entombing the rest of the grid of houses and gardens. Max and I peer in through a window-frame sticking out of the lava and see twisted copper pipes, a bath-tub, the belly of a toilet. I point the torch on my phone into the darkness and we glimpse half a radiator and something that might be an electricity meter half-eaten by the volcano. There's a photo of the house, which wouldn't look out of place anywhere in European post-war suburbia, and a list of the people who lived there. Two parents and three children. Nobody died, not in the eruption itself, although one of the rescue workers inhaled a fatal quantity of poison gas during the cleaning operation in the following spring. It's not a grave-yard, but it's not quite a museum either.

We skid down the edge of the lava flow to the half of the street that isn't in the underworld, and find that there are plaques outside these houses too, showing what they looked like during the eruption or when the family returned in the summer of 1973 to find the windows gone, the rooms full to the ceiling with ash and the roofs bending under its weight. Some houses have gauges outside showing the peak height of the ash, like the signs outside fund-raising churches at home. Eldfell peers down over our shoulders, still there.

Later, Max and I go to watch *The Volcano Show* at the local cinema. This film is shown several times a day, with English, French or German subtitles, and the outside of the cinema building is covered with a mural of a spewing volcano. Inside, it reminds me of the cheap, local cinema where I saw most of the brat-pack films of the 1980s, a relic of the 1930s with red velvet seats from which the plush had been worn by two gen-erations of Mancunian bottoms, where they still stopped films half-way through so that a girl could come out and sell Cornettos from a tray slung round her neck. There is a sweep-ing staircase up to the box office of Heimaey cinema, but the paint is peeling off the walls and the banister is sticky to the touch. We creep into the darkened auditorium, late, and see

that it is empty. We are the audience. When we tip the creak-
ing seats and fold our coats, the curtain rises, purple and gold
as if revealing *Gone With the Wind*, and the film begins.

Among the emergency workers, apparently, was a camera-
man. We watch the mountain explode, orange as an oil flare
against the winter night, and a glacier of molten lava inches
down to the town. Smoke and ash hang in the air, and bearded
Icelandic men in wide-cut trousers wield shovels. Cigarettes
hang from the corners of their mouths while they dig, as if
there wasn't enough glow and smoke on set, and occasionally,
as the lava laps their shoes, they stand back and allow a slight
ruefulness to flicker over their faces as their houses collapse
and red flame leaps across the screen. Nobody runs or raises
his voice. There are no women in this film. Snow falls. Lava
slithers. At the harbour, in front of a fish-processing plant that
isn't there any more, men stand holding snaking hoses in both
hands, as if engaged in a gargantuan pissing contest. A cat
threads the burning ruins.

The music changes. The mountain is still steaming, but
there is no more lava. People appear on the slopes, and in the
graveyard and on the roof of the school and the medical
centre. They have spades, and are shovelling ash. Where the ash
is going is not apparent. Foreigners came to help, recalls the
voiceover, not specifying which foreigners, and there they are,
flower children in dungarees and floppy hats with daisies
around the brims. I wonder how the men from the pissing
contest regarded these volunteers. I cannot imagine Icelanders
as willing objects of foreign charity, especially when it came
wearing CND badges. Students with flowing hair strew seed
across the new-born hill, to stabilise the bare ash and reduce
the likelihood of a landslide, but some of the mountain is still

too hot. On fast-forward now, houses emerge, the cemetery reappears, its population unchanged, though in nine months some of the old people must have died and been buried on the mainland. Birds sing. A dusting of green is seen on the ash above town, where the foreigners' seeds have germinated.

4

Back to School

It's almost the beginning of term. Max is going to the International School. If we decide to stay permanently in Iceland, he can move into their bilingual stream, but for now it seems more important to minimise his immediate sense of alienation than to maximise his chances of eventual integration. The other children, and most of the staff, sound (but are not) American; we still haven't learnt that International English is not the same as the language we speak at home.

Icelandic children start school aged six, and stay in the same school until they are sixteen, when they move to a college, which takes four years to prepare them for university, or into vocational education. Childhood and adolescence have a different shape here. Fifteen-year-olds are in the same category as seven-year-olds, both children, both part of that tribe old enough to go around without adults but not old enough to drive, the only people who walk and take the bus, while nineteen-year-olds, although able to drive, vote and drink alcohol, share their daily space with sixteen-year-olds. We hear no-one demonising older children here, nothing akin to the English fear and loathing of teenagers. When I tell a group of students about the high-pitched sounds played to stop 'yobs' congregating outside English shops, they don't believe me. What kind of country would allow businesses to control children's freedom of movement?

The International School is housed in the local state school, and the buildings, so new that the swimming pool is finished as term begins, look more like those of a new art gallery or the headquarters of a particularly avant-garde corporation than a state institution. The classrooms are all open-plan, widening off light-filled spaces too broad and curvy to be corridors. The children skid in socks around pieces of sculpture, trees in pots, fish-tanks and glossy wood-fronted kitchen areas, complete with ovens for baking classes and coffee pots for the teachers. It isn't just the obvious expensiveness that's exciting, but the way the architecture suggests an entirely novel idea of childhood. The library and many of the classrooms have glass walls over the sea, as if it matters that the children should be able to see the horizon. There are no doors, no way of shutting people in or out, as if children and adults together could be trusted to move or be still. There are no stalls for the children's toilets – the part of looking round schools in England that always makes me think about home education again – but single bathrooms used by staff and students and kept clean by all concerned. There is nothing to stop a child wandering off and fiddling with the cookers or pulling boiling coffee off the counter, but they don't. And most importantly, there is nothing to stop anyone entering or leaving the building at any time. No fences, no gates, no boundaries, and the spinning doors open to all. English schools, Max says after a few weeks, are like prisons. They think they have to lock the children in.

Max sets off uncertainly in clothes of his own choosing and returns with tales of his six classmates, each bearers of at least two passports. Two embassy children, one Norwegian and one American. Two girls with Russian mothers and Icelandic fathers, girls who, Max recounts, take ages after swimming to put their make-up on and rearrange their hair. The daughter of a Filipina mother and a Polish father, and the son of a Finnish academic researching economic collapse. The builders are still finishing off the play equipment in the first week of term. There is nothing delineating 'school grounds', nothing to keep anyone in or out. Children play on the log climbing frames, swings and stepping-stones after school and at weekends just as during the school day. Adults use the basketball courts in the evenings. (I remember the CCTV cameras trained on the perimeter fence of Max's primary school at home.) That land, those facilities, belong to everyone. And because most children make their own way to and from school, there isn't exactly a moment of departure, nor a 'school gates' culture among parents. We learn about Max's classmates' families only via the gossip of seven-year-olds, at least until a sequence of birthday parties shows us all quite how foreign we are to each other. Only the British, it seems, do birthday cards. The Americans send out for pizza for the birthday tea. The Norwegian version of 'Happy Birthday' has more verses than the British national anthem, and the Icelanders at the International School do children's birthday presents on a scale I have not previously imagined (although we have an unrepresentative sample here: Garðabær-dwellers are regarded by the rest of the city as vulgar and nouveau riche, the footballers' Cheshire of Iceland, and within that group the International School hosts those whose families have spent time abroad or who plan to do so very soon – a discordant blend of academics, diplomats and 'entrepreneurs' with Russian connections). School-children's days seem largely disconnected from their parents' movements. They finish their lessons and move out to the playground, and after a while adjourn to the beach or the pool. No particular need to go home, for parents are still at work. The streets of suburbia belong to the children, who make perfectly sensible citizens.

Nevertheless, we have trouble letting Max go. What are you worried about, asks his new friend's Icelandic mother, when we want to escort Max and her son to the play-beach down the road. Traffic, we say, watching another driver go by steering with her knees because she needs both hands for texting. Water. Rocks. Abduction. Other children. Everything. That stuff doesn't happen here, she says. I don't know why but it just doesn't. Come on, I say, seven-year-olds fall off things everywhere, things like sea walls built up out of piles of concrete blocks and ending in shallow water and rocks. I don't believe Icelandic children just somehow have better balance. More practice, she says firmly. They learn to take responsibility for their own safety, which is pretty important with this climate in this landscape. Relax, you're in Iceland now. Honestly, there's no recorded case of a child being abducted here. You've seen how we leave babies in their prams in the street? Not one has ever been taken. Think about it, where would you go? Everyone knows everyone. They don't know me, I say, suddenly understanding why foreigners might be treated with suspicion. I could abduct a child. I know you, she says. Pétur knows you. Mads and Mæja know you. And we know lots of other people. We'd notice if you suddenly disappeared, and where would you disappear to? You haven't even got a car, and if you did, do you think the people at village petrol stations don't notice strangers coming through? It's not possible, not in Iceland.

We try letting Max go to the beach a few times and she is right, nothing bad happens, or at least, nothing bad happens outside our heads, where things are pretty terrifying. The pavements outside the cafés and designer boutiques of the city centre, we remind each other, are indeed lined with prams, each containing a sleeping infant inside layers of quilts and waterproof covers. Then there are a few stormy days when Max doesn't want to go out anyway, and by the time the wind dies down we are back in our right minds. No, we say. Because however often we might decide that our better judgements are based on foreign foolishness in relation to parking or fruit-eating or assessment methods for postgraduate work, your safety is more important than cultural relativism. No. And I hear in my voice an echo I haven't heard before, the echo of thousands of immigrant parents raising kids in a society they don't fully understand or inhabit. I don't care how things work here; I know what's right and you'll do what I say because I love you. Max goes along with it, for now, for the cold months when he doesn't much want to be out there anyway, but he has tasted freedom, understood that it is cultural preference rather than a fact of life that says he can't go out alone. His parents are fallible, their law a matter of cultural relativity.

Finding a nursery for Tobias is harder. At first we thought we wouldn't need one, since Anthony intends to stay at home with the children until Tobias starts school. In Canterbury, Anthony and Tobias had a weekly round of Drama Tots, Monkey Music, playgroup and swimming. Once we'd worked out where these sorts of activities took place in Reykjavík, we thought, Anthony and Tobias would start to make friends. We ask around, try the Intercultural House, which is there to support recent immigrants, and the local council, check the leisure centres for adverts. There is nothing. You need to sign him up for playschool, the nice woman in the council office explains. It's important. All children go. Look, he has priority because he comes from a non-Icelandic speaking home. She looks over her shiny wooden desk at the mud-spattered pushchair and our wet coats. It's highly subsidised. You don't pay much.

We go home and think about it, but there isn't much to think about. Tobias can't spend all day, every day, alone with Anthony in the flat, playing with his shoebox of toys and reading a couple of dozen books. We go down the road to see the nursery by the play-beach, warmly recommended by Matthew's friend's cousin, Hulda Kristín's neighbour and Pétur's daughter's colleague. It is newly built, clean, with exposed brick walls and pale lino floors. The rooms radiate around a central atrium, which has a low wooden stage and big crash-mats for bouncing. The head, a fluent English speaker, shows us round. Small blonde children gather around low tables, concentrating on the movements of water and sand. Some are outside, where hills to run up and roll down have been built in a small field. There is a vegetable patch, and a cook who uses only fresh ingredients. We ask the usual questions, feeling competent in nursery selection after Max's pre-school years, and are told about low staff turnover, simple rules calmly enforced, naps and toilet training to individual requirements. We ask why there are no books, and why the walls are bare. Because we are a Hjallastefnan establishment, she says. Did you not know? It is very popular here in Iceland.

It is why the children have this uniform. We notice, now, that the children are all in navy tracksuits with a logo on the front. And it's hard to be sure among two-year-olds in navy tracksuits, but all of the ones in the room we can see look like boys.

Yes, says the head. We have separate rooms for girls and boys, because that way they have a place where they are not always defined by gender. We have simple toys to give them space to be creative, a space away from all the Disney and advertising and pink for girls and guns for boys. They wear uniform so they don't think about clothing, so the differences are only in character. It is very popular here. You should read about it.

We wander around a bit more and then go home. Well, we say, he has books at home, after all. He doesn't know he's a boy, so maybe he won't notice the separation from girls. It's just down the road. It's only part-time. The anti-capitalist bit sounds good. And what really matters is that the staff are lovely and the children seem happy. I check with colleagues in the coffee room at work, who assure me that the absence of books is in no way sinister, that it's not the Nordic way to offer books to the very young. That comes later, the professor of French tells me. We almost think children should be protected from reading until they are six. It's the time to be outside and to play together and to learn these hard things about friends and enemies and sharing and fighting. Pens and paper come later. I remember Max's nursery encouraging the children to 'learn their letters' at three, ready for the Foundation Stage, even though none of the staff thought it was particularly useful. Would England be a better place if we insisted that people learn the hard things about sharing and fighting before

teaching them to read? All the Nordic countries have more lit-
erate and better-educated populations than the UK, and most
of them appear to be better at distributing resources and not
fighting. Maybe it is a better way, we think. Maybe Tobias will
learn to be Nordic and calm and good at sharing.

I can think of little to say in our defence. Tobias lasts three
weeks. Anthony goes with him; parents are encouraged to
stay until children are happy to be left, which in our case
doesn't happen. The children don't actually do very much,
Anthony reports. They spend half an hour watching their
teacher cutting up fruit. The teacher sings but the boys don't
join in. The boys have to move around in crocodiles, each toddler with a hand on the shoulder of the child in front, to teach
them conformity and group identity. The staff are nice, but it
feels weird.

I find the English section of the Hjalli website, which I
should have done weeks earlier. Hjallastefnan is a movement
established by Margrét Pála Ólafsdóttir, an Icelandic nursery
teacher who began to develop what she describes as 'rather
unusual pedagogical methods' when she became director of a
pre-school in Hafnarfjörður in 1989, and is now the director
of a private company running eleven nursery schools and three
primary schools in and around Reykjavík. Ólafsdóttir writes
that,

In Iceland, as in other parts of the world, little girls are
brought up 'nicely'. They are dressed in pink and cuddled
lovingly in the first months of their lives. Their future is
clearly laid out; they start their public life in a mixed sex
nursery school or kindergarten where they learn that girls
are entitled to no more than a quarter of the teacher's

attention and guidance. They learn to take a minimum amount of space and stay mainly in the corners of their classrooms and playground. They learn to be modest, 'nice and gentle,' waiting patiently and quietly for their turn. They are trained to develop a victim's attitude toward themselves, in which they are passive in dealing with their surroundings. This training is necessary for what is awaiting them; minimal participation in a male dominated society in which women go on waiting patiently for the recognition that they exist. (http://www.hjalli.is/information)

Little boys, by contrast, are made of slugs and snails and puppy-dogs' tails, and can't wait to get their jackboots on and start kicking people:

Little boys have another fate. They are bounced around energetically from the first moment of their lives. They are strongly encouraged to get up on their feet and to grab at whatever comes to them. They do not spend long in the arms of any adult because that is suitable only for those who must become victims. Just like the girls, the future of the boys is carefully planned from the very beginning. They walk into their public life when the school door opens and where the action awaits them. They do not have to wait for attention and guidance because they get it without having to ask. They are not afraid to occupy space and take the playgrounds over (with their fists if they have to). They are the future directors and governors of the society.

The solution to this problem is to separate boys and girls from infancy so that 'we can give our full energy and attention to encouraging the girls to become active and assertive and to teaching the boys to become sensitive and non-aggressive.' The children have no toys or books because,

> we make a point of being able to take care of our own things; the teachers and the children make the clay and chalk we need, we write and draw our own books and write our own plays to show to the other children in the next department. We take care of the garden and repair broken things. We are self-supporting people.
>
> We do not use normal toys. For the sake of the children's imagination and creativity we refuse junk just as we abolish all things and methods that cannot help us to reach the goals. We do not have one jigsaw or one pearl. [I think she means 'bead'.] Instead, we have unstructured material, such as everlasting wooden blocks, sand, water and the tables and chairs. This choice of resources also helps to create more calmness because the temptation of the garish toy 'fix,' or the fighting and competition to get the best piece is nowhere to be found.

Three weeks, I'm sure, did no harm beyond delaying the beginning of Tobias's integration into his Icelandic world. Anthony didn't leave him there alone for more than an hour or so, surely not long enough for a two-year-old to learn that because he has a penis he is violent and aggressive, or that people with vaginas are victims who need to be trained to get angry. Not long enough for him to think that books are the tools of the enemy or that conflict must be avoided at any price. We were stupid. We assumed that because this is Iceland, the gender politics would be intelligent, and we didn't see that what's posing as feminism is just another way of saying that girls can't cope and boys are violent. I am sure that these are errors we wouldn't have made at home. We are so careful to be good foreigners, to suspend judgement, to believe that our views are culturally specific and therefore irrelevant, that we betray ourselves. And our children.

I phone the nice woman at the council and explain that things aren't working with us and Hjallastefnan. Can she suggest an alternative? Oh, she says, but this method is very popular in Iceland, very popular indeed. Especially with writers and teachers like yourself. I know, I say, I'm sorry, it must be a cultural difference. Is there anything else, anything a little more – well, mainstream? Well, she says doubtfully, there is the state nursery at Lundaból, but it's a long way for you to take him every day when you have no car.

It is about a mile, a pleasant enough walk through sleeping suburbia. There are gardens consisting of grass, rocks and rowan trees behind white picket fences. You can peer in through 1970s windows to see shiny wooden floors and tidy kitchens, and sometimes a dog barks. The nursery is on a slope from which you can see across the houses and over the top of IKEA to the mountains. There is a metal gate with a latch out of reach of toddlers, and then a tarmac playground with a spider's-web climbing frame, surely the same model as in my local park in the early 1980s, and certainly of a kind long uprooted in England on health and safety grounds. There are swings, not baby swings with holes for the legs and a frame to hang onto but big swings of the sort that at home are considered unsuitable for the under-fives. The yard is busy with children pedalling tricycles up a concrete slope and free-wheeling down, and the tricycles have platforms on the back so that one child can stand and hang onto the shoulders of the one peddling. No helmets. No knee-pads. There is a flight of concrete stairs off to the side of the slope. Anthony and I exchange glances and go round to the porch, where we knock a few times, wait, peer through a window, knock again.

You should have just come in, explains the teacher who eventually comes, conducting us past an electrician who is being watched by a group of four-year-olds as he works on the fire alarm. No signing-in book, nothing to stop people with samurai swords or guns coming in and taking the toddlers hostage, or indeed taking one away. When we lived in Oxford, I explain, the nursery had a video-entry system and two doors and the outer door was always answered by two members of staff together. Yes, she says. We hear that these things happen abroad. And now here is Katrin.

Katrin is the head, and she shows us around. Each room has areas for drawing and painting, for messy play, for playing with model farms and zoos and dolls' houses, for building train track and Lego. They have singing every day, and a dance teacher comes once a week. The children spend at least two hours a day outside, no matter what the weather, so they must have proper winter clothes. The food is Icelandic, traditional Icelandic, no pizza or pasta or any of that, they eat far too much of that at home. Independence is important and children are expected to fasten and unfasten their own snowsuits, gloves, hats and scarves. (In the event, we discover, the children help each other, four-year-olds doing the zips for three-year-olds and three-year-olds putting two-year-olds' boots the right way round.) All the other children attend 8 a.m. to 5 p.m., five days a week, but if we want a different arrangement that is certainly possible. And here is Herdis,

who would be Tobias's keyworker. She's Icelandic and has just
returned from a year studying child development in Germany
with her own young son, so she knows about being a temporary foreigner. This is Tobias, I say, because that is what it says
on his birth certificate, and although we've called him Tolly
from birth we'd always agreed he'd be Tobias when he went to
school. No, I'm Tolly, he says. Tolli is an Icelandic name, Herdis
tells him. That's me, he says, Tolli. Having re-named himself an
Icelander, our son sits down with Herdis and the toy farm
and doesn't want to leave. It doesn't take him long to learn to
climb the spider's web and sit crowing on the top, higher than
I can reach, or to learn to ride one of those tricycles, or to ask
Herdis in Icelandic to push him 'as high as the sky' on a swing.
After the first couple of weeks, he begins to use Icelandic
words at home. I try to reply in Icelandic, to help him name
his bath, his cup, his book, but his pronunciation is better than
mine, and three weeks later he stops speaking Icelandic at
home and stops speaking English at nursery. By Christmas, he
is bilingual, and sounds like an Icelandic child speaking
Icelandic, getting the grammar and syntax right. I try not to
ask him, my three-year-old, to translate for me at the pool and
shops when I'm embarrassed by my own linguistic inadequacy.
He comes to terms with Icelandic food, and when Anthony
tries to collect him after lunch, according to our special
arrangement, he howls in protest. He wants to stay for *kaf-
fitími*, coffee-time. We extend his hours, but not much, not to
Icelandic levels, because we still know best.

By the end of August, term is about to start for me too. I
think you could feel the seasons turning in a university without knowing anything at all about students or teachers or the

rhythms of the academic year. There's a stirring of the air, a fluttering of pages, a sense of something beginning to seep along the corridors and lap at office doors. I've spent afternoons in the National Library without seeing anyone but a soft-footed librarian, but now there are murmured conversations somewhere on the other side of the modern languages section, a mobile phone ringing, doors swinging, and, once, fresh bloody handprints on the door at the top of the stairs. (In England I would, I think, have called over a librarian if not actually the police. Here, I assume someone had a nosebleed or a menstrual disaster and hope the cleaners will be along soon; I am not thinking like a citizen.)

The university had planned to demolish the building that houses the Faculty of Foreign Languages, because it's old and single-glazed and you have to use your hands to open the doors, because it's un-Icelandic. All state building programmes are now suspended, and we will have to make do with what we've got. I taught for several years at a mid-ranking English university in a Portakabin erected as a temporary measure in the 1970s, which, thirty years later, had not only a rotten floor and leaky roof but pigeons and the occasional squirrel in residence, and I can see nothing wrong with Nýi Garður. There are four floors, each with a bathroom at each end – for both men and women, which I find unreasonably disconcerting, as if it's worse to be heard peeing or seen putting on mascara by male colleagues – and offices off long corridors. It's warm and smells faintly of floor polish and clean clothes, and my office is across the corridor from Pétur, next door to Matthew and two down from Hulda Kristín. I feel buttressed there, surrounded by friends and people who know where I'm coming from. It's the only place in the country where I

feel entitled to be. None the less, I leave my office plain, its
lino floor and white walls echoing at each other. I bring in a
shelf of books, only what I need to teach, because I need the
others to help us feel at home in the Big Flat (named by the
children to distinguish it from the hotel room where we spent
the first days in Iceland). Then I sit there and do my job, in a
white box that looks out onto a wall, where on bright days I
watch the shadow of my own building creep up and then down
the other building. Other offices along this corridor are thor-
oughly inhabited, with oak desks, velvet sofas, indoor trees, oil
paintings, for these jobs are for life. British academics are a
mobile bunch, tending to move hundreds of miles with every
promotion, and most departments include several people who
commute from the other end of the country, or even from
another country, because their families have refused to move
again or because their partner specialises in a kind of medieval
history or neuroscience that happens at only one institution.
People's offices usually have a few boxes in the corner, full of
things that never got unpacked or that are awaiting the next
move. It's not surprising to see a suitcase under the desk.
There is no sense of this provisional, conditional way of living
at Háskóli Íslands, no flicker of sideways glances at other institutions offering other jobs that might be nearer home or have
a better library or saner colleagues. There is the University of
Iceland, and, unless you work in Business Studies or
Computing in which case there is the private University of
Reykjavík, that is The University. All the MPs went there, all
the lawyers (by definition, for where else would you read
Icelandic law?), almost all the doctors and social workers and
teachers. They all know each other. Until recently, doctors
were required to complete their clinical studies abroad, partly

because Iceland's population isn't big enough to provide suffi-
cient teaching cases of unusual illnesses, traumas and
complications, and until recently Háskóli Íslands offered doc-
toral degrees only in Icelandic Language, Literature and
History, but now you can go from kindergarten to professori-
ate without leaving Reykjavík 101. Some people don't think
this is a good idea: I'm beginning to recognise the usual
Icelandic tension between independence and insularity.

As teaching approaches, I wake earlier, take longer to go to
sleep, need to extend my evening walks out beyond the Álftanes peninsula before the chatter in my brain goes quiet and
I can see the wind on the water and the city lights over the bay
without having to hold back a curtain of egotistical anxiety.
My usual late-summer nightmares start up again, a month
earlier than usual. I dream, annually, that all educational qualifications lapse after ten years and that I therefore need to
retake every exam. I scramble for GCSE Latin, Biology,
Religious Studies, for my lost A-level surefootedness around
the treaties that ended the War of the Spanish Succession, for
the French pluperfect subjunctive, for undergraduate Anglo-
Saxon and the point of *The Faerie Queene*. I rediscover every
September that I have forgotten my education, just as I am
supposed to begin again to pass it on. But this time it's worse;
not only do I not know exactly what was changed by the Act
of Union or the Corn Law Reform but nor do I know whether
I am supposed to take a register, if the students are expecting
lectures or seminars, or indeed how to find the lecture hall.

The university, like most, has older and newer buildings,
but here they are linked by a web of surface and underground
corridors that I never come to understand. There is no campus
map, a state of affairs that begins to feel typically Icelandic: if

you already know your way around, you don't need one, and if you don't know your way around, you shouldn't be there anyway. Sometimes Matthew is in his office next to mine, happy to explain the coding on the timetable by which 'A' can mean one of three buildings, two located at opposite ends of the main campus and the other on the far side of town, but on my first day of teaching he's not there. I set off for class, which cannot be more than two hundred metres away, half an hour early. I rule out the first two buildings I try, which turn out, after I've climbed three flights of stairs and walked five corridors, not to contain enough storeys or rooms to make sense of the room number. I still have fifteen minutes. I hope the students' English is good enough to follow the material I'm planning to discuss. I hope my corduroy skirt and cotton jersey top are not unusual wear for a university lecturer here. I hope I haven't smudged my mascara. I work my way back to a corridor I've traversed before, and glimpse the building third on my list of possibilities, but now I can't get out. The door I want doesn't open when I walk up to it, and there is white writing on a green sticker across it that almost certainly means 'emergency exit' but has extra words as well, probably warning that alarms will sound, alerting the whole institution to my foreign-ness and incompetence, if I take matters into my own hands and push on the door handle. I go back down the corridor. Doors slide. There are people going along but no-one else trying to get out, although there are several of these green-stickered doors. I go the other way but there is no way out towards the building where I think forty-five students may be waiting to hear my thoughts about English Romantic poetry. I go back, round, out through the student cafeteria, but I can't see the building. I traverse a car park, late now, the wind whipping my hair over my head, rain hurling itself over my glasses, up a flight of concrete stairs. The hour has struck and there are fewer people moving around. I approach a door that does not open and has no green sticker and, thinking that I have a whole car park into which to run if alarms sound, haul it open. Someone behind me coughs and presses a button in the wall that causes the door to glide towards me. The rooms on the ground floor have the right letter code but the numbers are too high. There must be a lower floor. I hurry along the corridor, my heels tapping an authority I lost at Gatwick. Most of the doors are labelled with someone's name and a job title that might be 'janitor' or 'vice-chancellor.' There must be stairs somewhere. I rush to the other end of the corridor, ten minutes late now. No stairs. Someone's door is open and I tap and put my head around, I'm very sorry I don't speak Icelandic, but where is room 49, please? Downstairs, she says. Yes, but where are the stairs? She looks at me as if I have asked where the sky is. At the end of the corridor, of course. Which end, I want to ask, but I don't dare. I run back to the other end and find that the penultimate door bears a small label in the same font as people's names and job titles, '*stigahús*'. *Stiga* could mean stairs, I think, and I'm fairly sure it's not the Gents or the president's office, so I open it cautiously, and there are the stairs, and at the bottom of the stairs, along the corridor on the left – though with the cars being on the wrong side of the road even my sense of left and right has become less reliable than usual – is room 49. I try to smooth my hair, wipe my forehead on the back of my hand, and go in. Here, at least, anthology in hand, I know what I'm doing.

And so, it turns out, do the students. Class sizes are at least twice as big as I'm used to, and my groups of around forty are

smaller than my colleagues'. But the students are incontro-
vertibly adult in a way that British undergraduates en masse
are not. Anyone who has finished high school has the right to
attend Háskóli Íslands, and there are state loans available for
subsistence and no fees to pay, so with rising unemployment
there are several reasons to go to university and no reasons not
to do so. The result is an unprecedented number of students
with no increase in university staff, and English is a popular
choice because it seems easy to people who have grown up
watching American television, reading British and American
magazines and listening to British and American as well as
Icelandic music. Many of the students plan to become English
teachers. Some see an English degree as a way out of Iceland,
and a few love English literature. The shortage of staff means
that we have to merge third-year and postgraduate classes and
that group sizes are rising to the point where a classroom discussion is becoming impossible. At home, there would be
outrage and despair. Here, we go to staff meetings where
people knit and agree that the situation is unsustainable, that
none of the possible ways forward is satisfactory and that
something – admissions criteria, budget allocation, contact
hours – will have to change. Then they shrug and go back to
work, teaching groups of forty and up without handouts,
which we can't afford to print, or scholarly texts, which we
can't afford to buy. There's always the internet. *Þetta reddast*,
everyone always says at the end. It will sort itself out somehow.

After a few of these meetings, I talk to Matthew. I'm torn
between admiration for my colleagues' sangfroid and horror at
the conditions they seem willing to accept. How can the students learn without discussion, I demand. How can we teach

75

them to engage in critical debate when the most recent books in the library were bought in the 1970s? How can we teach them to write when there is no time to read their writing? He shrugs. I know, he says. I know it seems impossible but we get by. *Þetta reddast*. Calm down. Do your best. At least you don't have to fill in any forms.

He's right. My Icelandic working life is almost entirely unregulated. If I want to offer a new course at home, I have to fill in forms specifying learning outcomes, teaching methods, implications for resources, contact hours and primary and secondary reading lists. I am bound to follow these specifications in the classroom. I must take registers and upload the data onto the system. I must set essays of the approved length, getting the titles approved by the external examiner before issuing them to the students, and return these essays at the approved time, having provided written feedback that fills the approved space. I must give grades in accordance with the official marking criteria, and these grades' conformity to the criteria must be confirmed by a colleague. I must report concerns about students' health and welfare to the Student Support Officer. I must fill in forms detailing how I divide my time between teaching, research and administration. Older colleagues at home find these systems insulting and burdensome, and complain of over-regulation and a culture of infantilisation and distrust. Most of it seems more or less reasonable to me, but I do believe that I would continue to do my job to the best of my ability without surveillance. I'm looking forward to a year of free practice, teaching what I consider important and setting the work I think useful without needing to report and justify myself at every turn.

*

The students are older than at home, and, if only in matters of style, more diverse. In England, there is a de facto uniform for undergraduates which changes every couple of years. When I left, I was usually the only woman in the room not wearing tight jeans with flat sheepskin boots. Here, there are people older than me dressed as if for a day at the office, women my age in skirts and sweaters, younger people in younger clothes. While I'm waiting for the students to read a passage, I look at the feet under the desks, and feel cheerfulness rising at the sight of hiking boots, high heels, brogues and Mary Janes. Icelanders leave high school at twenty, and so without interruptions to their education would be in their mid-twenties by the time they reach my combined third-year/MA classes, but most of the women have had interruptions. Icelanders have children much younger than Europeans and North Americans. It's normal, the students assure me, when they ask about cultural differences and I tell them that students at home are rarely parents. We don't understand why you'd wait until your thirties when you're interrupting your career and the pregnancy's more likely to be complicated and you must get more tired, they say. It just makes more sense to start in your twenties and then make a career. There are so many assumptions built into this comparison that I don't know where to start. I explain about the cost of British childcare, and about employers' discrimination against mothers, and about the expectation that women will spend years at home with the children. There are no stay-at-home mothers in Iceland, which is why there are no toddler groups. Everyone takes nine months' parental leave, divided between the father and mother, and then there is forty hours a week of highly subsidised, high-quality childcare, and since no-one commutes this is enough for parents to

work full-time. Students can have babies without undue financial hardship. There is no particular expectation that the
person with whom you have babies in your twenties will be
the person with whom you live in your thirties, the students
explain, no stigma around the separation of parents or the
mutability of love. Gender discrimination, it seems to me at
the beginning, is simply not an issue in Iceland. I have a year's
holiday from the guilt that blights the lives of working mothers at home.

So many in the class assembled to learn about English
Romantic Poetry are parents, and it does make a difference. A
great deal of Wordsworth's early poetry is about children, and
for the first time I am not the only parent reading it. Mothers,
I find, have less patience with Keats. Older women are more
likely to notice Austen's deep scepticism about marriage, less
likely to insist on reading her as a romantic novelist. Everyone
who turns up in class does all the reading, and those who
don't turn up are no concern of mine. There is no register.
Icelandic students attend class or not, as they see fit, and in fact
in the absence of regulations are much more careful about
sending apologies than students at home whose attendance is
monitored and recorded, and who can expect threatening e-
mails and summonses if they miss too many sessions. Icelandic
students do not seem to confide personal problems to academic staff, although as the weeks pass I begin to think that it
is not an Icelandic habit to confide personal problems to
anyone. University lecturers are in no way *in loco parentis*, and
freed of my institutional obligation to be police-officer,
mummy and teacher in one handy package, I find myself more
interested in the students' lives. For me and for them, it seems
at the beginning, lack of regulation coincides with greater

personal responsibility. Maybe, I think, this is how Iceland works, and the abominable driving and indeed the economic crisis are the dark side of an unfamiliar but sometimes functional approach to rules and responsibilities. The children at Tobias's nursery, unfettered by what would be basic safety precautions at home, are not smashed on the concrete but confident and independent in their own estimation of their limits. The students turn up well-prepared and open-minded. Nobody abducts six-year-olds making their own way to school. Playgrounds are not vandalised, teenage girls are not wolf-whistled, no-one fears mugging or car theft. Babies sleep in prams on the pavement while their parents try on clothes or sit over coffee with friends. I hear myself sounding much more right-wing than usual and remind myself that Iceland, even if it is not the classless society claimed by many Icelanders, has a far smaller gap between the rich and the poor than Britain, that low crime rates are usually associated with socio-economic equality, that there are complex reasons and a unique history behind Icelanders' differences from the rest of Europe. There is, I hypothesise, six weeks in, something more like social equality, more trust, and better behaviour, at least until people find themselves behind a wheel or running a bank.

By the end of September, the sunsets that have been inching back a few minutes every day have reached Max's bedtime, and most days it's not 'sunset' but a more familiar darkening of grey skies. It rains as much as at home. We're all wearing winter coats and I am beginning to be glad that school and nursery insisted that the children have proper Arctic winter clothing from the beginning of term. If you wait, Katrin told us, all the snowsuits will be sold, and don't expect the shops to import any more. Toddlers' winter clothing is seasonal and imported from Denmark, and no-one's going to risk importing anything they can't sell.

I'm still taking my evening walks along the shore, even on days when the rain on my glasses refracts the low-level lighting along the coast path so that the city lights across the water are jumbled and kaleidoscopic. Almost all the birds are gone now, and I rarely encounter another person. Icelanders, says Matthew, take to the gym in winter. Another colleague tells me that she and her husband bought good waterproof coats only when the *kreppa* forced them to sell their second car. As far as I can see, most people don't go outside at all in rain or wind. I understand why people prefer to be inside on a wet night, but I want to follow the year's cycle out here on the shore, feel the rain and wind as well as turning my face to the sun at midnight and standing shivering under the aurora. Even in the dark, the half-finished buildings stand black against the horizon, like shells of bombed churches.

5

Pétur's Saga

The first snow comes in early October. It doesn't exactly *fall*, because it's coming horizontally, borne on a wind so strong that I have to hold on to Max as we walk 300 metres down the street to school. Tobias, it seems, can't go out, since the wind would flatten him and neither of us can hold the pushchair against its force. Dodging down the sides of buildings, Anthony carries him to the bus stop to get to nursery, but we're beginning to see Icelandic car-dependency with more sympathy. We can't manage without one.

I wonder how people coped here before cars. The 'ring road', Route 1, which makes a circuit of the island, was finished only in 1974, and even when Kathy and I first came in 1994 there were people living in the countryside without cars, dependent on the daily bus (which has now been replaced by a summer-only tourist coach service at four times the price). I've been reading, with horror and fascination, an autobiographical novel that I found in the university library about life in the north of Iceland in the 1940s, just before wartime and post-war prosperity made Icelanders drift from the farms into sedentary, urban lives defined by earning and spending. Valgarður Egilsson's *Waiting for the South Wind* was published in 2001, although its nostalgia for the wartime years seems to speak from the last century. The book's relentless romanticism makes me want to move to Tokyo or New York and buy shares in oil companies, but it also suggests how much Iceland has changed:

> For generations these people had lived at the Stonechurch farm, strong men, peaceful Vikings, who instinctively knew how to carry out any kind of work, whether it was building a house or a boat, shoeing a horse, building a bridge or a church or a ship – or even dealing with polar bears.

While the 'strong men' are indulging their instincts in matters of bridge-building and polar bears, Mother cooks, cleans and washes for her husband and seven sons while singing opera over the mops and pans. The family live on blood porridge and *skyr* and thrive because 'in cold weather, all food tastes good out in the open air. It is only at twenty-seven degrees Celsius that people become connoisseurs or gourmets with regard to food. Here the temperature was seven to eight degrees Celsius.' Iceland, it should be noticed, does not reach twenty-seven degrees Celsius. Gourmets are foreign. The Stonechurch boys soon learn to ignore the cold as they go about the spring work of breaking ice with their bare hands so that sheep don't fall through it and yomping along the cliffs in a blizzard. The Fjorders are real men and real Icelanders:

> No authorities had ever visited the Fjords, the landscape protected the Fjorders from them, it was too steep, considering

outsiders were not surefooted. The Fjorders, on the other hand, obeyed only God and the song of the golden plover, as well as fate and earthly forces.

On their way across the Fjord Heath – treading paths between rocks and tussocks that were only two horse hooves wide – the Fjorders had to keep their ankle movements and reflexes in order, their muscles were striated and not atrophic, their blood was still red and streaming, their minds – and their brains – were unspoiled by money or any other pollution, their fertility was not spoiled by pollution either . . .

I think again, with gratitude, about our underfloor heating and almost-free gushing hot water, which seemed distastefully extravagant in August, about steaming Jacuzzis at the pool and the way I need to turn the radiator down and keep the window open at work even when there's a blizzard outside. I am glad that my brain is spoilt by money which means I have bought a down snowsuit for Tobias and thermal underwear all round. Most of all, I think, atrophying my muscles as I curl up on my IKEA garden chair with my laptop, I am glad not to have to eat *slátur*, blood pudding.

Our friend Guy plans to come to Reykjavík for a long weekend. He's a car-lover who, he assures us, would relish nothing more than a day spent negotiating the second-hand-car showrooms of Reykjavík. I am not entirely sure I believe him – my disinclination to engage with the tedious world of car-buying is one of the reasons we are still walking to Hafnarfjörður to buy tinned tomatoes – but I am so grateful for the suggestion that I react by planning a menu to compensate him for his day rather than questioning his willingness.

Guy comes to meet me at my office when I finish teaching, and we set off. Two buses, and the final kilometre on foot, along a dual carriageway through the industrial quarter. A blizzard has blown in from the sea, and we clutch each other as we bend into the wind that's pulling my coat away from my body and hurling chips of ice into our faces. I suggest to Guy that we might take something for a test drive in the first show-room we reach and then use it to get to the others. He eyes up a Porsche, I suggest borrowing one of a row of Volvo police-cars left with the keys in the ignitions along the edge of the forecourt. By the time we reach the showroom's office and discover that all you have to do to test-drive a car in Iceland is ask for the keys, we can't make eye contact without giggling. We spend the afternoon driving around in a sequence of bor-rowed cars and nobody once asks for any proof of identity or signature, much less a driving licence. The combination of unfamiliar cars, the blizzard, the need to drive on the wrong side of the road and fear of Icelandic drivers makes me lose my nerve entirely and Guy does all the driving, with the aplomb of someone who learnt to drive in Texas and now insists on driving across central London every day. You will, he warns me, need to come to terms with this. I'm back at work on Tuesday, I can't stay and be your chauffeur. I know, I say, I know. But not yet.

Late in the afternoon, when it's been dark for a while and I've given up trying to keep my feet and trousers dry, we find a Volvo. I've never driven an automatic before and am alarmed by the prospect, but the car is of recent manufacture, cheap, in good condition, with a full service history and winter and summer tyres. It will drink fuel, Guy says, but it's the only one within your budget in which I'd happily take children on the

road round here. We take it to an empty car park and I get
behind the wheel. Yes, I say, it's fine, I can reach the pedals and
see out of the windscreen; it's comfortable. Start the engine,
says Guy. Go on. I drive it about twenty metres, stop, and
make Guy take it back. Yes, we say, we'll take this one, please.
And less than an hour later, having signed two forms, we
drive – Guy drives – back to the Big Flat. Insurance is sorted
in one phone call, tax arranged as part of the purchase. Still
no-one has asked to see that I have a driving licence. By the
time Guy leaves, three days later, I have driven across
Reykjavík and back, white-knuckled and swearing. The following weekend, we drive to Pétur's house. Pétur comes out
to see our new purchase and I set off stylishly, waving, on the
wrong side of the road. I've been driving for fifteen years in
England, I am fine on the M25 and around the mountain lanes
of the Peak District, can cope with ice and, as long as my
mother isn't watching, reverse-park with pride. But I'm infan-
tilised again by my foreign-ness here. It will take me weeks to
brave driving in the dark, even though dark is now most of the
time, and for the first half of the winter we will use the car to
stock up on food when the roads are clear and then walk and
cycle as long as there's snow and ice underfoot.

The greenhouse-grown Icelandic salads are over for the year
now. There is still fresh cabbage, but apart from that all the
vegetables are imported, expensive, and long past their best.
Fruit is waxy apples or squashy bananas, although a king's
ransom will buy you tasteless, mushy plums in Hagkaup. I
rub legs of lamb with smoked paprika and cumin from my
hoard, and roast potatoes with butter and shards of rosemary
picked in our garden at home. We have found good food in

Reykjavík. There's a French bakery on Laugavegur and a Vietnamese noodle bar just down the hill from Hallgrímskirkja and a sushi counter on the top floor of the bookshop that has American magazines. There are more formal restaurants that boast of tapas and pierogi and mole poblano, though the chilli tends to be dumbed down to toddler levels. There's a Thai grocer by the bus station and an English cheese shop near the zoo, and the rumour of a Polish bakery out in Hafnarfjörður. Mads has directed us to the treasured farm shop near Laugardalur, which has bacon from pigs reared outdoors and smoked trout and muddy potatoes, and in summer a cornucopia of greenhouse-grown Icelandic tomatoes. Mads and I exchange leads on lime leaves, poppy seeds and miso paste, like addicts following the rumour of a fresh supply. I've learnt how to cook here. That's not the problem. But it seems the coward's way out, expatriate arrogance, to strain every nerve to realise a simulacrum of what we'd eat at home, like Brits who move to France and then drive miles to buy cheddar. I will try to be more adventurous. As long as it doesn't involve blood pudding.

At the supermarket, I pick up a cellophane package of what I believe to be reindeer meat. Tobias is pulling on my arm, begging for vanilla *skyr* and sweet barley cakes. I cook venison often at home, but this is an unfamiliar cut, a slab of dense, dark muscle. It's only as I put it away at home that I read the label properly. *Hvalur*, not *hreindyr*. Whale meat. No wonder it was cheap. What shall we do? I ask Anthony. Imagine what our friends at home would say if they knew we'd eaten whale. Whaling is one of the subjects that Brits in Iceland should be cautious about mentioning. (The others are the Cod War and Gordon Brown's use of anti-terrorist legislation to freeze

Icelandic assets as the banks went down in 2008.) When I discuss whaling with my students, most see it as a problem only
inasmuch as the practice might compromise Iceland's applica-
tion to join the EU. They don't understand why anyone who
eats meat and fish should have ideological anxieties about
catching whales, and point out that Iceland has a much better
track record on managing marine stocks than the EU does. I
argue that whales are intelligent mammals subject to a particularly brutal and long-drawn-out butchery. I wouldn't buy or
eat whale meat by choice, but since we have now paid for it, I
suggest to Anthony, it would be worse to throw it away than to
eat it. Let's eat it, then, he says. Max is always keen to try
something new, and hovers in the kitchen trying to decipher
the back of the packet. I think you're supposed to serve it with
potatoes and brown sauce, he says. I blench, put it in the
freezer and revert to cooking with tinned American chickpeas,
cod and smuggled chorizo. I still don't understand how
Icelanders survived Icelandic food before the great post-war
shift into the modern world.

I ask Mads, who says that of course many of them didn't and
many of those who did emigrated at the first opportunity, but
adds that no-one really knows how much Icelandic moss and
seaweed people were eating. I recall the almost complete
absence of vegetables from seventeenth- and eighteenth-
century English cookbooks; some food historians used to
think that this absence showed that people rich enough to buy
books didn't eat vegetables, but it now seems much more
likely that eating vegetables was so obvious that no-one bothered to write about it. Maybe people were somehow meeting
all their vitamin requirements from cabbage. I suggest this to
Matthew, who replies that when he first came, an elderly

couple asked him what he missed most from England. Salad, said Matthew, and fruit, and especially spinach. And broccoli. The old man looked him up and down. Sheep food, he said. In Iceland we leave the grass for animals. I ask Pétur, who first came to Iceland in the 1960s and lived on a remote farm, working as a cow-hand, what there was to eat.

'I had to get over my pickiness,' he says. When he came to the farm for the first time, he was twenty, he'd been travelling for days and he was hungry. But he arrived on a July afternoon when the farmer was expecting rain, and everyone was working hard to get the hay in before it got wet. He went straight into the fields, and stayed there, working, until late in the bright night, until the work was done and everyone could go up to the house for food and rest. And then, he says, 'the worst imaginable kind of food I could ever think of was put on the table, steaming salted fish with a terrifying smell to it, and hot sheep fat, and potatoes. That's all there was. And I knew I was going to be there for six weeks, and I would have to eat it or starve. I told myself, you wanted to come to Iceland, you wanted to find out what it's like here, you bloody well eat their food, and I forced myself to eat it. And it was delicious, absolutely glorious. It's one of my favourite dishes today.'

'Not with the sheep fat?' I ask.

Messíana is vegetarian. It's a wheat-free, sugar-free household, with soya milk and olive-oil spread in the fridge (though they will always buy in Coke and ice cream for the grandchildren, and Pétur makes fine buckwheat waffles on Sunday afternoons, served with lots of whipped cream and low-sugar French jam).

'Oh yes, it's glorious. I could have had butter, the younger kids were having butter, but I thought I'd try the sheep fat. In the old days people used cod liver oil on the salt fish. I tried that and it was quite palatable, not half as bad as you'd expect. The sheep fat would be hotter than boiling point, so hot you'd pour it over and it would crackle, and there'd be little bits of suet in it, brown and crunchy.'

Rick Stein, I remind myself, cooks chips in beef dripping. I still don't want to think about suet.

'Presumably there was no fruit and very few vegetables?'

'That was exactly the situation.'

'Then why didn't people get ill?'

'Because we ate a lot of fish,' he says firmly. 'And Iceland moss, swede, and white cabbage. A lot of white cabbage. It was the fish, though, I think. And of course a lot of milk, and *skyr*, there are a lot of nutrients in *skyr*.'

'*Skyr* contains protein,' I point out. 'But it doesn't solve the vitamin C problem.'

'Well, it is a bit of a conundrum, why they didn't all get scurvy. People drank a lot of Iceland moss tea, and they were probably using many more grasses and herbs than is recorded. That knowledge has gone.'

'The people on the farm were widely read,' Pétur says. It mattered to his hosts to keep up with new developments in science and literature, and this matches both what I've learnt about Icelandic rural life and what I know about the Scottish islands and the Faroes. Mid-century farmers were not ignorant about nutrition and Pétur remembers discussion of vitamins; the old people bought and ate whale-fat ('it tastes good,' he adds, teasing me, 'nice and sour'), but the children didn't eat it. There were three girls, twelve, eight and six when he arrived, still his friends fifty years later. 'They were absolute goddesses and they'd walk around the farm like goddesses and milk cows like goddesses, and they would come in and sit down at the table for tea like very hungry children. It would be glasses of milk and those round biscuits, *kex*, and that was what they ate. No fruit at all, and they all grew up fine.'

Be that as it may, I think, Pétur and Messíana take care of their own family's diet. The pile of marking on his desk is tall enough to suggest that he might be willing to be distracted from a Sisyphean task.

'What else was it like?' I ask. 'Was Iceland what you were expecting?'

He smiles at me, because we both know how hard it would be to expect Iceland if you hadn't seen it, if you had no basis for imagining lava fields and simmering earth. 'No,' he says, 'not at all.' Pétur came to Iceland to see a land without trees, because he'd grown up in the South Downs where the curves and bones of the land were always hidden by hedges and woods. He wanted to live with bareness, to inhabit a place without softness and blurring. But he hadn't imagined his own presence in this stripped landscape, his own exposure. In Iceland, you can see five times as far as in England, but you can also be seen for miles. Pétur had found a job on the farm in Borgarfjörður, out to the west, and he'd expected remoteness, isolation. He found that wherever he went, not only could he see six or seven farms, widely spaced but unsheltered by any kind of vegetation, but he could be seen from those six or seven farms. It felt more densely populated than rural England, which in fact has a higher population density but more hiding places. 'I felt naked,' says Pétur. 'I felt completely exposed.'

He left at the end of that summer, back to Cambridge, to

return to Iceland after his degree with the intention of staying a long time, perhaps not forever but at least until he felt ready to leave. That next autumn was a time of disappointment. During the summer, there had been no need for artificial light in Borgarfjörður, so when darkness fell in September and the lights at all the farms in the valley came on, it was a shock. Everyone knew when everyone else rose and slept, went out and came in. He came for emptiness and absence and found more presences than in an English city.

And then as winter drew on, the community stopped seeming like an insult to the landscape. ' I would wake up in the morning in heavy frost, completely still weather. I'd go out into the courtyard, onto the front steps, and you could hear — over the river, two miles away — you could hear somebody coming out of their house over there, and you could hear someone talking to someone back in the house. You couldn't hear what they were saying, but you could hear the talking. And it was lovely. A very intense community but also a very distant community because you didn't see people so much, you just had contact with them. The old farmer used to tell me that he would go down to the river and shout across, and the guy on the other side would be giving him news, and they would be exchanging the news between the two *sveitir*, the two parishes, and they had news from further afield, and the news would be shouted across the river, and of course it was a noisy river so you really had to shout. There were distances between people but you were always in contact with the nearest farms, there was always a jeep standing outside from the next farm and somebody drinking coffee. And when the milk lorry came it would give you three books for that week, and you'd give him the three books that he gave you last week, from the library, and he'd take those to the next farm, so there'd be a continual march of books around the *sveit* with the milk lorry. And my farmer told me to read the books, he said read this and read that, and I did it because I was told to.'

And that, says Pétur, is how he learnt Icelandic, from the farmer's reading list and from the farmers in Borgarfjörður, and also how he learnt Icelandic manners. Iceland was not, as it first appeared, a simpler place than England. Iceland has complexities so subtle that their existence is invisible to an inattentive foreigner. One of the Icelandic clichés about Icelanders is that, by foreign standards (as if 'foreigners' had one standard), they are rude. There is no word for 'please' in Icelandic. 'Thank you' and 'sorry' are used much less than in British and American English. Nevertheless, it has been clear to me from the beginning that Iceland is a place where the most intricate and important things are unarticulated, partly because intricacy doesn't need to be spelt out in a place where everyone has always known how things are done, and partly because it is unIcelandic to explain yourself. Self-explanation suggests some entitlement on the part of your audience to know your interior life. Icelandic drivers don't indicate, Pétur once told me, because they don't see why anyone else needs to know where they're going.

'Though people were very shy of the fact that they were on a more primitive level of civilisation than they thought I was,' Pétur says, following my thoughts.

They still are. It's one of those contradictions in Icelanders' collective ideas about foreigners; Icelanders want to be seen as tough, as people who take no nonsense, with centuries' experience of going without (without salad, fruit, waterproof shoes, paved roads, trees, Father Christmas and all the other luxuries pertaining to effete foreigners). But at the same time, there's a need to prove that Iceland can have anything it wants, that Icelanders know what to do with salad and pizza dough and Christmas trees just as much as anyone else. More than anyone else. It's typical, I find, generalising as I am generalised, for Icelanders simultaneously to despise foreigners' judgement and to go in fear of being found inferior.

'And were they on a more primitive level?' I ask. It seems probable that Icelandic farms in the 1960s were at least technologically behind suburban Sussex. There's a plane taking off outside the window, and a skein of geese going the other way. It's one of those Icelandic mysteries, that having a runway beside a wetland nature reserve seems to be unproblematic.

'Well, in some respects, yes. Table manners, for example. I'd just come from Cambridge, where you use the right fork, and you tilt the spoon to get your soup, and no-one knew about any of that in Iceland. I remember watching them putting soup spoons in their mouths and thinking, why do they do it like that? And then one day I thought, because it's not as stupid as the way I do it. And none of this please and thank you. Pass the salt, and here comes the salt. It was unnerving, but of course there were things I wasn't doing correctly. I found it very hard to stand up at the end of the meal and say *takk fyrir matinn*, the same way I couldn't say *takk fyrir mig* when I left.'

Takk fyrir mig means literally 'thank you for me', which is what Pétur's ten-year-old granddaughter says in English with startling grace when she has been round for tea. I, too, know these phrases but feel horribly awkward about using them. The artificiality of another culture's set phrases is painful where my own, similarly rehearsed, praise for the cook and requests to be 'excused' for reaching across the table, are entirely natural. It's just so false, says one of my students, all this thanking people and apologising all the time when there's nothing to be grateful or sorry about. It's like Americans telling you to have a nice day when they've never even met you and they really don't give a damn about your day.

'There were manners of course, but the manners were sometimes not to say anything. So I'd say, "Excuse me, but please would you pass the potatoes." They'd pass them and I'd say, "Thank you." And they'd look at me, because you don't say thank you when someone gives you a potato. That's why you're there, and why the potatoes are there, so you can eat them, and you know that and they know that you know that so why would you say thank you? There's not very much of that kind of thing in Icelandic, it's at a lower level in the same way that the flowers in the fields and the trees on the hills are at a lower level. They're smaller and more subtle and they make more sense.'

The flowers and trees are smaller than at home because they grow more slowly so far north, because it's harder to live here in the cold and dark.

'So there were often guests?' I ask. 'As well as all the networks, the milk lorry and shouting over the river?'

'There were,' he says. 'But the networks were often where you found out what mattered. The phone was very important. There was one line between farms – it only changed about twenty years ago – so there was a code for each house, one long ring and two short, or whatever, and when it rang you'd pick up and hear click, click, click, all down the line, and this watery noise and you'd have to shout, "Put down the phone, everyone. I can't hear!" I was there during the winter, when the farmer's wife was having her fifth child, so they moved down to the village and I stayed alone up there with the old man and his wife. It was amazing; you milked the cows, you were out doing a lot of work during the day, and then in the evening you'd come in and read and write – I wrote so much during those weeks – and the first thing the old man would say when he came in and sat down at the table, he'd say to his wife, "So, what did you hear today?" Because she'd been at the phones, listening. And she'd always reply on the intake, "Nothing."'

Icelandic women – though not, as far as I know, men – do indeed speak on the in-breath. Tobias has picked it up from the staff at nursery. I find myself practising at moments of solitude, but I can't really do it. Not like an Icelander. It's a kind of feminine Icelandic woodwind technique.

'And we'd start eating and after a while she'd say, "Guðmundur was phoning Siggi." And then there'd be a pause and we'd eat some more and she'd say, "I couldn't hear all of it." It was a recognised way of keeping in touch; it meant everyone knew everything.'

'It sounds like Facebook,' I suggest.

'It was a little like Facebook. If you had no e-mail or phone and had to put everything on Facebook. The telephones were little box things on the wall with a handle on them, and a button you could press so that people couldn't hear you, and one farm had a little weight they used to put on the button, but at the next farm their button didn't work. They didn't know, so you always knew when she was there because you could hear her breathing heavily, but it was an accepted thing to listen to everyone, and it was a great backward step when the private telephones came in. They felt it.'

There were other 'backward steps into the future'. Pétur regrets the enormous, cast-iron solid-fuel stove that dominated 'old Johanna's' kitchen. The stove fuelled the boiler and had a tap for hot water as well as being the cooker, and it kept the kitchen warm through the hardest winters when it was too cold to sit anywhere else in the house. Everyone gathered around the stove, and then one of Johanna's sons sold it, gave her an electric cooker and installed a modern boiler so the family didn't sit together any more.

Johanna liked to talk. At first, Pétur struggled to follow her, but as the winter passed he understood more, and lingered in the kitchen for stories of her youth in the early twentieth century. She told him about the arrival of rubber boots in rural Iceland, when for the first time it was possible for people who spent their days working outside to keep their feet dry. The old people, she said, didn't like it, found dry feet uncomfortable and were sure it must be unhealthy. They used to pour water into their wellingtons before they went out. (Along the lines of a wet-suit, I muse; your feet would be wet but not, after a while, cold.) And she remembered the building of a road up the valley, the novelty of being able to walk all the way to the next farm without having to look at her feet. 'Before the roads were built,' Pétur says, 'there were very few places in Iceland where you could look around while you walked, or even run, because before they made big fields to be farmed by big machines you were always going over or around rocks, streams and ditches.'

'Or lava fields,' I add.

Lava fields seem impassable until you get used to them, a landscape like a rough sea, arrested in stone. You scramble up a wave of rock, and think you see a way through, and then climb down the other side and are lost again. Sometimes you can pick a path along the troughs of the waves, but rarely for more than a hundred metres and rarely in your intended direction. Something else occurs to me.

'I thought Icelandic women used to knit while they were walking?'

Pétur lifts his hands, as if any idiot can knit while crossing the lava. 'Well, you can do that, can't you? You don't have to watch your knitting.'

Icelandic knitting usually involves several colours, and therefore several balls of wool at once. I can imagine no way in which even someone who could normally combine knitting and walking could combine Icelandic knitting with crossing a lava field.

'Was everything still hand-knitted?' I ask. 'In the 1960s?'

'The old woman had her *rokkur*, her spinning wheel, and this magnificent German steel knitting-machine. But we did a lot of knitting. We'd all sit around and she'd run off the big pieces and we'd knit them together, or sew them together. She'd run off these mittens with two thumbs on them, one on each side, and the idea was that you'd use one side when the other side wore out, but of course you never had any idea which side you were using. But you'd always see people walking around with two thumbs on their hands. And socks, we'd darn socks a lot. The barn was full of old-fashioned things. There was a lot of braided horse-hair rope there, and the old equipment for throwing rope over hay and binding it onto a horse. The horses were still very important, although they weren't used much for work any more. They were used for herding the sheep. And the old man would sit out there every morning sharpening the saw, and he had a special pair of pliers for angling the teeth. He was brought up in the old days. When he'd finished his porridge, you couldn't see that the plate needed washing. Every time. And he had flu, we all got flu that winter, and he lay in bed with his bad flu. It was a blizzard outside, but he did all the work, he got up and did the work, and in between he'd lie in bed. And then he'd get up, go out, and go and stand in the snow and throw up, and come in and lie down again. And he'd do this three or four times a day, and he'd always go out to pee and so on.'

'Were there no toilets?' I ask, mildly horrified. I remember al fresco peeing from Kathy's and my camping trip and it was no fun even in summer, without blizzards.

'They had one. He wouldn't use it. They built a new house, which was as modern as the one I lived in with my parents in Sussex. But you could find farms all over the place where there was no bathroom, no lavatory, where people went out into the cowshed instead, places where people were living as they had done fifty years earlier, with mud floors and chickens wandering in and out of the kitchen. Even later, in sixty-eight, a friend took me up to the north to visit his parents there, and when we arrived we sat down and had a slap-up Sunday dinner. All families had the same Sunday meal: it was always a leg of lamb with brown potatoes and sauce and red cabbage, and the potatoes were sweetened with brown sugar, horrible.'

Pétur doesn't like sugar, for a range of sound ideological and physiological reasons. I do, because it's what gets me through the day, but even I don't like Icelandic caramelised potatoes. Or the sweetened mayonnaise that Icelanders put on salads, or the sweet brown paste labelled 'mustard'. Being in Iceland has given me my first opportunity to feel superior about sugar.

'But it was a beautiful meal, and I said thank you for the meal, and then I asked where the lavatory was. Everyone sort of looked into their plates and looked away – it wasn't a question I should have asked. And they were fairly modern.'

'How did you find out what you were meant to do?' I ask, fascinated.

'Jon took me out to the barn and showed me the cowshed. There were three or four cows on the farm, in a stone and turf building. They'd be bound in their stalls all winter, and there was this run that they'd shit in, and you'd do the same, why not? Or go out onto the *tún*. But you know there was a lot of doubt about running water in houses when it first came, lots of people didn't like that idea at all, thought it must be unhealthy.'

'So they just heated water on a stove? For washing?'

He grins. 'One of Messíana's friends once tried washing her hair in cow urine. That was the way they did it in the old days. Apparently hair looks beautiful if you wash it in cow urine.'

Messíana looks about sixty. 'When was that?'

'Oh, in the 1950s. Up on the farm we were still making our own soap in the late 1960s, boiling sheep fat down with caustic soda. And we made our own *svið*, singed sheep's heads, using the old forge. Torfi would have used it in the old days to make horseshoes, but we burnt sheep's heads in it.'

If you look into the meat section of an Icelandic supermarket, burnt sheep's heads will look back at you, milky eyeballs peering out of brown skulls. Apparently they come cut in half, so you don't have to saw through the skull at home. Max wants us to buy one. I am pretending I don't think Tobias has eaten sheep's brains at nursery. Icelanders regard *svið* as an easy week-night supper and my students are amused by my horror. You eat lambs' legs, they say, why not the head? They are right – I can see that it's moral as well as logical to eat the whole animal once you've killed it – but I'm still not going to touch one, much less take it home and scoop its brains out.

'We blew everything off with a blowtorch, and then we used a hot poker to get into the areas around the ears.'

I can't suppress a whimper.

'And I would go out every now and then into the outhouse, and take a new sheep's head and saw it in half and drag it back for us to eat. Torfi would recognise the sheep, and to us the meat was very good.'

'So people say.' I sound like Queen Victoria responding to a dirty joke.

He smiles.

'So you learnt to fit in.' I look at Pétur, whose shoulder-length curly grey hair is twisted and pinned with small barrettes, on whose bookshelves Derrida in French jostles Virgil in Latin and collections of medieval and modern Irish poetry. Most people look happy at the mention of his name, but I don't think anyone could say Pétur 'fitted in' in contemporary Reykjavík, and nor would he wish to. 'How long did it take for you to be accepted? As a foreigner?'

The farmers of the valley accepted him, he says, as he learnt Icelandic, and worked in the fields. Always as a foreigner, but they accepted him. Pétur and the farmers shared opposition to the American military presence in Iceland and to the Independence Party which was in power then and until the 'Pots and Pans Revolution' of 2009. They shared support for the co-operative movement. I am repeatedly surprised when the people who have known Pétur longest refer

to him by his English name and not the Icelandic patronymic
he embraced when he became an Icelandic citizen, as if they
are unable to recognise his Icelandic identity, but Pétur
knows that foreign-ness is permanent, and not necessarily a
disability.

Winter comes, though I don't feel as if we've had autumn. I'm
not sure you can have autumn without trees. In mid-October,
I buy a bicycle. I tried all summer to find a second-hand one,
but even with Hulda Kristín and Matthew's help couldn't do
it. The manager of one bike shop asked Hulda Kristín why on
earth anyone would want a used bicycle. Matthew said there
were bikes in the storage area of his apartment block that
hadn't moved for a couple of years and he was sure the owners
had moved out months ago, but neither of us quite had the
stomach for that. This still feels like a place of excess to me,
like a country where everyone has more stuff than they know
what to do with. (Rich words from one who has left her own
country to escape Great-grandma's embroidered linen tablecloths.) New bicycles cost about twice what they do at home,
until October when Hagkaup sells off all the things Icelanders
buy in summer, patio heaters, ride-on lawnmowers and jet-
skis, to make room for skis, winter tyres and snowmobiles.

I start riding to work, ten kilometres along the coast
path. At first, the sun rises around the time I drop Max at
school. On a clear day, the frost feathering the pavement
and dusting the grass glistens pink as the sun comes hesi-
tantly over the hill behind the city. Other days, it feels as if
there's no convincing source for the grey pallor of the sky,
as if the sun is a rumour like the *kreppa* or the swine-flu pan-
demic. I cycle past marshland, where there were geese a

few weeks ago and now are none, along the side of the free-way, where I see more accidents requiring ambulances and leaving broken glass and bits of car thrown up the embank-ment. Up a hill, along a quiet road lined with houses the size of aircraft hangars, each surrounded by a pool of grass and concrete. There are no flowers in the gardens here, no trees, certainly no vegetable plots or currant bushes, although the people in the painted wooden houses in the city have found ways of coaxing most of these through the winter. Each of these houses has three or four cars, each about the size of the sitting room in an ordinary British house, beached on the drive in front of the garage door, and there's often a pram parked out there as well. Two of these houses, the two white ones with terraced circular patios lapping like waves at the French doors, have tinted win-dows, which don't stop me peering in. I glide back down to the shore, the path squeezed between the freeway and the sea. Although the traffic is loud here and exhaust smoke heavy in the air, it's where the birds congregate. There are always seagulls, screaming and fighting, but the others come and go as the autumn passes. I greet various kinds of Arctic duck, some with curled feathers on their brown heads, some black and white, visible as navigation buoys against the water on a blue day. I labour up the hill, past a retirement home which has a gym on the ground floor where I often see a nurse helping old ladies to use the machines, and a sit-ting room with a glassed-in verandah where the residents sit in velvet armchairs, lifting their faces to the sun. I usually get off and push the bike up this hill, trying not to mind when the real cyclists, men with proper Arctic cycling clothes and balaclavas under their helmets, ring their bells at me to get out of the way. I pass through Kópavogur, a cityscape more comfortable than Garðabær, a town with smaller cars and a gathering of shops around a series of car parks, with a church perched high on the end of the peninsula. It's a church that appears to be inspired by the shells of the Sydney Opera House and it's floodlit through the dark, making a surreal landmark visible across the city and far out towards Hafnarfjörður. Down the hill on the other side of the church, checking the brakes because the slope is as steep as the slide in the school playground and then I'm on the road again, around drivers who don't encounter cyclists from one month to the next and use the mirrors only for applying make-up. I cross the road and freewheel back down to the shore, and from here the ride is a reliable pleasure, half an hour of my day stolen from both my employer and my children. The track passes below the graveyard, one of only two burial grounds for the whole city, its stones spreading out along the hillside like suburban sprawl as the population grows. Icelanders don't do epitaphs, only names and dates. And then I'm in the parkland under Perlan, pine trees rising on one side and the water in the inlet usually placid on the other. It's always windy here, sometimes a fight to keep going up the hill and to balance the bike against the gusts, and windier as I round the headland and pass the end of the runway at the little airport. Planes come down so low that it feels as if I could touch them if I stood on the sea wall, and the two-seaters are often parked on the other side of the chain-link fence, where I can see men tinkering with them the way dads used to play with their cars at weekends, all boiler suits and oily rags. There's a hole in the fence and the tarmac is temptingly smooth; I wonder what would happen if a foreign woman cycled along the bit that says 'Civilian Apron C'.

I ride along the ends of the gardens of houses overlooking the sea. There are no fences here. Anyone could wander off the path and up to the windows. These are older houses than the ones in Garðabær, although still expansive as cruise ships, docked between the city and the shore. Their eccentricities are pleasing: a vaguely Mexican place, with a scattering of blue tiles set in its apricot painted walls, a white house built bunker-like into a slope, with a hot tub, swaddled now in tarpaulin, set at its feet; a glass cube three storeys high which, despite my growing nostalgia for Victorian brick curlicues, I find myself coveting. The króna is still weak enough that if we did decide to move here permanently, we could sell our terrace in Canterbury and buy one of these, put up swings and a trampoline in the garden and let our books spread out along hundreds of metres of concrete walls. It's open sea on my left now, buffeting the stones, and I slow down and don't look where I'm going because sometimes I see seals here, hauled out onto inshore rocks. It's hard to tell in the half-light of mid-morning which dark bulk is a seal and which is weed-covered rock or a huddle of cormorants, and I don't know exactly why it matters, but seal mornings are better days. Nearly there now, past the wooden fish-drying hut from which I still catch a whiff in an on-shore wind, and round at last to the road. There's the only few metres of bike-lane in Iceland here, along the side of a dual carriageway that doesn't go anywhere in particular and isn't much used. The students keep telling me I should stick to the pavement, which is legal here. It has to be, they say. Because it's only foreigners who cycle and they'd just get killed if they went on the road. (The men in Proper Cycling Gear, I think, don't count, because their cycling is a sport rather than a means of transport, rather as the few Icelanders walking the coast path do so with Nordic walking poles and Lycra rather than shopping bags and city shoes. It's one thing if your chosen form of sport chances to cover distance, quite another to choose not to drive.)

And a left turn – get off and walk over the pedestrian crossing – and I'm on campus. I lock the bike to the railings, which is apparently unnecessary but a lifelong habit I can't break, and go upstairs to my office. I'm back on the radar – teacher, colleague, employee, mother and wife at the end of the phone – but in a few hours I'll get back on my bike and disappear again.

I'd like to know more about the olden days, the pre-vegetable years before the Americans came. I should talk to some more people, but I can't, not yet. On bad days, I still choose to go hungry rather than go into a shop and have to talk to Icelanders. I am ashamed to require Icelanders to speak English and too embarrassed to try to speak Icelandic, even though I know the words. I am afraid I can't pronounce them properly, afraid people will laugh at me, afraid of the paralysing horror of standing there in a shop making incomprehensible noises. Sometimes I don't swim because I can't face the mortification of buying a ticket for the pool. There are days when I don't use the staff lunchroom because I think Icelanders will resent feeling obliged to talk to me. I hadn't expected to find my foreign-ness so disabling. I come from a wandering, academic family and spent almost all my childhood summers outside England. I have the usual British diffidence about imposing myself, but I've never before been unable to summon the nerve to buy a sandwich. Pull yourself together, I tell myself, but often I can't.

So I take refuge in narrative. I take out all the Icelandic fiction in translation from the National Library, barely a shelf, and more in German and French than English. There's a film archive, above the Culture House where the saga manuscripts are venerated. I can do libraries and museums. I know how to keep quiet. The film archive holds every film ever made in Iceland or by an Icelandic producer, and there are booths where you can sit in a leather chair, put on headphones and pass the afternoon in front of the screen. It's warm up there, above the sex-shops and neon-lit bars off Laugavegur, and snow swirls past the low windows. I begin at the beginning, with the jerky sepia-and-white of the interwar years which need no subtitles because there are no words, and work my way through the headscarves and sharp-cornered cars of the 1960s towards the echoing footsteps and blood-sprayed walls of contemporary Icelandic film. I will be indiscriminate, I promise myself. I will watch everything. And when I've done that, armed with whatever it teaches me, I'll talk to some people from beyond our circle of fellow-strangers.

Many of the films are set in the Middle Ages. They blur in my mind with the documentaries of Icelandic life in the first half of the twentieth century; both show people wrapped in grey and brown wielding rakes on rainy hillsides, their hair and clothes whipping in the wind. Lines of heavily-laden horses snake over mountain passes with people trudging at their tails. Rain drips from everyone's hair. Children run in and out of turf houses through low doorways, like rabbits emerging from and disappearing into burrows, and every so often one of the men says something apparently proverbial, like 'the dark horse runs longest' or 'the fog hides many secrets' and hits another man on the head with an axe. Then there is another procession of wet horses, sometimes carrying a coffin. It's like listening to a tale told by a drunk; I am fascinated, mostly by the landscape, but have no idea what the narrative logic might be. The subtitles are little help because there seems to be no relationship between what people say (not much, mostly about farming) and what they do (mostly farming but sometimes murder).

Over the weeks, as darkness draws back through the afternoon and snow becomes a fact of life rather than a special effect, I progress through the decades. The settings change a little. Mid-century, the films are all about people leaving the farm for the city, or not leaving the farm for the city, or occasionally leaving the city for the farm. I imagine Pétur going, as ever, against the flow, appearing from Cambridge on one of these bleak mountainsides and settling down for the winter as if Borgarfjörður were where all the twenty-two-year-olds wanted to be in 1964. Wet horses are still important, but there are also wet buses. There is usually a father who stays on the farm and at least one son who wants to leave. Cameras go inside now, and there is chipped Formica, dirt-floored rooms with a few wooden chairs, and women who knit and cook but say even less than the men. Two or three times in each film, one of the men says something like 'the folk over the fells are fleet of foot' and then stabs his brother or son with a butcher's knife or clubs him with an agricultural implement. I begin to play a kind of Icelandic film cricket, guessing who is going to do what to whom. I always lose. I watch some of them again, hoping for retrospective insight into the motives for violence, but even in hindsight I can't imagine why, or see any narrative build-up or tension. I cannot make connections between actions and words, can't recognise motive or discern character. I feel stupid; I've found a genre I can't read.

6

Winter

By November, it's been winter for a while. We recognise winter not just because the colours of land and sky and sea have changed, although the greens and blues have turned to shades of grey, but because there is less light, even in the middle of the day. The sun rises at a shallower angle every day, every day the zenith is a little lower, every day sunset is a little further south, as if the sun is running out of power. Winter is like watching film shot by natural light, like watching Lars von Trier after Spielberg's summer. There is snow, and then rain again, and then more snow. The Christmas holiday is shorter in Iceland than at home, and there are no half-term breaks from school, although the International School, true to its American roots, closes for Thanksgiving. Icelanders work now, putting their heads down, getting things done so that when summer returns, when the days begin to lengthen again, we will be able to go out and sit in the sun. I try to remember the midsummer light, and to know that as the days are shortening now they will lengthen after the solstice. Life will come as surely as death. It's hard to believe, my Arctic theology.

Anthony has moments of despair as dark falls earlier and earlier, 4 p.m. at the beginning of November, 2.30 by December. We're losing, he says, five minutes a day. But those times are sunset, I remind him, not darkness. Winter sunsets, like summer sunrises, go on for hours. The sun sidles over the horizon, but the sky stays pale for a long time. I walk the coast path long after the last light has drained from the sky and think about darkness, and I like it. I like the way it's impossible to ignore the passing of time. Today is darker than yesterday, tomorrow will be darker than today. Dust we are and to dust we shall return. It makes me feel alive, makes me feel my life like heavy cloth on my hands.

I'm still cycling to work, past the digital thermometers at the roadside reading minus four, minus five, minus six. Sometimes its hard to keep moving fast enough to keep warm enough to keep moving, and I know I'll have to stop soon, but there's such pleasure in moving silent and solitary along the edge of the Arctic sea that I want to keep going. The track has down-lights at waist-height, so I can see ice and puddles and stones under the wheel but there's no glare in my face as I watch the darkness pale and deepen. It's never really dark, even on a cloudy night. I find myself coming to know the phases of the moon as I know the days of the week or time of the month. I know how the stars wheel through the days and nights.

My last ride is the week before Thanksgiving. It's nearly 9 a.m. and sunrise is still a couple of hours away. There's pallor in the south-eastern sky, but out to the north-west, over the sea, the sky is navy, full of cold stars. A full moon seems to have been circling the city for a few days and it rolls out, heading south along the horizon, throwing a shifting pathway over the sea. Everything has a shadow, for the first time in weeks, but they are moonshadows, black on white, and they all point due south, towards that false pink promise behind the mountains.

I'm getting to know my students well now, but there are still surprises. I'm teaching a course on contemporary travel writing. The students aren't used to studying non-fiction, or contemporary literature, and we're all enjoying thinking about how much where you come from shapes what you see when you leave. Home, I tell them, is the paper on which travel writes. Travel writers are always writing home. They tell me that the Icelandic for stupid is *heimskur*, one who stays at home, and that there is a saying: 'He is as stupid as a child reared at home.' This is a nation where travel is the precondition of intelligence. But there's another saying they told me right at the beginning: 'Iceland is the best in the world.' Unemployment is highest among 'foreigners' because immigrants were the first to be sacked when the *kreppa* began. The university is on an official mission to enter the top one hundred in the world, and staff and administrators like to hear how things are done in universities that are already in this category, but – as in most large institutions – there are always reasons why nothing can actually change. I find that I am becoming frustrated by the absence of exactly the regulations I thought I was escaping. I don't understand how the students are supposed to know how to do well when there are no marking criteria, no public statement about the difference between a bare pass and an excellent mark. I am shocked that one of my colleagues assesses his literature courses by multiple-choice exams, so they can be marked by a computer. There is, I discover, after weeks of teaching my own courses

by discussion, no tradition of student participation here. My
colleagues don't usually expect the students to use class time
for discussion, and spend the weekly hour-and-a-half standing
at the front lecturing to rows of quiescent faces. Icelandic
students won't speak in class, my colleagues tell me. It's not in
the culture here, people are too afraid of making fools of
themselves. They do for me, I reply, and then realise that since
nobody told me otherwise, I have required Icelandic students
to behave like British ones. They've shared their writing and
argued about the meaning of *Kubla Khan* and fought over
Austen's feminism. If Háskóli Íslands wants to play with
Europe's universities, some things will have to change, and
everyone is interested to know what those things are. As soon
as anyone mentions 'abroad', *útlönd*, the outlands, in a meeting, people fall silent and take notes, as if it's self-evident that
what happens *í útlöndum* is exemplary, as if Iceland's self-
esteem depends on its ability to mimic foreign ways. But
when I suggest that we might actually follow examples of
other practices – double marking, for example, or a system of
external examination so that someone from another institution would confirm that what we are doing meets accepted
standards – I'm told that it's not possible to do things differently here, because this is Iceland, and the reason I don't
understand this impossibility must be that I am a foreigner.
Foreigners may know how to do things abroad, but only
Icelanders understand Iceland. This country seems both out-
ward-looking and insular, a nation of deeply provincial
voyagers. 'Insular', Pétur reminds me, is the adjectival form of
'island', and not incompatible with 'well-travelled'. I try, and
fail, to explain to the students why English has two words for
'foreign' and 'outlandish'.

We've been reading Jonathan Raban's *Old Glory* and talking about how to write about rivers. Raban takes a small boat down the Mississippi, inspired by his childhood reading of *Huckleberry Finn*. I talk about *Three Men in a Boat*, and about the rivers in *The Waste Land*. The students discuss the idea of the river as highway and border, taking people and goods up and down but keeping them apart. I know by now to assume no limit to their geographical experience. Juliána, who lived in Paris for a year, talks about city rivers, the Rive Gauche: the river as socio-economic boundary. Ólafur remembers how New York used to pretend its river wasn't there when he was a child: the river as sewer, taking away sins. Jón fishes in the river that crosses his family farm every summer, joining his father, brothers and male cousins in a ritual of returning to the land and to primitivist masculinity after nine months of urban professional life: a river of (seasonal) plenty. The discussion is going well, but they're ignoring Raban's encounters with people on and near the river, and I realise that we've talked a lot about landscape this term and hardly mentioned inhabitants. What about the way he writes about meeting strangers? I ask. How does that feel, when you're travelling and you start to hear people's stories? How does Jonathan Raban use strangers' tales?

There's a silence. I wait. The silence goes on. Find an example, I suggest, and they ruffle pages obediently. But they are exchanging glances, in a way that usually means the crazy foreigner is at it again. Maybe we should write about encounters with strangers this week, I say, practise telling second-hand stories. I can hear the intake of breath. OK, I say, tell me. What have I said? The Danish student and the Americans are looking around, as puzzled as I am. Yeah, says Rosa, it's weird, isn't it, the way some people will just, like, *talk to strangers*. Like, people they've never met before in their entire lives. Oskar nods. My great-aunt's like that, he says. But then she is Danish. She'll just start talking about the weather or something. *In a shop*. He shudders. Really? asks Disa. Really people she's never even met? In the city? Yeah, says Oskar, shaking his head, as if the Danish great-aunt is in the habit of pinching policemen's bottoms or drinking on the steps of parliament. Like in America, adds Ólafur, they'll tell you anything. It's just embarrassing.

Icelanders, it turns out, don't chat to shopkeepers, or complain to each other when the bus is late (though it isn't, usually), or exchange comments about the weather. There is outright mutiny when I suggest that those who have never spoken to a stranger should go out and do so as part of this week's writing exercise. In the end, the international students all turn in elegant little vignettes about finding that the other person on the train was going to the same ballet for the same reason, or about being invited to stay with the person in the next seat on the plane, while the Icelanders write about rivers. I wonder if part of the anxiety about 'strangers' is that Icelandic social and familial bonds are so dense that there aren't many strangers, that, like Jewish people from the same English town or Oxford graduates of the same cohort, any two Icelanders will eventually be able to name a common acquaintance and so the only true 'strangers' are foreign. In any case, I am gratified to have found people keener on minding their own business than the British.

One of my students comes to find me after class, a British woman who, like most of the immigrants we know, fell in love with an Icelander in London and found, a few years later, that he couldn't conceive of raising a family outside Iceland. (I sometimes think that all these beautiful, intelligent, multilingual twenty-something Icelanders with a sideways take on the world ought to come with a health warning when they arrive in London and New York and Buenos Aires: marry at your peril, for the *útlönd* years are just a phase. The rest of the world is only a finishing school for Icelandic graduates.) Charlotte's outsider status in Reykjavík is doubled because she is black. The first few times she visited her husband's family, she says, people used to turn around in the street to watch her go past. Children would hide and point. When she was driving one day and saw another black driver at a traffic light, they waved and smiled in astonishment and it took her only two days to find out who the other person was. That was ten years ago, she says, and it's better now. She wouldn't have come to live and raise her children here if things hadn't changed. Anyway, says Charlotte, there's a book I found very comforting when we first came to live here, and I wanted to lend it to you. Reading it was a big thing for me when I first arrived; it made me feel that someone had been through it all before. She presses a worn paperback into my hands and goes off to run her business for a few hours before taking her daughters swimming.

Ripples from Iceland, by Amalia Lindal, was first published in 1962. Lindal was an American who came to live in Reykjavík with her Icelandic husband when they were ready to have children in the 1950s, and wrote about her painful assimilation. It is partly the story of the narrator's own erosion, where the damage of motherhood overlaps with the emigrant's loss of identity. As in so many travel books, writing seems to be therapy for the trauma of alienation. It's a trauma that takes familiar, domestic form for Lindal:

114

I think one of the most difficult things for newcomers to Iceland to adjust to is the food. Such items as bacon, ham, pork, veal and beef immediately disappeared from our menu when we arrived because of the high prices ... Icelandic lamb is our staple meat: fresh, ground, salted, smoked, or in sausages or frankfurters, and mixed with spice and potato flour in a meat paste which can be fried up into stiff meatballs.

A recent United Nations report listed Iceland as having the highest protein and calorie consumption of western Europe and the United States. The conclusion was drawn therefore that Icelanders eat very well. I agree that the protein intake is high, with all the fish, meat, skyr, dried peas and eggs used in baking ... The carbohydrate consumption is also high, with potatoes, bread and cakes daily, and much use of sago, cornstarch and potato flour for thickening. Icelanders are well filled, but not well nourished, unless they take vitamins and cod-liver oil, or are wealthy enough to afford imported fruits and expensive fresh or canned vegetables daily.

Lindal writes a lot about vegetables. She dreams of American supermarkets and wakes up as she pays for trolleys full of peaches. Get over it, I find myself unfairly thinking, able to identify someone else's whingeing where my own complaints are obviously those of a normal person presented with weirdness. Go watch the light on Esja and remember why you came, but of course that's not why she came. She came for love, which is less reliable than mountains.

It's not just the vegetables that annoy Lindal. Coming from

an American Protestant background, she has no patience for the Icelandic attitude to money:

> In the fishing industry, one may make 100,000 krónur in a season whereas another, not so lucky, makes only 10,000. It's always a gamble, and so the fishermen and the merchants engaged in exporting and importing think in terms of big money and the big chance and have no feeling for a relatively stable and dependable income. The farmers, on the other hand, have an attitude about money much closer to that of large industry, but modern Iceland's economy is based on the elusive herring rather than farming.

This is clearly what is known in our house as a Grand Unifying Theory of Everything, a kind of key to all mythologies that finds one explanation for a complicated and ongoing process, but the idea is appealing. The banks fell because Icelanders have fishermen's attitude to risk. Big money and big chances. It's not true – many of the people who have lost houses and cars claim to have had no idea of the risks the banks were taking, and in any case Icelandic fishing is going rather well because the boats are landing their catches in Norway and Scotland and selling their fish for pounds and Norwegian kroner – but there's a storyteller's logic that works. The bankers are known in Iceland – even by the majority who disapprove of their actions – as 'Viking Raiders', stripping assets from útlönd. Vikings, fishermen, men who treat money like fish.

The winter weekdays are full, and mostly happy. I work, Max goes to school, Tobias goes to nursery and Anthony bakes a lot of bread – but then there are weekends. Icelanders, we gather, spend winter weekends visiting their extended families. With nearly eighty per cent of Icelanders living in the Greater Reykjavík area, almost everyone has parents, grandparents, cousins and a proliferation of step-children, ex-partners and in-laws within a few minutes' drive. (It's one of the reasons Icelandic marriages don't last, a sociologist at work tells me. With such dense social and familial networks, there is no chance of keeping an affair secret. He might have been joking.) Grandparents, we learn, often take the children at weekends; we suspect this may be one of the reasons why Icelandic couples are so relaxed about parenthood. My students tell me that in most families, one household, usually the grandparents', will hold a weekly open house on Sunday afternoons, with coffee and a table of cakes and the expectation that everyone will attend or send a convincing reason for absence. It sounds comforting, I say, envying the idea of a nuclear family buoyed on a sea of other people's interest and concern, because it feels as if Anthony and I must paddle hard to keep ours afloat until Monday morning. Sometimes, Pétur and Messíana let us pretend to be theirs, and Anthony and I can sip coffee and talk to their real children while Messíana reads to Tobias and her two-year-old granddaughter and Max plays with their nine-year-old grandson, jumping from behind a wall into the wind coming off the sea into the garden and then taking shelter again behind the house. But most weekends, Icelanders live their Icelandic lives and we roll up our sleeves, trying not to count down the hours until the outside world opens again.

We invent arts and craft projects using the previous weekend's newspaper, of necessity since prices are still rising in Iceland and the weekend *Guardian*, on subscription, is now the only thing coming into the house that isn't eaten within a few days. You can make lots of things with old newspaper, we find, not just papier mâché which uses up flour we can't always spare. We have themed collage competitions, spelling games with letters cut from the headlines. We decorate caterpillars made from egg-boxes with pictures from the gardening pages. We roll out play dough and cut out endless horses and elephants. The plastic smell of play dough is still on my hands at bath time. We make paper snowflakes and Blu-Tack them to the window, though it's clear that everyone else in the block has decided at one of their meetings that we will all hang white star lanterns in the windows this winter. (I tell one of the students about our joke that the residents of each block get together every year and agree on co-ordinated Christmas decorations. Yes, he says, they do. Yes, new ones each year, that's right.) We have wheelbarrow races across the grey carpet, Anthony wheeling Max, me wheeling Tobias.

I bake as if I'm the pastry chef in an Edwardian stately home, because butter and cream are cheap, it makes me feel I'm doing something productive and the rest of my cooking is now no more than an attempt to make it possible to eat the available ingredients. Swede and turnip are our only fresh vegetables, and we eat wizened apples, shipped from Central America on the slow boat and picked from a slimy heap in Bonus, more as an act of faith in the principle of fruit than because we believe them to have any real nutritional properties. Sometimes there are oranges, big, shiny oranges which are pale and dry when opened, the flesh hanging in bloodless strands. So I make brownies with chocolate from home, sour-cream vanilla cake with a *skyr*-based icing of which I am rather proud, gingerbread with Danish glucose syrup instead of treacle. Icelandic supermarkets, we discover, sell all the sweets at half-price on Saturdays. It's called *Nammidag*, 'yummy day', and the candy section is *Nammiland*. When Max studied the UN Convention on the Rights of the Child at school, his class put 'candy on Saturdays' high on their list of children's rights. Icelanders eat more kilogrammes of sugar per capita than almost anyone else in Europe (although dental health is relatively good, a contradiction that reminds me of their high meat, low vegetable diet and good cardiac health). *Nammiland* is the only place in Iceland to see a winter crowd. Early in the day, young children push and whine, stuffing carrier bags from the pick-and-mix while their parents stand back by the baking goods. Later on, the aisle is full of teenagers shoving and shrieking, shovelling Icelandic chocolate liquorice and Polish cola gums into plastic bags until they're each cradling a haul the size of a well-grown baby. Late on Sunday nights, when the frenzy is over, the floor is scattered with crushed sweets, bright as stained glass, and gobs of caramel feel like pebbles under my shoe. Some weekends, Max and I enter the fray, looking for alternatives to expensive Danish chocolate chips to put in our cookies. Baked goods and painting; bread and circuses, though for whom I am not sure.

But there comes a time, every day, when we have to get out, when the children are not just chasing each other up and down the flat but chasing each other with forks and malicious intent. We go for walks. We go to the Zoo and Family Park, which has to stay open all year because, like children, the animals need feeding even when there's no other reason to get out of bed. We swim several times a week. There is, I think, a slow pace to Icelandic winter weekends that I can't match. Only the thought of Monday morning quiets my panic.

*

In early November dawn comes at around nine-thirty. One Saturday there is sun. Esja turns gold, and from the table where we're having second cups of tea we can see an oddly straight-edged dusting of snow on the top third of the mountain. Winter sunshine commands our presence in the same way as the late-night sun did in July. Get it while it's here. Don't waste your chances. You'll want to remember this day when the wind is so strong the children can't walk down the street and you haven't seen Esja all week. We know now how fast the weather changes, that by the time we've made a real plan and got everyone into the car we'll be too late for the sun, so we head for the lava field. The land glows like well-polished furniture in candle-light, the sea glinting an almost Mediterranean blue, and frost melting except where the shadows of street lights and boulders block the sun, a shadow theatre on the ground. There are swans in the bay, and sharp-winged gulls move so fast through the air that at first I imagine the terns, *kríur,* have come back, winter is cancelled. But it is only the beginning.

We drive into town, to the market by the harbour for fish and *flatkökur.* We park at the university and walk down to the lake so the children can feed the ducks, but there isn't the usual gang of geese menacing passing toddlers and we hear the whooper swans fluting from the other side of the lake. When we come closer we can see why: the lake is opaque as milk, the ducks confined to one side by ice that stretches across the water towards where the swans occupy the other unfrozen area by the bridge to the town hall. It is duck-ice, so thin that it bends and creaks when a few brave or hungry birds are enticed across it by 'bagels' so un-bagel-like that even the children have rejected them, and the ducks crash through it as they come to the edge. Watching ducks fall through ice is unreasonably funny, slapstick without the cruelty. Tobias likes the idea of jumping in too. At last, after eleven, the sun comes over the horizon and the ice shines pale yellow, with the standing ducks' shadows cast in black.

On Sundays, when everything else is closed, we swim, usually at Garðabær but sometimes at Hafnarfjörður, which has a bigger set of outdoor pools. I drive tentatively over hardening frost. The indoor pool is crowded; I can see people's heads in the steam rising from the outside pool, so Tobias and I scurry across the concrete and hurl ourselves into the toddler pool, which is pleasant enough as long as we keep our necks and shoulders submerged and occasionally splash warm water over our tingling faces. Anthony and Max join us after some persuasive waving and beckoning and Max sticks a foot into the bigger pool but says it is too cold. I should take his word – he's almost impervious to cold – but can't believe all the people swimming with serene expressions are secretly shivering so after a while I steel myself to rush across and try too. Max is right, although that doesn't stop him, twenty minutes later when we are about to leave, making a rush for the slide and swooping down, his body steaming as he runs up the stairs but cooling to air-temperature as he comes down the slide wearing an expression of pure glee.

Our perception of cold has changed, although Reykjavík is much warmer than other settlements on the same latitude because of the Gulf Stream, and it's a relatively mild winter; the temperature is rarely below minus ten. English winter coats are just about adequate, at least for the adults. It's not *that* cold, I keep telling friends at home. And then one day in early December the temperature rises to two degrees. The warmth is as surprising as an electric blanket when you were expecting frosty linen sheets. My cheeks and chin don't go numb, even though the bus to work is late and I have to stand still for more than five minutes. My hands still hurt with cold, but my feet, in woollen socks and leather boots, remain comfortable and it doesn't feel as if I've been slapped when my scarf slips down my face. The ground, though, is glazed from two days of snow followed by overnight rain and a hard frost. I spend the day marking, watching the moon set, the sky pale, and, somewhere around midday, the shadow of my office building begin to creep up the building opposite, first a soft pencil line of pink and then, for perhaps an hour, a sharper, yellower outline. Going to get coffee, I glimpse through Pétur's window the marsh between the university and the airport steaming, and Esja, revealed for the first time in several days, covered in snow and pink as a raspberry meringue.

At night, I take long baths, glorying in cheap hot water and the underfloor heating in our tiled bathroom. I always check the sky on my way across the flat to bed, and at midnight one night in early December see bright green clouds hanging over the northern horizon, visible even through our windows mottled by dust from the abandoned building site. I put long socks, a cord skirt, jumper, scarf, coat and hat over my pyjamas and slither along the road to the pile of builders' rubble at the end of the peninsula and yes, there they are, higher in the sky and brighter than usual. The bath was hot and I am able to stand there for nearly half an hour, watching the green curtain reach across the sky and contract, like the convulsive grasping of a palsied hand. It is the movement that makes them uncanny, as if there must be some consciousness directing the stroking and grabbing of the sky. I stand, and watch, and shiver, and watch some more. I want to stay until the end, but after a while find that there is a limit to how long an intelligent adult can be enthralled by green lights, and go home.

Mæja recommends the Advent celebration at Árbæjarsafn, the outdoor museum outside the city. Árbæjarsafn has a collection of wooden houses moved from the city centre as the concrete office blocks went up. Each house has been reassembled and furnished to represent the domestic life of a particular trade or class in a particular decade of the late nineteenth and early twentieth centuries. In summer, high-school students dress up in breeches or aprons and long skirts and practise their English and German on tourists, but the museum is usually closed in winter, opening only for the three weekends of Advent when Icelandic families come to celebrate Icelandic Christmases past. You'll see all our traditions, Mæja says. The leaf bread and the special singing and maybe even the Yule Lads. She doesn't mention the birth of Christ, and nor does anyone else. Christmas in Iceland seems so far to have no religious content at all; at the heart of the fairy lights, advertising and office parties is an apparently atheist celebration of the solstice, dogged by the thirteen Yule Lads. Max is learning about the Yule Lads in school and remembers far more about them than he does about conversational Icelandic or basic arithmetic. The Yule Lads seem akin to trolls or the Faroese *huldufólk*, 'hidden people' living secretly around farms and settlements and coming out at night to steal and harm anyone who catches their attention. They come in the dark weeks to take away the Christmas food, steal the candles, peer through windows, slam the doors. Occasionally their parents come too, and then you have to be especially careful because they have left their mountain fastness to snatch children to eat. The story is more like *Beowulf* than the Nativity, but when I think about Icelandic farms in winter, about weeks of darkness outside and blizzards pounding the low turf houses, I see why you would want the children to be afraid to go outside. It's a tradition that goes back centuries, although in 1749 the Danes made it illegal to frighten children with these stories. It was only in the 1970s that the Yule Lads began to bring presents for good children who left a shoe on the window-sill. As one of my (Danish) students comments, the rest of Europe buried these creatures or Disneyfied them beyond recognition a couple of centuries back. Slightly twee versions of these characters appear on the milk cartons from late November, and Max has been asked to cut out these figures and take them into school. He tells me their stories as we open out and wash the cartons, prefacing them by pointing out his own immunity from the last of the Lads, because 'I'll be back in England by then and they don't leave Iceland.' There is one picture he cannot look at, showing Grýla the mother of the Yule Lads, who comes for children in the night, ties them up in her black bag and takes them away to eat. Cats with sharp teeth slink around her feet. When we come to stick them in his Icelandic Culture Book, I have to handle Grýla and Max insists that we make a fold-down paper cover so he can open the book without having to look at her.

There's nothing scary at Árbæjarsafn. People huddle in the lee of buildings, wearing Icelandic jumpers, and watching other people hold hands and dance in circles. Inside the houses, candle-lit as the grey afternoon darkens and snow begins to drift, women wearing long woollen dresses cut leaf bread, sheets of pastry, into lace patterns ready to be deep-fried and dredged with sugar. There are blood puddings hanging in the chimneys, and a craft fair in the Visitors' Centre. Children gather in the courtyard and sing a song that Tobias has learnt at nursery, and when another child takes his hand for the dance he begins a conversation in Icelandic. The other three of us stand in the dusk and watch him dance into the circle of Icelanders, singing.

I finish my pile of Icelandic fiction just before Christmas. The more recent books, mostly detective fiction, are obviously written with translation in mind, giving extraneous detail about Icelandic transport systems and seasons and in some cases including plugs for particular hotels and restaurants, but at least the killers have motives. Some of the more literary novels cause me the same puzzlement as the films. I simply don't understand why the characters do what they do, can't see the connection between speech and action. In apparently gentle novels of bourgeois life, characters rape and kill with no warning, no reflection and little reaction from anyone else. I find the violent episodes entirely unpredictable, never know at the beginning of a paragraph if the person coming through the door is bringing coffee or a crowbar to the person sitting at the table. I wonder why a society distinctive for its low crime rate should produce novels and films in which ordinary family life is invariably punctuated by bloodletting. Are Icelanders simmering with rage under their jumpers? Does the tradition of independence and self-containment leave people battling to contain emotions for which they have no vocabulary? (Maybe it is significant that the National Library doesn't have the complete works of Freud.) I watch people carefully. There are no rude words for sexual or bodily functions in Icelandic. When Icelanders swear, they have to borrow from English. Most parents, as far as I can see, have enough childcare and practical support from extended families that they don't get particularly angry with their children. I don't have enough experience to know whether there's a taboo on expressing anger, whether Icelandic life is arranged not to be infuriating or whether I'm too much of a stranger to see ordinary expressions of feeling, or indeed whether I'd need to go drinking downtown on a Friday night to see a wider range of Icelandic behaviour. I still feel very foreign.

We go home for Christmas, two weeks back in our own house with our own things and friends eager to see us. England's having a cold winter. Our house is Edwardian and draughty. Even once we turn up the heating, we can't get the house warmer than 14 degrees, and it's much colder than that upstairs and at night. One morning, I wake with numb fingers and see that my chilblains have turned aubergine purple. We put on another jumper, and another, and some gloves. We drink a lot of tea. The railways close because of the snow. Pensioners are told to keep one room warm, whatever the cost. People are advised not to drive, and some of those who do drive find themselves snowed in at service stations and church halls. You must be used to this, our friends say. You must think this cold is nothing. They're wrong; we look forward to going back to Iceland, to be warm again.

But it's good to be home. I take my credit card out and it makes me feel better. A lot better, about everything. We have no disposable income in Iceland. I know that nobody needs disposable income, that part of the point of going to Iceland was to free ourselves from the stuff we have at home, and indeed that I have missed buying things far less than I expected. Nonetheless, I buy more toys and books for the children than we can possibly take back to Iceland. I buy things I know they don't particularly want, things made out of plastic which will still be on the planet long after the human species falls into deserved oblivion, and made by children as young as mine in countries that haven't ratified the UN Convention on the Rights of the Child. I buy lots and lots and lots of food, wandering around Sainsbury's in a fog of happiness because there are five different kinds of tangerine and none of them are rotten and because I can buy peppers and aubergines and squash and bags and bags of salad that I don't even have to wash. I order locally reared organic meat and vegetables online and then go back to Sainsbury's the next day, and to the farmers' market in the afternoon. I buy four new cookbooks in glorious Technicolor, two of them pertaining to cuisines I know nothing about and have never eaten. I buy an embroidered merino cardigan one day because I'm bored by the one I'm wearing. I buy two knee-length cord skirts in muted colours to complement the three I already have. I go to Waterstone's and to the bookshop in Whitstable and back to Waterstone's, buying so many books that each trip ends with several bulging bags. I buy shoes. I have an expensive haircut. And it all makes me feel very happy.

And then it's time to return. I'm looking forward to oblique light along the coast path, the wind coming over the lava field, the weekly contingents of birds: seagulls and then ducks and then geese and at last the terns. I'm looking forward to feeling the Earth tilt back towards the sun, back towards life, in the knowledge that this, too, is only for a season.

It's an easy enough journey this time. There's a delay because they're having to de-ice all planes leaving Reykjavík, during which Anthony and I have a row and I stalk off to duty-free, Tobias in tow, and buy a large bottle of a perfume I've been wanting for years but have hitherto considered too expensive. We don't come to terms until landing, when I realise that I need Anthony to co-operate, need his inscrutability, because under all the new clothes and books in the suitcase are two whole salamis, a wheel of Kentish cheese, five packets of spring bulbs which promise 'fragrance', approximately three kilo-grammes of chocolate, from Cadbury to Valrhona, two Christmas cakes and a stollen, half a dozen russet apples, a bag of unwaxed lemons and a couple of dozen tins of anchovies, capers and vine leaves. I haven't checked the details because it's always preferable, in my experience, not to know when you are breaking the law, but I've heard colleagues and students complaining about protectionist legislation that makes crimi-nals of the most casual gourmet travellers. People swap stories about how to get fresh herbs into a country where you can't even buy the seeds, reminisce about the owner of the first pizzeria in Iceland who used to smuggle mozzarella on a friend's fishing boat in the days before Icelandic dairies started to produce 'pizza-cheese' which comes in greyish rubber blocks and tastes like salted plastic. I send Anthony first with the suitcase and pointed instructions to look arrogant, and follow holding both children's hands, trying to look harassed and speaking English loudly. It's Icelanders who get stopped. Tourists don't need to smuggle because they can go home and buy anything that pleases them for half what it would cost in Iceland. I smile at the customs officers, looking up through my hassled-Mummy hair and chirping at the children to come on and hold hands and stop wandering off, which they aren't. There are sniffer dogs. Trained for sausages or heroin? You can't conceal fear from dogs, and it would be egregious to go up to one of those uniformed men and explain that I'm scared of the dogs because they're dogs and not because I'm carrying contraband. The worst that can happen, I remind myself, is the loss of some food. I can feel heat in my face and my heartbeat banging high in my chest. Max, who knows what we're doing, grips my hand, looks anxiously into my face. He'd make a lousy chorizo mule.

And then we're outside, the air a cool flannel on the face after a long run under a hot sun. There's snow, a drift of crystals each the size of a dandelion seed, and, at 2 p.m., sun on the snow, the slanting late-afternoon light that's the Icelandic winter zenith. The snow is so light that when the children kick it, it drifts down again like feathers, and all the lines in the land are softened. As the bus sets off, the low sunlight is pink, the mountains and the swaddled outlines of the lava field the colour of candyfloss. Ghosts of steam rise from the pools at the side of the airport road and hang there, swaying a little. There's no wind. The few motionless clouds are the colour of pink carnations. Tobias goes to sleep, and I cradle him in my lap, watching Esja shining rose from head to foot, the smudge of the forest above Bessastaðir that marks the furthest Tobias will walk from the flat, the sea below the aluminium smelter steaming as if coming to the boil. There's something odd about the light, about the water, a stillness I don't understand until we wake Tobias, get off the bus and begin to haul our suitcases along the snowy footpath down the coast. The snow's too deep for the wheels and the cases are so heavy with gluttony that we can't carry them, and meanwhile Tobias is struggling because the snow comes above his knees and our footprints are too far apart for him to use. Follow the suitcases, I tell him, watching them scythe the snow. We come down past the school, where there are footprints of the children who come to play on the snowy basketball pitch and frozen swings. The sea is silent. There are no birds. Most of the sun is below the lava field now, and the eastern sky is darkening. Careful across the icy playground, we come down to the shore, and there's no movement in the sky or along the beach because the sea is frozen. Instead of waves, there are grey slabs, piled up against each other like fallen gravestones, from the black rocks of the beach to the dimming horizon. I hadn't thought this would happen, hadn't understood that the movement of water and light, the rise and fall of waves, the shifts between lapping and pounding, the coming and going of the tide, could simply stop. The land looks less solid than the sea: individually-frosted reeds poke through folds of snow and the low light is provisional beside that rubble of ice. The sea looks like a flattened township, like buildings after a landslide. Even in the dusk, the sky looks different. There are no reflections. We exchange glances and go quietly back to the flat, which is so warm that we open the windows and take off the layers of jumpers and scarves that have cocooned us through the fortnight in . England. Tobias races up and down, introducing new toys to old, and Max disappears to re-read the books he hasn't seen for a couple of weeks. A yellow moon the size of an Icelandic car sails out from behind Esja as the last light fades at the other side of the sky. The city lights come on, but there's no twinkling in the sea. I start cooking; a homecoming, of sorts.

7

The Icesave Thing

Back at work after the holiday, I'm preparing my teaching when the hum of people going up and down stairs, making coffee, stopping by for a chat, goes quiet. Radios come on, people listening to the news on their computers, and then there's a collective gasp. Pétur and Matthew come to my office to tell me about it. The President of Iceland has refused to sign the Icesave agreement detailing how the Icelandic nation should repay the British government for compensating British investors in the bank that ran the Icesave accounts. Matthew is doleful; now things are going to get even worse, he says. People will have to realise that they can't just blame politicians and bankers for everything. (Why not, I ask, there was no referendum about not regulating the banks.) We're already at breaking point, says another colleague, coming in to make sure the foreigner is properly briefed. It's desperate here now; Icelanders have nothing and are going to have nothing for generations to come. Can't they see that? Pétur, who likes a little anarchy and can't see capitalism fall far or fast enough, is elated. Now we'll see some proper action, he says, twinkling and rubbing his hands. I know I don't really understand the detail of the financial issues issues and I'm not sure most Icelanders – or Brits – do either. Pétur wanders off. While Matthew's trying to explain, there is a series of explosions outside the building. Our eyes meet. Bombs? In Iceland? There's reason to protest, of course (exactly what reason will have to wait for another day), and people are angry but – fireworks, says Pétur, putting his head round the door. Not the revolution. Pity.

I haven't seen fireworks in Iceland before. They turn out to be marking the 'last day of Christmas', which – since we are on the edge of the Judeo-Christian tradition here – means not Epiphany but the day the Yule Lads return to their lair on Esja. It's the tradition, says Matthew, to use up the fireworks left over from New Year. The fusillade goes on, getting louder as the sky darkens, until as midnight approaches the whole city is ablaze, the sky screaming. These aren't the low-level garden displays put on at home for Bonfire Night. It's all higher, brighter, louder, more, going on longer, from mid-afternoon dusk until the early hours, the air across town heavy with smoke. These are only the remnants from the real celebrations a week ago. The next day, I check the price of the fireworks left in the supermarket. The smallest box costs about £70. *Morgunblaðið* reports that Icelanders let off an average of three kilogrammes of fireworks each (including children) between New Year and the trolls' retreat. This information intensifies my curiosity about the *kreppa*, of which I have still seen no outward sign that I can recognise. There's far more poverty visible in Canterbury than Reykjavík, and has been far more poverty visible in every British city I've lived in, including Oxford and Bath. But I've been in Iceland long enough now for it to occur to me that it's perfectly plausible that Icelanders would spend the last króna they don't have on some really big fireworks.

There is a run of bright days in January, days when I go into Pétur's east-facing office with a cup of mid-morning coffee to watch the sun rise red into a clear sky and hear the latest about what everyone calls 'The Icesave Thing'. I leave work early to catch the last of a slow purple sunset on the way home. Cycling out along the peninsula one afternoon, I look back at the city and see that there is a pale green mist hanging over it, filling the space between Perlan and the church at Seltjarnarnes and trailing out over the sea beyond. At first I take it for another Arctic natural phenomenon – it has a beauty of a kind, this strange colour wrapping itself around the city's landmarks and hovering on the lower slopes of Esja, as if the Northern Lights have somehow crept out by day – but when I read *Morgunblaðið*'s English website I understand. Not aurora but smog. *Morgunblaðið* says the smog is here 'because there's not enough wind', and when I ask the students the next day they confirm this. It always happens, they say, when winter days are still. It's because of the weather. But it's not because of the weather, it's because of the cars, because Icelanders have almost a car each, because many of the cars are huge 4x4s and because some of them drive around for seven months of the year on nailed tyres, doubling their petrol consumption, even though the city roads are gritted as soon as snow falls and so far there have been five icy days in seven months. Most of the time, there's enough wind to carry the resultant pollution away from the city, off to fall as acid rain somewhere else, but when the wind drops we sit in our own waste, asthmatics wheezing and the rest of us tasting exhaust fumes deep in our throats. But you should be used to it, the students tell me. London's always in smog. I don't think they believe me when I say that we have, at least, whatever our sins and failures elsewhere, dealt with that problem.

My head of department in England sends me an e-mail. He is planning next year's teaching, and asks me to confirm my return at the end of the year. I don't reply. I know what the answer is, really. I know that we are surviving on my Icelandic salary only by acts of self-denial to which no sane person would commit herself in the long term when there is an alternative on offer. The obvious and responsible choice is to return to the life we left, pick up the car from Anthony's sister at the airport and go home as if we'd never left. I will tell Anthony that it's time for us to make this decision. Later.

The Icesave Thing rumbles on through January and February. The debate, in theory, is over the interest rate and speed at which Iceland repays the governments of the UK and the Netherlands for their compensation of British and Dutch Icesave investors. There are protests in the parliament square, low-key Icelandic protests in which people pass around hot drinks and talk to their friends. Colleagues speak of 'going to protest for an hour' between classes or on Saturday afternoons, but even they can't explain to me exactly what they are protesting for. They don't like the situation, they are frustrated with the new government that replaced the Independence Party which had been in power from 1944 until the coalition it dominated collapsed in the Pots and Pans Revolution of 2009. Some don't think that the state should bear responsibility for debt incurred abroad by privately owned banks, but no-one seems to have a plan for the kind of action that might result from this or any other principle. Early in March, two months after the President refused to sign an agreement that had passed through parliament, and thus triggered a national referendum, the voting papers go out. It's a very Icelandic affair; the Law department at the university, charged with writing the pamphlet to explain the issue and procedure to all Icelandic voters, postponed doing so because they expected the referendum to be cancelled, which wasn't unreasonable because the agreement at issue had been superseded by one that's better for Iceland. But once the process has begun, there is neither a mechanism nor a popular will to abort it. So Iceland conducts a referendum over a paper that is already acknowledged by all concerned to be defunct and irrelevant, and ninety-eight per cent of Icelanders, reasonably enough, reject it. All the English language sources of Icelandic news and opinion concur that the referendum was nevertheless worthwhile because people feel good about having voted and it makes them feel better about the situation to have been consulted. I can't help wondering if they wouldn't have felt better yet had the money spent on organising the vote been given to the voters instead.

The same news sources offer daily stories of Icelanders having homes and cars repossessed and seeing their debt repayments rise far in excess of their income, partly because people took out mortgages and car loans in foreign currencies during the boom years and are still having to repay them in foreign currencies now the value of the króna has halved. I can see food getting more expensive week by week; turnips are now a treat and the sacks of frozen fruit and vegetables on which we rely, which came from Belgium in July and Poland in October, are now imported from China. But I can't see

Icelandic poverty. Mine seem to be the only children in Iceland with patches on their trousers. It's rare to see anyone old enough to drive on a bus. Very few of my students and colleagues bring their own food to work. There are the cars, and the fireworks, and the absence of a second-hand market for anything but vehicles. Mine is among the oldest laptops on campus, although I make common cause with a student whose screen works only when she places clothes pegs at exact intervals along the edge. Max is given homework, which is actually homework for me, of eating meals made only from ingredients grown in tropical rainforests for a week. (This in a country about as far from a tropical rainforest as it's possible to be, where imported food is highly taxed as well as expensive because of the transport costs. We make cocoa.) I've been wondering for a while, but now I begin to ask people why I can't see the *kreppa*, offering the possibility that I'm just a stupid foreigner who doesn't get it and can't see what's staring her in the face. No, say the students. Many of them have been wondering the same thing. No, say my colleagues, though if you'd seen the boom you'd be able to see the bust. So where is it, I ask, where is this crisis?

It's the first time I feel able to ask a stupid question in public. You should talk to my grandson, says Pétur, his face softening as it does when he thinks of any of his grandchildren. Ása Björk's boy, you know? He knows everyone in the young Left-Greens. Tómas Gabríel is Pétur's oldest grandchild, son of Ása Björk the priest, and he was at the forefront of the demonstrations that brought down the right-wing government in a hail of stones and burning benches last winter. I'm keen to meet him because those demonstrations, leading to the Pots and Pans Revolution, took place between my acceptance of the job at the university and our coming to find an apartment and a school in May. It was hard to follow the detail from outside Iceland, especially without reading Icelandic, but I knew that the events of December 2008 and January 2009 were unprecedented in Iceland, and that some of my Icelandic acquaintances experienced those days of political activism as a time of personal as well as national revolution.

There had been protests outside the parliament building every Saturday afternoon through the autumn of 2008, sometimes as many as a few hundred people listening to speeches, holding placards and occasionally throwing eggs and toilet paper at the windows of the debating chamber. People were protesting against a government very closely allied with the 'Viking Raiders', the small group of bankers who had brought Iceland to the point of sovereign bankruptcy. Almost all the banks failed, their debts far in excess of Iceland's GDP. The news during those months worsened from one week to the next, as unemployment rose from less than one per cent to ten per cent, average household debt was revealed to be 213 per cent of disposable income, and foreign currency transactions were suspended, jeopardizing the import of some medicines as well as books and fruit. University staff were asked to minimise the use of printers and photocopiers because the state institution could no longer afford ink and toner cartridges. As the value of the króna crashed against other currencies, the cost of Icelanders' foreign-currency car loans and mortgages rose far beyond the value of the collateral as well as beyond the reach of the debtors. It became clear that Icelandic banks had been lending to Icelandic consumers without any consideration of their customers' ability to pay. It was reported that

Icelandic banks had lent money to their own employees to enable those employees to buy shares in the banks, using the shares as collateral for the loans. The suicide rate climbed sharply. Internationally, Britain used anti-terrorist legislation to freeze Icelandic assets, and the provision of aid from the International Monetary Fund was blocked by the Dutch in the hope of putting pressure on Iceland to repay Dutch investors in high-interest Icesave accounts. The extent of the government's involvement with the Viking Raiders began to be apparent, although as I write in the winter of 2011 investigation of this corruption is still under way.

The government remained in power as its complicity with the Viking Raiders was exposed, and took the usual four-week Christmas recess despite Iceland's state of acute crisis. When parliament reconvened on 20th January 2009, an angry crowd gathered. It was reported that the parliamentary agenda for that day included the possibility of paying organ donors, rearrangement of traffic priorities and discussion about allowing grocery shops to sell alcohol. (Most alcoholic drinks must be bought from the state monopoly 'wine shops' under current legislation.) The crowd grew. It was the day of President Barack Obama's inauguration in the US, and Icelandic protestors had banners saying 'Yes, we can!' People brought household implements to make enough noise to force MPs to stop discussing wine shops and recognise their presence and their demands. There were old ladies banging spoons on pans, younger people with spades and wheelbarrows, fishermen with fog-horns. Some people lit emergency flares. Protestors banged on the windows of the debating chamber, and when the riot police arrived they were pelted with eggs and *skyr*. The police retaliated with pepper spray, using it indiscriminately and sometimes over walls and around corners to attack people they could not see. The protestors set up a nursing station to bathe victims' eyes with milk before taking them to hospital. The crowd grew as the night wore on. No-one wants to stand still outside for very long in Iceland in winter. Every Christmas, Norway gives Iceland a Christmas tree for Austurvöllur square, where the parliament building is. The tree was still there, and made a good bonfire.

It took a week of protest to topple the government. Around 30,000 people, ten per cent of the Icelandic population, joined the demonstrations. Most of the people I know were there, with pans and banners, and those who were abroad at the time recall their shock at seeing pictures of angry crowds, tear gas and police batons in Iceland. I would like to hear from someone on the front line.

Tómas Gabríel lives just over the road from campus, and I pick my way there through heavy rain, over ankle-deep slush, as the sun goes down one day in March. He comes to the door, a thickset young man in a black T-shirt, and stands patiently while I pick with cold fingers at my boot-laces.

Tómas Gabríel lives in a block like Mads and Mæja's, one that looks to British eyes like unloved 1970s council housing, where the outside space is worn grass with rubbish blowing around and – even here, even in March – the occasional used condom caught on low bushes. There are pebble-dash walls, and that kind of subdivided double-glazing that speaks of beaded macramé plant-holders and brown plastic upholstery. But not here. Inside, there are white walls, gleaming wooden floors and a comfortable clutter of well-designed modern furniture, plants, musical instruments and books. A pair of desirable embroidered shoes lies on the floor where someone has kicked them off to curl up in one of the chairs, and there are ironed white linen cloths on the table. Tómas Gabríel brings me coffee. His arm is in a sling, following, he says, surgery on a dislocated little finger. It sounds like one of those mishaps which fills you with wonder that such an apparently peripheral part of the body can cause so much trouble.

So, I say, tell me about your politics.

He tells me that he was raised in a strongly socialist household. No-one from Pétur's clan could say otherwise: we need to get rid of money, Pétur says, and go back to barter. But Tómas Gabríel's mother relied on example to show him what was right; she never told him how she voted, so when he came of age he did his own research and came to his own conclusions. Tómas Gabríel 'fell in love' with the Left-Greens, the party that formed a coalition government after the Pots and Pans Revolution. When he started his philosophy degree at the University of Iceland, he made friends with the students running the youth branch of the party, and in autumn 2008 he joined the managing committee. It seemed, he says, like a way of changing things for his country and his generation, as if all that he and his friends needed to take power was courage. The idea of standing for parliament in your early twenties is not as fantastic in Iceland as it would be in the UK, especially since the elections in 2010; the youngest member of the Alþing is in his early twenties and there are government ministers younger than me.

'I went to all the demonstrations at the beginning, when they were peaceful. And then things started boiling up in November and December. My friend was becoming more of an anarchist, and it was a wild ride getting to know everyone – not the people behind the scenes because there was no 'behind the scenes'; they were at the scene, the people you saw in all the pictures and footage of the demonstrations. And then one of the activists, someone who became my friend later, made this really good protest. He took the Bonus flag, you know?'

Bonus is owned by the corrupt banker who owns most other Icelandic chains and indeed owned half the British high street. The same man owns Hagkaup, and there are well-substantiated rumours that when the produce in Hagkaup gets too old to sell, it is sent to Bonus for poorer people to buy. The Bonus flag, which flies in every Icelandic village and suburb, is daffodil-yellow with a bright pink pig on it, presumably not intended as a symbol of greed.

One Saturday in December, Tómas Gabríel's friend climbed up the parliament building, one of the taller buildings downtown, and replaced the Icelandic flag that flies there with the Bonus pig. The crowd of protesters roared, but the debate in the chamber went on. There were only two police officers present, as it was the first mass demonstration and the police were taken by surprise. The demonstrators helped the climber to get away, having been alerted to the imminent arrival of the 'Viking Squad'. (The Viking Squad is Iceland's armed response unit, not to be confused with the Viking Raiders, although these multiple claims on 'Viking' identity are revealing.)

Ordinary citizens have a right of access to the parliament building. This right is important to Icelanders, symbolic of communal responsibility as well as rights. There may be broken windows but there will be no bombs or guns. You can park right outside the door, less than a metre from the debating chamber. I regularly take a shortcut between campus and

the city centre that passes between two parliamentary buildings. (It's also under the flight path of the city airport, less than
a kilometre from the runway, the one used by the planes on
which you're allowed to take firearms and up to five kilogrammes of ammunition.)

Tómas Gabríel continues. The following week, his friend
was arrested on questionable grounds to do with his membership of Saving Iceland, a charity and campaign group
concerned to protect Iceland's pristine landscapes. Tómas
Gabríel's friend had been protesting against the building of the
Kárahnjúkar dam in 2006. Most of the people I know
protested against that. One of the last projects of the discred-
ited government was to flood a huge swathe of the highlands,
bulldozing some of the oldest archaeological sites in Iceland,
to provide hydroelectricity for an enormous, American-
owned aluminium smelter. The contractor used immigrant
labour to build the dam, and is alleged to have kept the workers underground for twelve hours at a time without access to
drinking water or lavatories; there are reports of people licking the tunnel walls for water. Kárahnjúkar was demonstrably
the most dangerous workplace in Iceland since records began,
and there are accounts of foreign workers being forced back
into tunnels before poisonous explosive gas had cleared. There
had been an outstanding warrant for Tómas Gabríel's friend for
three years, and the police came for him as he left his philosophy class on the Friday before a large demonstration planned
for the Saturday.

'So he had an outstanding warrant and he had to choose
between doing jail time and paying a fine, and he chose to do
jail time because he didn't want to give any more money to
that government. We have a long waiting list for jails in

Iceland, and the law states that you have to have three weeks notice when you get to the top of the list, so that you can put your affairs in order with your family and at work.' (There are so many uniquely Icelandic assumptions in Tómas Gabríel's explanation that at first I don't understand what he's saying. There is a waiting list for Icelandic prisons, because there aren't enough spaces in the prison for everyone who receives a jail sentence. So, after conviction, criminals go back to work and home, and when a space comes up in prison they are given three weeks notice of their incarceration.) 'But they didn't give him the three weeks notice. It didn't escape anyone that this was an attempt to take control of the protesters. It backfired, because after that demonstration we marched up to the police station. It had been peaceful until then, and we spent hours waiting outside, with slogans and speeches, but then it reached boiling point and the door got kicked in. And that was the beginning of everything, that day in January. After that we knew it was real. They sprayed the crowd with pepper spray, with no discrimination and no warning. They're supposed to warn you first, but we were all in the lobby of the police station – we had kicked in the first door, so they might have felt threatened – and this hand just reached round and started spraying. There was a sixteen-year-old in hospital with burnt corneas. It was – hilarious.' He doesn't sound amused. He sounds disbelieving, betrayed. 'I had great respect for the police. I used to think about joining the police, to help people. They handle very dear matters, very delicate situations. If someone dies at home, they are first on the scene. They help grieving families and people escaping domestic violence. But you expect the people who uphold the laws to follow the laws, and when they don't – well, the social contract is breached. It's a different situation. If the police don't respect the law, why should we?'

Tómas Gabríel is speaking fast, his eyes on the wall above my head, as if he's seeing the scenes from last year projected there. I sip my coffee, wait for the next instalment. Traffic swishes through the slush outside; we're getting towards rush hour. He tells me about the beginning of the protests, the anger and excitement among his friends. After their philosophy class, they walked around the lake to parliament.

'We barricaded it, front and back, and let no-one in and no-one out, and it went on until the police broke it up at 3 a.m.. The police kept pushing us back. That's when I got pepper-sprayed the first time, a direct shot in my eye. It hurt. Quite horrible. That made me really angry. Before that, I was just protesting but after that – well, I was focussed. I had to get back at them. It was such a good feeling you had from being there, watching the politicians being carried out through secret tunnels. It was the first time in my life I really felt proud of being Icelandic when I saw all those people, thousands of people, gathered round the parliament, taking part. Some just watching and some up against the riot shields.' He tails off, as if the images are fading. People talk much more about 'being Icelandic' than I've ever heard anyone talk about 'being British'. Britishness seems to be largely an accident of birth, whereas being Icelandic, like being American, requires the observance of certain events and practices. The Pots and Pans Revolution may be one of them. 'I don't know. It got out of control. People went too far, police and protesters both.'

They went back the next day, 21st January, and again on the 22nd, determined not to stop until the protests were heard. Excitement crackles through Tómas Gabríel's voice, remembering those days of bonfires and shouting, when to hope was to act. The exact chronology, through that sleepless week of darkness, blurs as he talks.

'I don't remember if they burnt a flag, but everyone was sweaty and tired and it was awesome. It was a really cool, cool day to be outside.' Tómas Gabríel is talking as if protesting is a sport, an outdoor activity that makes you feel sweaty, tired and good. I don't know if the coolness of that January day is literal or metaphorical, but I recognise the feeling of being young and taking control. Wordsworth's account of the early days of the French Revolution murmurs in my mind:

> For mighty were the auxiliars which then stood
> Upon our side, we who were strong in love!
> Bliss was it in that dawn to be alive,
> But to be young was very heaven!

'Then I remember I went home and I got a phone call around midnight. My friend said, "Tómas, are you real about this? Are you willing to go to the end for the demonstrators? Are you really into this?" I said yes. And she said, "OK, come down to parliament. They are shooting tear gas."' He stops. Tear gas. In Iceland. The Icelandic police gassing the Icelandic people. In Austurvöllur.

'I jumped into warm boots, got a good coat and a scarf to cover my face and ran down the whole way, the whole way across Reykjavík. It was freezing and I kept slipping but I ran. And when I got there it wasn't Reykjavík, it wasn't Iceland. It was dark, this disgusting smog in the air. There were people, teenagers and young people, walking away and cradling a friend of theirs and everyone choking and puking and crying and it was – I was – I kept going. And when I got there I saw this barricade of riot shields. On the other side of the square there were people gathered together, and I was standing there like an idiot in front of the riot shields, maybe ten, twenty metres away. And something landed at my feet and I look and I go, shit, that's tear gas. They shot a canister at me because I was the only person standing there. I looked at it and thought, no. Walk away. I held my breath but it got in deep and I was coughing up and my throat and eyes were burning away. I have asthma and lung problems and I felt I was suffocating. That was when everything turned, everything went surreal. It didn't feel as if it was happening.'

I notice the detail of Tómas Gabríel's topography, the way his story moves around the few hundred metres of Reykjavík's centre. His apartment, the university over the road, the parliament buildings across the park. His city is gathering new stories before my eyes, the meanings of space changing. These demonstrations were domestic in more than one way, an expression of alienation from *home* for which it's hard to find international comparisons.

'That night we went from parliament to another place, it's by the sea. And there were people there who were way out of line, people who'd been clashing with the police before the riots, drug-dealers and felons. They'd gone off and found some rocks and come back to throw them at the police. At which point the police were running really low on pepper spray and they'd said, all right, that's it, gas masks on, we're going in.'

Things often run low in Iceland. Things are there and then not there again for a few weeks: limes and walnut oil, children's ibuprofen, my preferred brand of tampon, nothing for which there is no substitute. Except pepper spray. Until then, someone had been making a decision about whether to use pepper spray or gas in each situation, but from now there was no choice. 'And it was – I remember standing there and seeing this guy just pick up a bottle, a big glass bottle, and throw it at this police officer. There were seven police officers, and I'll hand it to them, those were some brave police officers. Seven of them, and hundreds of us, and they were getting rocks and glass thrown at them. It was getting really unpleasant until one of the activists walked up to them and took a loudhailer and said, "Look, we can be angry, but let's not take it out on these poor souls. They didn't do this. We can paint the city red but we don't go hurting people." And then some of us ran up to him and stood with him and made a kind of blockade around the police. And after that the night turned into a sort of tug-of-war with the police and we were lighting benches and setting them on fire. There were some injuries, a friend of mine got shoved into a bench by a police officer and broke his sternum, there was bleeding, and they were hitting people on the head with batons which is illegal, they're allowed to hit your arms and legs but not your head. The hospital was on standby because the police had told them, right, expect serious injuries, we're not going to stand for any more of this. But the day after that was Wednesday, Wednesday the twenty-second, and that was the day the orange ribbon came out. If you wore an orange ribbon it meant you were protesting but you were peaceful, you didn't want violence. I celebrated it this year; I called it "Gas Mask Day". After that the police weren't really needed at the demonstrations. Things quietened down. There was no more burning. There were a few others, smaller protests and demonstrations, but I didn't partake in those, I just watched. And shortly after that the government fell.'

And after that, Tómas Gabríel says, he became disillusioned. He talks about the weaknesses of democracy, about people voting for the wrong reasons and about the compromises made by anyone who takes power, but I wonder if his disillusion has more to do with the way 'things quietened down'. The quietening down was uniquely Icelandic; the police were overstretched and under-prepared, exhausted by back-to-back shifts and night working. The Reykjavík force had called in back-up from all over the country, putting administrators and new recruits on the streets with front-line officers, but the protests were unprecedented and no-one in Iceland had much experience of managing crowds and public order. According to the *Reykjavík Grapevine*, on 22nd January 'protestors wearing orange armbands offered to relieve the police from their duties in guarding the parliament building. This was accepted, and the police in riot gear left the scene.'

Tómas Gabríel revives. 'I feel really sorry for the people who missed it. I can always say that I went there, I did what I wanted to do, I shed tears, I bled blood, I now know what tear gas and pepper spray tastes like and I'll tell my children and my grandchildren. That's what 2009 was like and it was great. It was a brilliant, brilliant moment and next year on January the twenty-second I'm planning on getting a gas mask tattooed on my arm, with the date, just to remind me.'

Tómas Gabríel is watching his memories on the wall above my head again, as if there's a re-run of the kind of sporting triumph that men seem to recall and discuss for decades afterwards. Tómas Gabríel wants something different from what there's been for the last twenty years (almost exactly his own lifetime), something new and better. But he must –

surely, at twenty-one – have a sense of the future as well as nostalgia for those three days fifteen months ago.

'Do you still feel that sense of hope?'

He shrugs. 'We're in a situation where there's not much we can do. Every account is heavily in debt, everything needs to be cut. But I feel happy that although this government will have to downgrade everything, it will be done with the people in mind. Not the private investors, not the big companies run by the Independence Party's buddies. So even with this great cutting knife that has gone through our healthcare, when I arrived at hospital with my finger deformed, in a lot of pain, I was treated immediately and well. Within a couple of hours I was on a surgical table and I had capable staff around me and that tells me that we are doing something right.'

It takes time, I want to tell him; the state is an oil tanker that takes five miles to stop. The new government promises to defend the principle of not nationalising debt, promises to make the inevitable cuts in the most humane and accountable ways possible, promises to protect what Icelanders value about their country while accepting what the International Monetary Fund offers and considering EU membership.

'So you're optimistic about the future for Iceland?' I ask. I shift in my chair. It's beginning to get dark out there.

'Well, the people who suffered most from the crisis are people who had good jobs, big loans, big cars, big TVs. We had so many people who were in a really tight situation, knowing that as long as they had their job, their overtime, they could keep up the repayments. Just. People who just trusted that things would go as they go.'

Þetta reddast, I think. It will sort itself out.

Tómas Gabríel reads my mind. 'Yes, it's very Icelandic. But

I wasn't raised like that. I don't take loans. I drive a twenty-one-year-old car, I study, I play sport and I work a few hours a week to buy gas and food. That's the way we should be, less extravagant, and I think this crisis will bring more people to that mindset. I hope so. I hope we don't just find new loans, pay it all off, party it up for five more years and then find ourselves here again.'

It's not the first time I've had a glimpse into the frustration of Icelanders who have been considered weird and even deviant for the last few years, people who throughout the boom eschewed debt of any kind, disdained shopping, reduced, reused, recycled, grew and made their own (potatoes, socks, garden sheds), not out of poverty but as acts of principle. They stand now as exemplars, Puritans, hoping a purged Iceland will see the light and join them in the City on a Hill. But people who have always seen themselves as mainstream consumers have also said to me that Iceland needed a lesson, that the *kreppa* is the overdue punishment for a decade of greed and arrogance. Matthew, who was raised in a broadly right-wing American tradition and owns the biggest television I have seen in a private house, says that we all have to take responsibility. He and his partner saved up to buy their television, but he is, he says, still partly to blame. He delighted in the new foods coming into Iceland, in the Israeli coriander and American cranberries. He loved to sit in glossy cafés with his new laptop and a cappuccino. When fresh spinach began to be imported five years into his time in Iceland, he went wild for it, and didn't ask what economic current had carried it to his table. It's time to go, and I walk back through the rain to the bus stop, hoping that the future holds something as good as the past for Tómas Gábriel.

*

The Icesave Thing

I keep wondering about the other side of the argument, because at the moment I can't imagine how anyone could begin to defend the bankers or the Independence Party. I'm sure my friends are right – or at least sure that I share their politics – but it seems a good idea at least to look over the fence at the other camp. English language sources of Icelandic news are rare and brief; the *Iceland Review*, mostly for tourists, has a rather Chinese policy on current affairs, carrying head-lines about wildflowers and ski-resorts on days when the Icelandic papers are all writing about the IMF. *Morgunblaðið*, now owned by one of the corrupt bankers, offers a few sen-tences of English summary. Otherwise, it's blogs – mostly left-wing – my students – mostly left-wing – and my friends – mostly left-wing. I should try talking to the other side. One of my students has a friend who knows Arni, the head of the youth division of the Independence Party. We agree to meet one Monday in March. I suggest my office, which is warm, quiet and central. No, he says, at the National Museum. We can talk in the café. The café has wooden floors, high ceilings, glass walls – a pleasant space where groups' chat, small chil-dren's play and the hysteria of coffee machines reverberates around the walls. It's not a good place for a nuanced conver-sation. Another café, I suggest? His office? No, he says, we will meet at the museum.

It is 'window weather', bright but cold. I notice the short-ness of my shadow as I cross the car parks between the university and the museum. It's minus five and I pull my scarf up over my face, but my eyelids and forehead sting in a wind so sharp it finds its way between my gloves and my sleeves, around the tops of my socks under my trousers. I can see from the car park that there is no-one in the café. There are a couple of tourists trying the heavy copper doors. Of course. Monday. The museum is closed. I pull back my glove and check my watch. I am, as always, five minutes early. Icelanders are always late, at least five minutes, for everything, but I can't adapt, because what if the time I'm late is the one time an Icelander is punctual? I back into the corner of the porch and the main building, where I'm well sheltered from that wind, and find that I can almost feel a breath of warmth in the sun on my face. I watch birds coming in to land on the marsh in front of the airport, because the birds are coming back now, and a jogger in a balaclava, head bowed into the wind, crossing the pedestrian bridge that arches cat-like over the eight-lane highway out of town. The painted houses downtown are bright in the sun, and after ten minutes Arni appears, a tall man with a red face darker than his blonde hair, hand outstretched in greeting. We apologise to each other for the museum's day off. Arni suggests the campus canteen as an alternative. I conduct him to the coffee room at the top of the Foreign Languages building, and make coffee while he sits texting. He can't put his phone away, sends and reads texts throughout our conversation. I can't really get Arni to say anything. He's wary, a politician on the record. I ask him what it means to be Icelandic, hoping for something which will reveal the crazed patriotism I've been told is typical of the Independence Party. (It's like a cult, two of the students told me, wide-eyed, people grow up in it and they have these stages for each age and they marry in it and never leave.) He tells me that Icelanders are creative and productive. 'We are a small nation, we come from small villages where everyone has to get up very early and work very hard, and that's a big part of being Icelandic.' Icelanders are 'homogenetic' and this spares them the dramas and crises over race, culture and national identity that rack other countries. Over the big issues, he says, such as independence and the rejection of the Icesave deal, 'we are unanimous, and this shared purpose is our great strength.' I wish I were the kind of person who can ask a confident man, at home in his own country, how it came about that a unanimous society had to throw his party out of government with bricks and burning benches. Instead, I suggest that immigration might have some effect on this cultural homogeneity. 'Well,' he says, 'we had this debate in 2006; some people who were influenced by some of the far-right parties in Norway and Denmark opened the discussion, but they didn't succeed, no-one took any notice and now it's a non-issue. When the issue came up, there were tens of thousands of people coming here from the Baltic area, Poland and the Eastern Bloc countries, in numbers that were a significant proportion of our population here. The general feeling was that these people are coming to work, which is why we came from Norway, back at the beginning. We're all immigrants, you know. They're welcome here, as long as they come to participate.'

'Really?' I ask.

He's texting again. 'Yes,' he says. 'Really. We have a strong sense of national identity but we have never had any National Socialist movement here.' This is only approximately true; some Icelanders, even during the war, saw Germany as Iceland's natural and traditional ally.

'The national movement is the cornerstone of our history. We all learn the history of the struggle for independence, because it is such a magnificent thing to see. We were living in the dark ages from 1300 to 1800, just a Danish colony, with such low standards of living, so much worse than elsewhere in

Europe. And then we began to go abroad more and it brought about this great change, there was contact with the Romantic movement and young men and women were becoming poets and writers and artists, and writing about the nation and really going back to the heritage of the sagas and the first centuries here when we were free and happy. That was our enlightenment, the rediscovery of the saga heritage. We have such a strong correlation between gaining our independence and seeing a lot of progress, because these came – telephones, electricity, roads – after we became independent. Our national movement isn't about being superior, but it is the thing that raised us, brought us into the light.'

Hence, of course, the fear of the European Union. I know, and he, I guess, doesn't, how hard it is for an immigrant to assimilate in Iceland.

'What about people who don't have the saga heritage and don't have feelings about Icelandic independence? How do they fit in?'

He smiles, someone who knows all the answers. 'It's going pretty well. We hear about these other cases, in Scandinavia and Europe, where there are a lot of problems but we don't have them here. People come on their own, or with a small family, but we are not seeing little villages of Muslim people with radical Islamic views. Iceland is in very tight control of who gets into the country, who qualifies for citizenship, and we're not a society that has very many foreigners, it's not as if there are areas of the country where they run the towns, and so for the moment this is not an issue here.'

That binary again, us and the foreigners. *They* don't run the towns. He's not going to say anything newsworthy about Icelandic racism.

'How does the financial crisis affect this?' I ask. There's a little plane coming in to land outside the window. 'People are talking about selling off natural resources to foreigners.' I mean, partly, what about 'foreigners' who aren't itinerant migrant labour, what about 'foreigners' who might occupy positions of power, might, for example, buy up your high street chains and take over your banks?

Arni shakes his head. 'That would be a very, very bad idea. But the lessons of this crisis are not yet learnt.'

There is, I think, general agreement that regulating the financial sector would be a good idea, and that allowing people in government to privatise national services and sell them to themselves causes certain difficulties a few years down the line; some consensus that loans against depreciating assets in currencies irrelevant to the transaction get people into trouble. Among other things. 'What are those lessons?' I ask.

'Well, I hope that Icelanders will take more notice of second opinions, get less carried away by the mood. On a political level, we're in a vacuum, fighting about whose mistake it was. And we may have to rethink our position in the world, for example in relation to NATO and the EU. EU membership was such a non-issue here before the crisis, because we were really the masters of the universe at that time. All the statistics looked good and we received a lot of international recognition for that and not everyone recognises that now. But of course these changes make you think about such things: can such a very tiny nation get by on its own?'

But those statistics, I don't say, were lies, because most of the money turns out to have been imaginary, a fiction of dishonest accounting. He continues, summarising the Icelandic debate about EU membership, with detours into fisheries policy and the future of the EEA. He makes scant reference to his own views ('we need to reconsider this question now'), none to the party line.

'What do you think the domestic responses to the crisis should be?' I ask.

'We need to stop playing the blame game and move on. There are very interesting things going on here now. It used to be that all the talented people here went into banking, and now they've lost their jobs or quit and they're building things of their own, really interesting things. So I think if we take the right stance and move out of this crisis in the right direction we will see a very different landscape in five or ten years, and a much healthier one. We've always had this problem here: what should the industry be? We had fishing, we went into aluminium in a big way, and then the huge banking sector. I would like to see more small enterprises. We have such opportunities here, we are well-educated, we are energetic, we are hugely creative. This is a big chance for Iceland.'

Although my instincts are to disagree with anyone speaking from the right-wing, and although he hasn't said anything interesting or unpredictable about the *kreppa*, my spirits lift at the last bit. Being 'energetic' and 'hugely creative' with banking hasn't worked, but there is something appealing as well as deeply irritating about a country that doesn't recognise rules. Whatever Iceland does next, whether led by Tómas Gabríel's friends or Arni's, it is likely to be interesting.

8

Spring

Winter goes on a long time. Matthew warned me, back in September when I was eagerly awaiting the first snow, that mid-winter is the easy bit. December and January bring parties, fireworks and aurora, early nights and late mornings. It's March and April, he said, when people start to get depressed. The light is back and it looks as if you should be able to go out, but it's still damn cold, the roads are still icy, the snow is grubby and stained by exhaust fumes and you lose hope that summer is really going to come back. Matthew doesn't have children, who wake at seven on Saturdays just the same as on school-days. Seven looks like midnight except that there are no aurora. We have four hours to fill before daybreak. Many Icelanders enjoy these weeks, time to read and knit and curl up on the sofa with a blanket and a DVD. In the Icelandic memoirs I've been reading, winter is the time when friends can stay for hours, lingering over coffee and cake because there's nowhere they need to be and nothing they need to be doing. People used to sing together, read the sagas aloud to groups of knitters and, in later years, since there have been ovens and wheat flour and butter and eggs even though the cows are dry and the hens aren't laying, embark on complicated baking. I like the idea of this, but the reality of two waffle-fuelled little boys in an open-plan flat has nothing to do with curling up or lingering. I remember a scene from Iceland's 'national novel', Halldór Laxness's *Independent People*, in which a child wakes before anyone else on a winter morning:

> The first faint gleam on the horizon and the full brightness on the window at breakfast-time are like two different beginnings, two starting points. And since at dawn even this morning is distant, what must this evening be? Forenoon, noon and afternoon are as far off as the countries we hope to see when we grow up, evening as remote and unreal as death . . .

The boy waits, desperate for his breakfast of half a piece of bread smeared with tallow and cod-liver oil. His mother is bed-bound for the winter, and the family live on porridge and dried fish; 'Never did the children long so much for a nice juicy piece of meat or a thick slice of rye-bread and dripping as when they had finished eating.'

A bit of seasonal hunger, I think, sticking down a collage of animals cut from our Saturday *Guardian* archive because Tobias has lost interest and run off to start a fight with Max at the other end of the flat, would have its functional aspects. I wouldn't mind at all if the boys had less energy at weekends. Icelanders deal with this problem with lots of organised sports. The leisure centres are full of little girls doing gym and little boys playing ball-games, but these activities, reasonably

enough, are conducted in Icelandic, and Max is sure he
couldn't get by, not yet. We never see Icelandic toddlers in
winter. They don't swim. They are not at the zoo. Nobody
takes children walking, winter or summer. They are not on the
buses or downtown, although there are still small babies sleeping in large prams outside shops and cafés all along
Laugavegur, snow settling into the creases in footmuffs and
hoods. They are not in the museum. (I ask my students: the
toddlers, they say, are at nursery for eight hours every week-
day and many spend one day at the weekend with their
grandparents. This information, each of the parents adds, per-
tains only to *other families*. They themselves spend a great deal
of time with their own children.) Perhaps, suggests Max,
Icelandic toddlers hibernate, and he and Tobias go off to play at
hibernating, although spring comes after fifteen minutes.

And at last the sky pales, although the sun isn't over the
horizon, and going out begins to seem less arduous than staying in. There are two possibilities: swimming or the zoo. The
underground car park is heated, and I fire up the heated seats
and the warm air before we leave the building, so although
there's a foot of greying snow on the ground, making gritty
fortifications along the pavement where it's been shovelled
off the road, and although the roadside digital thermometers
insist that it's minus seven out there, we don't have to confront
the reality until we park. I take the keys out of the ignition and
start to wrap my shawl around my woollen cardigan, wriggle
into my coat and gloves, pull my hood over my hat. No-one
else has moved. Max turns a page. Come on, I say, maybe
they'll be feeding the seals! Anthony pulls his sleeves down
over his hands and stares out at the icy car park. I changed my
mind, remarks Tobias. I want to go home now. Me too, says

Max, I don't like the zoo anyway. Anthony and I exchange glances. We could just drive home. We left the building, which was a lot of the point. We passed time putting everyone's shoes and coats on and finding all the gloves and hats and snacks and water-bottles. I squint up at the windows of the Range Rover parked next to us, its sides rising past our windows like an oil tanker passing a yacht. There's a family of five sitting in there, listening to music and passing around crisps. Maybe driving around and parking is a normal way to pass winter weekends. I open the door.

Your feet, I find, go numb almost immediately, but hands take longer and hurt more. I hold my hands out to the children. Come on, I call, if we move fast we'll soon get warm! Tobias wants to be picked up so he can see into the field where there were cows in summer, to make sure they haven't come back. Reykjavík Zoo limits itself to native and sub-Arctic fauna. The Arctic foxes are performing the crazed waltz of caged animals. Next come the seals, too many of them in a concrete pond smaller than most swimming pools. At feeding time, children are allowed to enter the enclosure with the keeper and throw fish from a bucket, while a cat slides around their legs. (Just as well they don't have tigers, Anthony mutters.) Then we can visit the hens, which is a treat because they are kept inside and there are heat-lamps for chicks fresh from the incubator. Tobias names rabbits, chickens, pigeons, teaching me Icelandic, and I spin out the conversation as long as possible, but at last it's time to go see the reindeer, who move like dancers, shimmying across the snow to a syncopated slow beat. They sigh companionably, not interested in us but not surprised that we're there, and I hold Tobias up against the railings so he can watch them slouching away. Storybook reindeer,

Spring

Donner and Blitzen, aren't reindeer but something fleeter, lighter, modern and European. These reindeer nose at the snow and then sit down with weary dignity, as if waiting, like the rest of us, for spring. Below the reindeer, there's a caged hawk, a bird meant to survey our ant-like scurrying as it drifts on the wind, hopping from its perch like an oversized sparrow. (No sparrows in Iceland, no robins or blue tits. Sometimes they blow in on a south-easterly gale, hurled along the Vikings' Atlantic route, and die of exposure and exhaustion, of lack of trees, in Seyðisfjörður.) Max's lips are turning blue but he won't wear a hat. Back to the aquarium, where cod and skate nose the glass and there's shelter from the wind even though the doors stay open, and then over to the stalls, where pigs lie as if dead on the concrete floor, so fat they look as if they might split open. Sometimes there are piglets, and when there aren't Tobias wants to know where they've gone. To stay with their grandparents, I say, on the farm. On past empty pad-docks (they go inside, we explain, for the winter, and think lovingly of the Volvo's heated seats) to admire a large wooden sculpture of a goat, which I imagine to have a hollow belly and a trapdoor, Trojan style. The nerves in my arms twang like plucked strings in the cold. Past the pond, where in summer there are pedalos, now frozen solid, to the adventure play-ground, which is the final test of willpower. Tobias runs up ramps, slides down the metal slide, impervious in his snowsuit and balaclava. Max swings and swings. Anthony stamps his feet and swings his arms. Tobias reappears on the deck of a pirate ship, small feet pattering over the bridge. I glance around and start to do small star jumps with my feet. The sinews in my arms have stiffened and I cannot think about movements that would disturb my coat. I pull my scarf over my nose and blow into it, but the brief warmth leaves the wool damp and chill over my face. Max swings, feet swooping as if he can't feel the wind around his ankles. Tobias comes down the slide with an expression of intense concentration, as if gravity works only as long as he thinks about it. It's getting dark again.

My head of department at home sends another e-mail, this time with a red flag. Am I teaching next year or not? After the children are in bed, whispering because in this bare, open-plan flat there are no secrets, Anthony and I consider our position. Tobias, of course, would want to stay. For almost half his waking hours, he's an Icelander, and he doesn't care at all whether his clothes are patched and there isn't much fruit. The International School is a good place for Max, better than his English school with its sub-clauses about the colour of children's socks and a curriculum determined by a regime of standardised tests unthinkable in the Nordic countries. But in Iceland we can't afford the books he wants, or music lessons, or a printer for his homework. He can't have skis, or trips to the ice-rink, and new shoes have to wait until we next leave the country. Money wins, in the end. Anthony looks out into the dark, which depresses him. In summer, we'll be going home.

Every night, Max and I check the online aurora forecast, run by the University of Alaska but also covering 'Europe' where, roughly, we are. The scale for auroral activity goes up to ten, which never happens, but we've found that on a clear night, anything over three is usually visible, even if only as a green wavering on the northern horizon. I check both the forecast and the sky just before going to bed, and we have a pact that

Spring

I'll wake him for anything over a five. And one day it happens: a six on the scale, and purple flames licking the sea. It's only half past ten. I shake Max awake and put out layers of clothes: thermal underwear, socks, trousers, thicker socks, over-trousers. T-shirt, polo-neck, jumper, gloves, coat, hat, hood. We creep out and ease the door shut, scurry like excited children into the car park and bundle ourselves into the car. This time, we're going to look properly, not blocking out the city lights by crouching behind the builders' rubble on the headland.

I drive out across the isthmus to the Álftanes peninsula. There's no thermometer in the car, which is probably just as well, but the warm air coming out of the exhaust fills the rear-view mirror and there's ice on the gritted road. There are no other cars, and the settlement ahead lies silently under the street lights and the curtains of green and pink light. I turn right, northwards, and we're bumping along a gravel track behind the last houses before the breakwater. I stop when I realise that I have no idea how we'll turn round and get back in the dark, and we get out. We should have brought a torch. We stumble towards the sea wall. I climb it, and haul Max up behind me, and we sit there. The sea is still rough after the last storm, refracting oblongs of lime and violet framed by white foam, and the upper half of the world is festooned with light, swaying in figures and swathes that remind me one minute of a crowd of ball gowns hanging to dry, the next of searchlights coming from above. The aurora are unsettling partly because they show the depth of the space, the falsity of our illusion that the sky is two-dimensional, and partly because it's hard to convince your instincts that something bigger than you and grabbing at the sky isn't out to get you. Salt spray spatters against my coat, and suddenly the lights are all around us, between us and the yards on the other side of the car, sweeping the sea at our feet. I clutch Max and we keep still, as if they might take us for rocks, these bright forms coming out of the sky. Max talks about aliens all the way home, and for once I can see why.

At the beginning of March, there's daylight at breakfast time and I'm cooking supper at sunset. It's not a treat to be outside in the light any more, and for several weeks it's not much of a treat to be outside at all. Rain falls on snow. I walk along the coast path to pick up the bus to work at Kópavogur. There are cycle tracks and a few boot-marks along the path, but on the pavements mine are the only footprints for days. The walls of snow shovelled off the roads rise higher, covering more of the pavement, and there are trenches in the slush where people drive in and out of their garages. But nobody, evidently, leaves any of these houses on foot from one week to the next.

The children have a day off school – there seem to be a great many bank holidays in Iceland – so I take them swimming. The sea is freezing again, as if there's a layer of silk lying on top of the water, and by the shore the waves wobble under the silk as if trying to get out. We hurry into the pool, and then the clouds part and for the first time in months there is sunlight in the water, translucent sunbursts and flames of light. Look, I say to the children, look, and Tobias comes over and tries to catch the darts of brightness. The old people are sitting on the steps, huddled like animals in the patch of sun, silent, heads tilted back and eyes closed as if waiting for death-masks to be made. When they leave, I take their place. The sun is so low it shines straight into my face and I close my eyes, seeing my eyelids' red as if for the first time. I lift my face to the light, the wind chill around my chin. I had faith, I think, and it is rewarded.

The bulbs I smuggled back after Christmas do nothing for a long time. Pétur, who gardens enthusiastically although his house is so close to the sea that the windows are marine-quality and in winter storms he finds shells thrown over the house into the back garden, has given me some spare plant pots. We fill them with a mixture of expensive potting compost and soil stolen from the abandoned building site across the road. One dark weekend, when it's too cold even to go out on the balcony, Tobias and I carpet the kitchen with newspaper and squat there with spoons, ladling soil and nestling the bulbs. I hang over them assiduously, moving them around the flat as direct sunlight comes back and again as its angles change. They spend mornings in the laundry room, moving to the bookcase after lunch and then at last, one happy day when the sun makes it round to the other side of the building before it sets, to the dining table. By the end of February, green blades have appeared. Don't touch them, I tell Tobias, if you poke them they won't grow, and we cradle them through the weeks of frost that persist long after the light is back. Oh, to be in England, I say, now that April's there, and whoever wakes in England sees, some morning, unaware, that the lowest boughs and the brushwood sheaf round the elm-tree bole are in tiny leaf. We were made to memorise it at school, as if we might be bound for the Raj, and even at the time I thought that there were a lot of places in England where you could wake any day of the year without seeing elm trees and brushwood, including the parts of Manchester where we were in fact living. We tramp along the beach, faces aching with cold, hopping from foot to foot as we wait for Tobias to finish watching the geese, who have come back, now that April is almost here.

We've been waiting to go to Hveragerði all winter, waiting for a day when it's warm enough to go more than a few minutes from home and dry enough for the idea of voluntary time outside to be appealing. Hveragerði, the tourist brochure promises, is in an area of geothermal activity where hot springs boil out of the ground and you can swim in a warm river. There's a hot springs hiking trail, and a bakery! A swimming pool and a pizza restaurant! Best of all, it's not Reykjavík, and so lets us feel as if we're travelling, at least gesturing towards intrepidity. In spring, we're going to explore all the places we've collected leaflets about, use the long days to visit archaeological sites and climb mountains and see geysers leap for the sky. It's not as if we've been snowed in all winter, but when the temperature's above zero it tends to rain and when there's a clear sky it's usually icy. In sheltered places, such as the patches of lawn between buildings at the university, there are needles of green poking through the yellow grass, and a couple of the houses down by the lake in the city centre have crocuses and snowdrops budding under leafless shrubs. If you went out without gloves, you'd come back in again. There's still a frost every night, and the roadside thermometers show minus numbers in the mornings, but there is the occasional jogger on the coast path again and ducks with bright plumage bobbing on the waves. And then one Saturday the infallible Icelandic Met Office promises nothing worse than showers, and by the time we've finished breakfast the real-time online road map shows that although the temperature over the mountain pass is minus four, the road is frost-free and fifty-two cars have passed through since midnight. If not now, when?

Later, it will seem funny to me that Route 1 ever seemed alarming, after I've learnt to drive on gravel tracks, to coax the car up hills so steep that you think you must have driven onto a hiking trail by mistake, not to look down as we follow pot-holed single track roads along the sides of hills so vertiginous that the car probably wouldn't even roll if you went a few inches that way, but plummet into the sea like a dive-bombing skua. But this is my first time driving outside the city. The road climbs across a snow-covered lava field towards jagged mountains and it feels too different, too strange, as if we're driving into the kind of landscape that tells you it's a fantasy film. The lava field's stone waves are like a frozen sea, each crest white on one side, where the snow has drifted, and black on the other. Down in the city, bright green is beginning to spread like mould across the dead grass of the empty spaces between roads and car parks, empty spaces that no longer seem odd, but here there's no sign of spring, or indeed of seasons. It's monochrome, the shapes of the land nonsensical to the European gaze. There is dark cloud twining around the mountains above us, and no cars in the rear-view mirror or on the road ahead.

Your fingers have gone white, says Anthony. I try to relax my wrists. We've just had the car serviced. We have two mobile phones, a packed lunch (not really a picnic because there is no question of eating it outside) and lots of winter clothes and we are, for goodness' sake, barely ten kilometres from home, not five from the edges of suburbia. Even Tobias could walk to the nearest bus stop. We drive on. The road is well made. We begin to descend the hairpin bends into what must be Hveragerði, where a grid of flat roofs folds out from the bottom of a creviced mountain. There are trees in the crevices, massed pines, and plumes of steam rising from among them and from the black scree paused on the hillside above, and from the bare red ground above, waving in water-colour lines and pastel scribbles into the sky.

The town is empty, the way Icelandic towns seem to be. There is a row of shops bordering a large car park: a branch of Bonus, a bank, a video rental place. I pull up in front of Tourist Information, which appears to be closed. Why are we here? asks Tobias. I don't want to see it. I don't want to get out. I want to go home. Anthony opens the door to investigate, and a block of cold air takes his place in the car, much colder than in Reykjavík. Max slides down in his seat, reading about the Romans, and I stare out of the window, wondering what it would be like to live here. Anthony returns with a map of the Hot Springs Trail and we set off again, past commercial green-houses where they grow flowers but no fruit or vegetables, to park in front of a garden centre which is somewhere between closed and abandoned. There are no other cars moving, no-one on the pavements or in the gardens. The houses are large by British standards but visibly dilapidated in a way that I haven't seen in Reykjavík, the paint peeling off corrugated iron walls and gates hanging off their hinges. We get out of the car like people lowering themselves into cold water, force Tobias into his snowsuit and set off, carrying him as he kicks and screams that he hates the snowsuit and wants to be cold. His tantrum is the only sound in town, maybe the only sound this side of Reykjavík. Max scampers ahead. There are more of those bungalows that would look equally at home – or equally out of place – in New Jersey or Wilmslow or Barcelona. But there are also the trees, pine trees that tower over us, breaking up the sky and murmuring at us, and we realise how much we have acclimatised to a world in which there is nothing between us and the sky, where trees, if any, are sociable things of human stature, rowans and dwarf willows. Consulting the map, we climb up past the church, a modern church with angled white walls and bright windows, and come out above the river. It must be the river that's meant to be warm, but the thermometer in town was showing an air temperature of minus five and it's not steaming. Can I swim, asks Max, who has seen the pictures. Try taking your gloves off, I tell him. Oh, he says. OK.

There's a narrow, arched wooden bridge over the river, vaguely willow-pattern. Tobias wriggles out of my arms and trots across, with me scurrying after him because it's high and narrow and there's room for him to fall under the rail. Halfway up the hill at the other side, we turn to look back at the town. Village, by English standards. There are wooden houses lining the river, and they all have jacuzzis hanging on to the rocks over the water, all covered with blue tarpaulins. There's no-one moving, not in the gardens or on the streets or in the fields between the river and the mountainside, although there are a few horses mooching around a red corrugated-iron farmhouse with white wooden lace under its eaves. Horses, says Tobias, look, horses in a field, eating grass! The ones in the zoo are still inside, eating hay, and I think he's stopped believing us when we tell him that spring will come and they will run in their field again.

There are clouds of steam drifting from the top of the hill, which is made of shale and red mud. As we climb, the ground under our feet boils and seethes, sulphur steam blowing into our cold noses. There is a path that winds between the simmering puddles, but they are always shifting, spreading, contracting, and sometimes the quaking mud has invaded the track. I take Tobias's hand, warn Max to keep back, as if hand-holding will stop the ground opening under their feet. There are boiled worms in the puddles, and earth the texture of baked custard. My hands are contracting painfully in the cold and I hold one over the steam, but of course what steams in an air temperature below zero is still far below blood heat. Iceland's geothermal *Sturm und Drang*, I realise, is exaggerated by cold. In a warmer climate, you'd see less steam. When Tobias stops talking about the horses we can hear the ground rumbling, as if there are stones being rolled around a cauldron at an angry boil. (This is probably exactly what is happening, somewhere below our feet where the trolls cook in their underground cave.) Steam hisses from under a rock. We follow the path, Tobias unusually docile about holding hands. The children poke their feet into puddles the colour of oranges, of fresh, sun-ripened oranges that you can't get here, and around us steam rises from the streams that skitter through rocks and shrubs down to the river, and from soft red patches where it looks as if the ground has been rubbed raw, as if the Earth's innards are poking indecently through. The heat has incubated spring, and there are patches of grass the colour of English lawns in May, and trees with bright new leaves and even buds on their low branches. The boiling and steaming is almost menacing, but I find myself reassured. Because there's something moving in this landscape that isn't me, because there's a precedent, a geological endorsement, for warmth and movement in an otherwise bleak and silent land. Tobias is getting tired and my feet are numb. We pick our way back to the car, passing – at last – some locals coming out of a house, who laugh at Anthony because he's carrying my handbag because I'm carrying Tobias. Icelandic men don't carry handbags. Icelandic women don't carry toddlers, who seem to move around only in cars. As we close the boot and the car doors, the sound echoes over the low roofs of Hveragerði, and we drive away like thieves in the night.

9

Eyjafjallajökull

On the 22nd of March, the Icelandic papers report a small eruption in the south. The farms in the valley below the volcano have been evacuated, and then the police close the roads in the area, not because there is immediate danger to travellers but to stop the tracks being choked by gawkers. Even Route 1 is only dual track for most of the way round Iceland, and the smaller roads aren't built to handle more than a few dozen cars a day. I phone Matthew, whose partner Hjölli is a seismologist working at the meteorological institute. Journalists are getting close to the volcano; could I? No, he says. It's between two glaciers and anyway there isn't much to see, just a little glow and some steam which could very well be cloud to most of us. The worry, he adds, is that it's near a glacier and could trigger a flood, and the real worry is that every time this one blows, Katla follows. And Katla offers ash plumes into international airspace, ash over most of the country and a lot of toxic gas. You'd be able to see that all right.

But four days later, the roads are reopened and the tour companies begin to advertise 'volcano trips' on the internet.

Eyjafjallajökull

It's still being called 'a tourist eruption', as if Icelanders themselves are so used to molten lava bursting over the horizon that they don't bother to glance up and it's only foreigners who feel the need to go and watch. I book a ticket. Max wants to come too. We won't be back until after midnight, but a live volcano seems worth a late night.

The bus will collect us from the Hilton. It's a useful landmark, on the corner of a big intersection, but I've never been inside before. We sit on a leather sofa and wait, watching the expressions of people coming in from their first taste of Iceland. Suitcases hurry like dogs at the heels of their well-heeled owners. People in dark clothes and sunglasses queue for the attention of two young women, blonde and made up like air-hostesses, behind a hardwood counter. The faces coming and going in the revolving door are uncertain, as if they're coming to apply for citizenship rather than check in. The lobby is built on the scale of a parliament or national museum, diminishing guests to insect-size.

The bus comes. I'd been hoping for one of the mini-buses we see sometimes heading out of the city with foreigners craning through tinted windows at Esja and the unused pavements and concrete apartment blocks of Reykjavík, but it's a full-sized coach, emblazoned with the tour company's logo. All year, I've been seeing these buses with envy for people who can look at Iceland and go home, uncompromised, pity for those who don't learn the changing moods of light and water, and, latterly, a little superiority to those who take home a tour-guide's narrative of Icelandic life. We climb the stairs and choose seats, and then sit there for an hour while the bus circles the city, picking up further passengers from hotels by a route that makes a maze of the ring roads, only to return to the main drag where everyone is instructed to leave the bus and exchange one kind of ticket for another. An hour and a half after Max and I boarded, we leave the city via Route 1, passing the Hilton on the way. Max and I open our books and lean back, but the tour guide starts to talk, over a PA system too loud for reading. Max puts his fingers in his ears and holds the book with his elbows. The tour guide tells us that the sagas are historically accurate, that all modern Icelanders descend from those who came from Norway in the ninth century and that Iceland has been a full democracy since the settlement era. No mention of the settlers' Irish and Scottish slaves, much less more recent immigrants. It's a clear day, the sun moving into the west over rush hour on Route 1. We pass the industrial parks and retail zones surging east from the suburbs, bits of heath and lava still asserting themselves between the car parks and warehouses. There are two British women behind me; after nine months in Iceland I want to turn and introduce myself but instead I hold my book open and eavesdrop, one of the pleasures I've missed most here. They've spent the last three days taking coach tours out of Reykjavík and have heard the same spiel on each one. The fat blonde repeats phrases after the tour guide, making fun of her accent and mispronunciations. I watch the reflection of the thin brunette staring out of the window, jeeps flickering past her face, until she turns to her companion and tells her to stop being so fucking miserable all the time. I wonder how long she's been wanting to say that. The fat blonde's indifferent response suggests this isn't the first time, and after the traffic lights change she starts up again. The tour guide is explaining that Iceland was actually responsible for the French Revolution. (I've heard this argument before, though only in Iceland; the poor harvests that exacerbated European hardship in 1796 may have been affected by an ash cloud from Katla.) One of the couple opposite us is reading a novel in Polish with American place names, the other the Lonely Planet Guide to Iceland in English. The guide begins to list the dates of every volcanic eruption in Icelandic history and Max, who likes that kind of thing, lets his book close. We come down the hill into Hveragerði, where steam is still rising from the places where steam rises. The guide tells us that before the earthquake in 2007, there was no steam here. If that's true, I think, they worked damn fast to set up a tourist trail as soon as the earth stopped moving. Which is entirely plausible.

Through Selfoss, and out, south now of our known world. It's the first time I see that some of the land outside Reykjavík, which is often described as more or less empty by city-dwellers, has a scattering of farms at least as dense as in Kent. This isn't wilderness. The fields are bigger and flatter than at home, and the mountains looming over them and the colours in the winter grass and the tilted sky don't look like anywhere else I've been, but the houses and barns, the horses and ditches, could be in Belgium or northern France. I wanted the strangeness I've seen in the films and that I remember from my summer with Kathy, I wanted flame rolling from a lunar landscape, not red-roofed barns and a flow of traffic suggestive of a bank holiday in Cornwall. There are cars ahead and behind, too fast and too close together, all going south as if we were fleeing rather than visiting a natural disaster. The tour guide points out a small white cloud apparently caught on one of the more distant and flatter mountains. That's it, she says, that's the eruption. It looks a long way away.

The sun is low now, the bus's shadow wavering half-way up

the hillside where the winter grass glows yellow. We're going to stop in ten minutes, the guide says, for a technical stop. Max looks up. She doesn't sound as if she's just told us that the bus is breaking down. There will be no further, er, facilities for a technical stop, she adds, so you should make your technical stop now. And if you want to eat this evening, you should buy some food too. I meet Max's puzzled gaze and explain that I think this technical stop has nothing to do with technology. The women behind have worked it out too and are mocking, but I can, sort of, see the problem. Icelandic is a language with no sensitivities about biological function, no rude words or taboos around body fluids. There is one word for peeing, weeing, making water, spending a penny, using the bathroom, urinating, doing a number one. *Pissa*. Icelanders speaking English, in my experience, use the word 'piss', even when excusing themselves from the dinner table or a seminar. If this is your tradition and you're talking to an audience likely to include Americans, I see the cause of wariness. But it's a very Icelandic solution. Rather than admit uncertainty and ask a native speaker for the appropriate term, you co-opt something you heard once and use it with scorn. Don't show weakness, don't admit ignorance, don't give anyone a chance to laugh at you.

The 'technical stop' lasts half an hour. It's eight o'clock and the sun is beginning to set, a process which takes several hours even in spring. A north wind slices across the plain. Max and I stand in the car park and try to eat the *skyr* I've brought, but it's too cold; with gloves on, the spoons slip out of our hands, without them, our hands are too cold to steer spoons. We've been told not to eat on the bus, where all the doors are open and the British blonde huddles in her seat, shaking and whining with cold. At last the guide comes back and walks the bus, counting and eating a sandwich. Two people are missing. The doors stay open. Max's teeth are chattering and his face looks blue. Across the aisle, an Englishman tells his Irish seat-mate that it's really good to be here because now he knows what it's like for the natives, the Eskimos, the Inuit and what-have-you. Someone else is beginning to devise public humiliations for the latecomers. They come at last, Italian, unapologetic.

The doors close and we set off again, through a different landscape. Streams glimmer down the sides of valleys lined with brighter grass. The farmhouses here are wooden, with painted lace under the eaves, and sometimes there is a white church on a knoll, with a bell shining in the low sun. I understand for the first time why this could have seemed like a promised land to settlers from the wilder bits of Norway: fertile green land with fresh water running off the hills, the land itself heated and sheltered fishing grounds close at hand. The light is dusty now, the sun resting on the edge of the glacial plain. The cloud we've come to see is nearer, pointing like a cartoon speech-bubble into one of the snow-covered hills. We leave the metalled road and begin to judder down a track, not the kind of track on which anyone would drive a bus in England. There are a couple of those wooden farmhouses on the hillside above the road, and their lights come on as we pass. I try to imagine how much I would resent all these cars tearing up my track and shining their headlights into my quiet sky and ogling the volcano that threatened my home and livelihood, but I don't think I can. And then the road is *lokað*, closed, and we turn off into what I take for a makeshift car park, complete with Portaloos for any technical needs, but it's just the stony floor of a glacial valley. There are perhaps a hundred cars here, and a throng of Icelandic jeeps and SUVs nosing at the river like goldfish waiting to be fed and then lumbering across the water and up the mountain. Right, says the guide, here we are, and there's the volcano. We'll be leaving in an hour and a half. The fat blonde whimpers. There's nothing to do here, she moans. She doesn't know what she's supposed to be looking at. What the hell is she supposed to do for an hour and a half?

Max and I put on all the clothes I brought and pull up three hoods each and put mittens over our gloves. Take a deep breath, I tell him, and we jump down into the cold. The wind funnels up the valley. But there's a sulphurous red glow now at the bottom of the speech-bubble of cloud, exactly the colour of my grandparents' living-flame-effect electric fire, and we set off on foot, across a makeshift bridge over the river which leaps and flexes with every step, jumping and paddling over a shallower tributary and across the boulders in the fading light towards the grassy side of the hill. Icelanders in snowsuits, ski-masks and moon-boots are spreading like ants up the mountainside, while tourists, like us cold and like us inadequately equipped, hover within sight of the lights from the car park. On and up. As long as we keep moving, we can keep moving. If we stop, we'll get too cold. I glance back, measuring our progress against the setting sun and the distance from the jumble of headlights and the silhouettes of photographers in front of them. Max notices what I'm calculating and gets anxious. Mummy, how much further, how long will it take, when do we need to get back, what time is it? Never mind, I say, look at the volcano. Look! Red light leaps into the fading sky, and as the sun slips away the cloud of steam is lit from below by the orange glow of the lava. The flame begins to slide down the hill, slow as tar, and a cloud of helicopters and light aircraft dances like midges in its light; richer tourists, who have paid a few hundred pounds for a closer view.

There's another half-hour 'technical stop' at the same petrol station on the way back, and again all the doors are left open so that the passengers, having just begun to warm up after standing outside to watch as much volcanic action as the body could stand, huddle shaking in our seats again. Even Max doesn't complain; as tourists on a bus we seem to be power-less, vulnerable as babies to the negligence of those charged with our care. At last the tour guide reappears and we set off. Max dozes as the temperature rises. The driver turns the lights off. People wrap themselves up, recline their seats and close their eyes. Max's head settles on my shoulder. I reach up the other arm and turn my reading-light on, find my page and continue re-reading *Adam Bede*, which I'm teaching next week. Adam discovers that Hetty has been seduced. There's a summer house, an English woodland. The sound system twangs and the guide starts talking again. Just before you all settle down for a nap, she says, and tells us when and by whom Route 1 was widened, before outlining other tours offered by the company in the coming days. Brits up and down the bus go so far as to murmur at each other, the Polish man turns up his collar as the expression of one who has a weapon and will use it later settles on his face and an Australian voice from the back swears. Max opens his eyes and gazes startled into my face. Don't worry, I say, it's nothing. Go back to sleep now. And he does. Darkness settles again. We're coming back through Hveragerði, where the geothermal greenhouses shine all night, alien spaceships between the road and the mountain. Just to let you all know I think I see the Northern Lights ahead! says the guide. Oh, just fucking fuck off, says the fat blonde, giving up all pretence at civility and tolerance. Just fuck the fuck off. But a ripple goes down the bus and we all crane to see out of the windscreen, where there's nothing but our reflected hope and the greenhouses. The bus climbs the switchbacks out of Hveragerði and pulls into a lay-by. The doors open. The blonde demonstrates the limits of her vocabulary until her friend tells her to shut up, there's a kid there. But Max is still asleep, and I leave him there while I get out and stand at the roadside. There they are, bright green, flickering across half the sky. Everyone's trying to take pictures, flashes grazing the dark. Just look at the damn things, I think, buy a postcard later. The aurora hang low over the mountain, lunge into the west, sweep the northern horizon. Late March, probably the last time I'll see them. I salute them and get back into the bus, where Max is still fast asleep.

A week later one of the students on my writing course hands in a story about growing up on the Westman Islands. Teddi's grandfather used to take him up onto Eldfell to feel the warmth of the ground, and once or twice to bake bread by burying it on the hillside. For a boy who preferred reading to football and walking to fishing, Heimaey was not an easy place to grow up. It was beautiful when we were there, I say wistfully, liking the idea of living on an island. It's all right, he agrees, in summer, for a visit. But no-one thinks about anything but fishing, there's nothing to do except fishing, and if you want to leave it's always too windy to fly so you have to get the boat and watch people puke for three hours except that it's always too rough to sail. Teddi is an older student, even for Iceland where most people are twenty before they leave high school, but not old enough to remember the eruption. No, he says, I wasn't born then, though my sister was two. But my grandfather carried people away in his fishing boat. A few weeks later, Teddi's grandparents are in town, staying in their Reykjavík flat for some medical treatment and he invites me over to meet them.

The flat is behind the mall, a nondescript part of town between Route 1 and the retail parks, apartment blocks inaccessible except by car and unrelieved by even the corner shops and fast-food outlets that punctuate the more desolate urban landscapes at home. We ring at a communal door with paint flaking around corrugated glass panels, and go up a flight of stairs covered in worn carpet. Teddi's grandfather, also Theódór, comes to the door. Inside, a wooden floor gleams like still water and white walls reflect on a kitchen so tidy that you would need to introduce artful disarray for a photo-shoot. It is the home of someone who has spent his life on boats; a place for everything, as if anything not fastened down or shut in would fly around in the next rough gust. Come in, says Teddi's grandmother Margrét. Sit down. Eat.

She pours coffee. There is cheese and biscuits, a stack of flat Icelandic pancakes and a plate of folded pancakes bulging with something that will probably turn out to be whipped cream. I can't work out the Icelandic lunch hour, which is sometimes half past eleven, and have just eaten a sandwich and too much chocolate. Theódór apologises repeatedly for his clear but heavily accented English, picked up while landing fish in Aberdeen and far better than my Icelandic, which isn't improving as much as it should. Occasionally we drop into German, which he speaks better than English and I better than Icelandic. I can usually understand Margrét's Icelandic and she follows some of my English. Between times, Teddi translates.

'He was just telling me that he'd bought a new boat the day before the eruption, actually got it at 8.30 p.m. And then four hours later they were woken by the telephone. That's how it was done: they called people to say that the eruption had started. Everybody went downtown, to the harbour, because that was the only way out. The airport was too close to the eruption site. Many of them were wearing only their pyjamas and bringing nothing, no belongings. A few had a suitcase, maybe, with some small things. And he was saying that many people went straight to his boat, because it was freshly painted and looked smart, and he didn't stop people coming, just let everyone in. He had 430 on board in the end, one tenth of the population. That's how it was done. He took them all over to Þorlákshöfn where there were buses waiting to take them to Reykjavík, to the big school there, and it was only there that everyone registered and was counted. But when the eruption began, people just went down to the harbour, and got away.'

I'm still trying to imagine this scene. I'm seeing, I realise, my own grandmother's wartime memories, mothers and children running for shelters that were often no refuge at all while the bombs rained on York and houses flamed out around the cathedral. 'So no-one organised it?'

'Not really. Everyone just got in the boats and left.'

Someone must have taken charge, I think. Someone made those phone calls.

Theódór and Margrét have followed this. 'No. It was just people calling their family and friends. People who noticed something was wrong. And then the fire-trucks started driving around with their sirens.' Margrét speaks. Teddi translates.

'She's saying that they went out half-dressed. My mother had a sweater and pants but no socks. My sister was only two.'

'It sounds very frightening,' I say. For the first time, it does.

'No,' says Theódór. 'Not for me. Some people were very afraid, but I have lost four ships. Three ran aground and broke up, one sank. I have many, many times gone to sea in bad weather. I sailed for years between England and Iceland, first in small boats and then in a bigger one. I have never been frightened.'

Theódór is a slight man, his pink cheeks and crisp checked shirt reminding me of my grandfather, who was an accountant who liked shopping and holidays and garden centres. Theódór looks as if he'd smell of Imperial Leather, not like a Viking at all, and yet I've never heard Icelandic masculinity so plainly articulated. I don't see how anyone who didn't want to die could fail to be frightened by the North Atlantic even without the volcano.

Margrét puts down her coffee, urges her men to take more pancakes. 'I was frightened. I grabbed the children, six children, just put them into whatever I could find and ran for the harbour and I didn't feel safe until the boat was outside the bay.'

It's a reversal of order for Icelanders to feel safer at sea, certainly for the wives of fishermen to feel safer at sea. How can you rest once you understand that the earth itself can explode under your feet at any moment?

I sip my coffee. 'Was there any warning?'

'No,' says Margrét. She looks out of the window. 'There was no warning. Nothing. There were no monitors then. There was no warning. It just happened.'

'Did you know it was a live volcano?'

'We knew the islands were volcanic,' says Theódór. 'We had a big eruption in 1963, when the new island, Surtsey, came up. My father was the first to see that one. He saw fire and smoke on the water and thought it was a ship burning, but when they steamed off that way they found that it was flames coming up out of the sea. And then the island came up, 123 metres high.'

'So was it still a shock when the volcano blew?'

'We hadn't thought it could happen on Heimaey,' says Theódór. 'Not until it did.'

'They never thought it would happen on the island,' adds Margrét. 'Even though it happened at Surtsey ten years earlier. They didn't think it would come this close.'

Theódór starts moving coffee cups and saucers around, a pancake for a volcano, a biscuit for the town. 'The fault just goes along like this. It's all in a line. Surtsey, Eldfell, Eyjafjallajökull. And then Katla. Just one line.' He looks up and switches to Icelandic. Something about a shipwreck. Teddi takes over. 'He's saying that as the eruption began he made five trips back and forth, first with people, then with people's furniture and belongings, and then for the fishing equipment. Five trips in six days. But the first trip was the hardest, of course. He was meant to take care of the engine, because he was the engineer, but there was no time to do that and the ship was so crowded it was hard to move around, so instead he was trying to take care of the people, everyone standing crammed close together, down below where the fish go and in the front and everywhere people pushed against each other. The weather was not that good and the boat was rocking and everyone started vomiting, so close together, so he was handing around buckets and bags but anyway they all got full up.

And he remembers, there was a woman there with two small children, and they were on the floor in a cubicle with a toilet. It had a very heavy iron door, and as the boat rocked she was trying to keep the door open to keep her children warm, because there was some heat coming from all the people and the children weren't really dressed. But the waves got bigger, and then one time she couldn't keep it open and it slammed on the finger of her two-year-old and snapped the top right off his finger. My grandfather tried to wrap something around the finger, to stop the bleeding. The child was screaming and screaming, so my grandfather mashed up some painkiller and gave it to him in a drink. The kid drank it and went out, unconscious. So my grandfather was a little bit worried and he called up a doctor, on the radio, and the doctor said, no, it's OK, it's better the child sleeps through this. So that's one of the things he remembers best, trying to bandage this small finger and then the child going out like that. It was rough, a very rough trip.'

Theódór nods, rests his hand on Margrét's shoulder and tells his grandson some more of the story. 'And then after that week, after those six trips to take everyone's possessions, the captain said it was time to go out fishing again. So he was away for the next month after that, fishing and in and out of harbours all over the place to unload the fish. And then towards the end of the month they had unloaded at Grindavik, and although the weather was getting bad the captain wanted to go out again. So they went out again, but the storm grew and the ship stranded and broke up on the shore. That was the twenty-second of February, and it had come into harbour at Heimaey on the twenty-second of January.'

Margrét breaks in, contradicting something, and they all

laugh. Theódór replies soothingly, reminding me again of my grandfather, who grew in calm in direct relation to my grandmother's fluster, as if there were a limited amount of anxiety in the house and she had hoarded it all. Margrét shakes her head and pours more coffee and then Teddi translates. As everyone squashed onto the boat in the early hours of 23rd January, Theódór went back to the house. 'Even though they hadn't taken anything with them, he went back for his gun and his stamp collection. And my mother got really mad at him, wanted to know what he wanted the gun for.' Across the table, Theódór sips, twinkles, shrugs. His gun, he wanted it. 'And of course he took almost all his things, his clothes and his gun and his stamp collection, with him afterwards, to the fishing. But when the ship stranded, there was no chance to take anything, so he went to his cabin and put the gun and the collection into a special bag, a waterproof bag that they have for such times. And the cabin had used to belong to a man who had passed away, so as he left, as the ship broke up, he asked that man to take care of the bag for him and promised to come back and get it. And then he went out from the ship. Most of the men lost everything they had during that stranding, but my grandfather managed to get back to the wreck a few days later. He went to his cabin, and everything was completely upside down. The gun was bent and broken. But the stamp collection was in the bag, hanging on a hook, and the stamps were fine. Dry.'

Theódór still has the stamps, not here in the city but safe in his house on Heimaey.

'So you lost everything?' I ask. 'Between the volcano and the shipwreck?'

Theódór nods, pats his wife's hand. 'A lot was destroyed.'

Eyjafjallajökull

I wonder if I am beginning to understand why Icelanders seem unperturbed by economic collapse, the swine flu epidemic which has swept Europe over the winter and the eruption of Eyjafjallajökull. Amalia Lindal's theory about fishing makes more sense after talking to Theódór. Fishing means that all plans and livelihoods are always dependent on the whims of North Atlantic wind and weather, and the alternative is farming on land that explodes from time to time. A limited sense of both responsibility and agency could be the only way of remaining sane in such a place; you can't live in Iceland without discovering the limits of human power, and it's not intelligent to try to take responsibility for what you can't control.

'Four hundred houses were destroyed,' says Theódór. 'And another three hundred filled up and covered over with ash. Two million tonnes of ash and seven million tonnes of lava went over the town. And then we had to clean it up. They took the ash away to the north, to make a new runway.'

'What was it like while you were waiting to go back?' I ask. I can imagine the night voyage, the emigrant ship making its way into harbour. But those months of limbo, watching television to see if your house is still there, if you'll ever be able to go home . . .

'We were one of the first families to go back—' says Theódór.

Margrét interrupts, listing families who returned before them.

'I said *one* of the first,' protests Theódór. 'We were among the first. Because our children were not happy at school in Keflavík. The people there were not glad to have families from the Westman Islands among them.'

Margrét speaks, telling something painful. Teddi translates. 'The children got picked on while we stayed in Keflavík. Because the kids there had heard their parents saying that the people from the Westman Islands who were losing their houses and their livelihoods were going to get compensation, so they'd be rich. So the children were bullied and they really didn't want to go to school there.' I meet Teddi's eyes. He knows about bullying. 'I was surprised,' he adds, shrugging. 'No-one has spoken about that aspect.'

'So they were treated like immigrants?' I ask.

'Yeah,' says Teddi. Margrét speaks. 'She's saying that when they lived in Hveragerði, the first weeks after the eruption, there was a school just for the kids from the island. With their own teacher. They didn't go to school with the Hveragerði kids at all, they didn't blend in, and so they didn't experience these problems there. They were never teased in Hveragerði.'

'What was it like for the grown-ups? Were they able to integrate?'

Hveragerði is less than half an hour's drive from Þorlákshöfn, where the ferry goes to the island. You can see the Westman Islands, and would certainly have been able to see the eruption, from Hveragerði.

'I was away,' says Theódór. 'Working.'

'At first, it was really cold.' Teddi is translating for Margrét again. 'We were staying in the summer houses. They weren't meant for winter. We all had to get used to being cold. But the children were very happy there. Of course it was a strange time, but we had our community there, the islanders, together for those months.'

The Westman quarter of Hveragerði. It takes fifteen

minutes to stroll with a toddler from one side of Hveragerði to the other.

'You must have been able to follow what was happening on Heimaey while you were away.'

Margrét nods. 'There was a programme on the radio every single day, telling us what was happening. Because there was someone there on the island all the time.'

I've been holding back this question, although I think I know the answer. 'Was your house destroyed?'

'No. Our house was standing but it took seventy trips with a pick-up truck to remove the ash. There were five hundred tonnes of ash in my house.'

'What was it like?' I ask. 'When you got back and saw it?'

Theódór frowns, turns his cup. 'This was very dark.'

There is a pause, which tells me that the darkness was metaphorical.

'Many of the people who were there at the beginning, trying to make progress with their houses, slept in boats in the harbour,' says Teddi. 'Some of the houses were undamaged, but people preferred to be on boats. That way, if something happened, you could just go. Start the engine and go.'

I turn to Margrét, who was always home, who was raising those six children while Theódór was at sea. (I would rather be at home, I think, even with six children, than fishing those waters.) 'What was it like for you when you saw your house again?'

She looks at her grandson. 'For the first days and weeks, I went many times to the window. We were busy cleaning, but I made many trips to the window, to see if anything was happening.'

'There was always smoke coming from the lava,' says

Theódór. 'We could go up there to cook our eggs! And we used the volcano for our heating systems. It stayed warm for the longest time, so we pumped the cold water up through the lava and then into our houses.'

'How long did it take you to stop checking?' I ask Margrét.

'As people started to move back, and things became normal again — you could see there were lights in the houses and people on the streets . . . The children were so happy to be back.'

'Do you ever worry about it now?'

I know what Theódór is going to say.

'No. I don't think about it at all.'

But Margrét does.

10

Vilborg

I have been applying for jobs again. It's a dreamer's tic, like lingering in front of estate agents' windows. What would it be like to have a different life? What would my story be if we lived in a house with apple trees in the garden, or if we moved to Denmark, or Japan? It's the same instinct that brought us to Iceland in the first place, and being here, having left England, I want to hold on to our emigrants' freedom. Going back to Canterbury now would feel like aborting a journey. I accept that we have to leave Iceland, I tell Anthony, but let's keep going. We know we can do it now, being foreigners. Let's stay foreign. I apply to universities in Switzerland, Singapore and Australia. I haven't yet told anyone at Háskoli Íslands that I'm going to resign at the end of the year, as if I think the elves might double academic salaries and allow us to stay. I keep listening to Icelandic stories, acting as if we won't leave.

You know, says Pétur, you should talk to Vilborg. We're in his office, and I'm distracting him from marking by asking for more tales about Iceland in 'the old days'. I'm like a child

191

who doesn't want to go to sleep – just one more. Tell me the one about the rubber boots. Vilborg, he says, remembers the Second World War, and she's a gifted storyteller. I'll get her to phone you, but it might take a while. She's busy, travels a lot.

I scent some more first-hand history. Before we left England, I read the memoirs and journals of some British soldiers occupying wartime Iceland. Iceland seems, for many, to have been a relatively safe and easy posting, where the weather and the land were more dangerous than the enemy. But despite their physical safety, anxiety sings through some of the soldiers' writing. The North Atlantic was a deathly place in the early 1940s, known intimately by both sides. Towards the end of the war, Iceland's mid-Atlantic location, its potential as a stepping-stone from North America to Europe, made other nations' hunger for power swirl around it like an Atlantic storm. I would like to hear a first-hand account of the Icelandic wartime experience.

I wait. Vilborg is busy. And then one Sunday afternoon when we've all gone round to Pétur's house for gluten-free waffles with whipped cream and French jam, she phones. Pétur's not saying much, but the call goes on. The rest of us wander up to Messíana's studio to play with the bags of feathers she uses in her costume design and to watch rainbows over the sea. (Is it not magnificent, Pétur said to me once, is it not more than a man could hope, to be married to a woman who buys coloured feathers by the kilo?) After about twenty minutes Pétur comes upstairs. Will you listen to this, he says, holding the phone out. She's talking about what the American soldiers thought when they first arrived in Seyðisfjörður in 1943. Amazing woman, amazing. And such beautiful Icelandic. He puts the handset back to his ear, reverent as an eavesdropper.

Vilborg

I've never heard a British person say that someone speaks 'beautiful English', not unless in patronising approbation of second language acquisition ('you'd never know she's French, she speaks beautiful English'). Anglophones merely talk, but several people here have mentioned someone's excellent speaking, as if conversation in the right hands is a recognised form of performance. But of course, says Pétur, there is an art of speech, of rhetoric, that isn't just about standing on a platform and going on or trying to persuade or convince. I hope it comes over in her English, he adds. Vilborg uses the language better than anyone.

It takes a few weeks before Pétur pops his head round my door at work and says Vilborg would like to meet a young English writer. I hope you two get on, he says. You'll either love each other or hate each other. She's a lot like you. A lot like me how, I demand, although I know it's a compliment of sorts. In a nice way, of course, he says, and he and Matthew, who's stopped by to explain the latest developments of Eyjafjallajökull and the Icesave Thing, look at each other and laugh. The answer, I think later, might be that we both talk a lot.

On the appointed day, late in April, Pétur e-mails me a map, as he does every time I'm going somewhere new. I walk from work into the city centre, around the lake. There are drifts of what look like miniature violets, or maybe some kind of gentian, under the bushes, and the first few Arctic terns of the summer slicing the air. We've all been waiting for them, the *kríur*. They follow the earth's wavering, winging the globe to avoid the dark. Northern summer in the Arctic, southern summer in the Antarctic, an annual round trip of nearly

60,000 miles that means the polar summers are always theirs. I'm not sure I like the terns. I admire their fish-like flitting through the air, the fine-line delicacy of their pointed shapes, birds that could be drawn only in the finest pen-and-ink, but I am afraid of their speed and sharpness, the way they share our seaside space and would razor open anyone who put a foot out of line. Sharing the walking paths with the summer birds again reminds me too vividly of last summer's disabling sense of foreign-ness, of knowing only that I didn't know the rules and didn't know either how anyone, any bird, might react to my ignorant mistakes. I don't, I think, identifying the terns overhead by their cries, feel like that any more.

I come out by the National Gallery, which I have still failed to visit, vicariously traumatized by Anthony's account of trying to take the children there on a day when they didn't like each other. I turn up one of the warren of streets behind Laugavegur, into the oldest part of the city where painted houses sit at companionable angles behind wooden fences, in gardens where there are trees and fountains and sometimes even a flowerbed. If we stayed, I always tell myself, we would live here. Sometimes Anthony and I pick out our favourites, and it's true that if we sold the Canterbury house we could have one of these, one with wooden lace over the porch on a road too narrow for stupid Icelandic cars. We could walk with Tobias to the pre-school by the lake and we'd have the French bakery and the bookshops and the Vietnamese noodle bar right on the doorstep (though Max would still have to get out to school in Garðabær, somehow). I check my map. Vilborg's house is one of a row that runs parallel to the street. It's made of corrugated steel, painted sky-blue. I pause on the doorstep, suddenly nervous about turning up at a stranger's house with the intention of taking her childhood memories. I smooth my hair, wipe my nose, and ring the bell. The door buzzes, I open it, and there's Vilborg, less of an old lady than I was expecting, leaning down a flight of narrow, twisted stairs towards me. She has long hair, the colour of Regency powdered wigs, swinging over high cheekbones. Come in, she says. I am Vilborg and you are?

Sarah, I say. Sarah, and you're expecting me, aren't you? Pétur said?

She ushers me in. On the coffee table, there's a plate of chocolate digestive biscuits and a steel salver in the shape of a lily pad, the sort my grandmother used to use to offer sausage rolls to the Masons' wives, holding slices of green and red pepper. There's a coffee pot and two cups and saucers on a tray. Young women, Vilborg says, often don't eat chocolate biscuits, so she has prepared the vegetables for me. She hopes I will take whatever I would like. Would I like to look around the house? She and her husband bought the house in the 1960s to save it from demolition. (Her husband, Pétur told me, was a major figure in twentieth-century Icelandic history, a publisher, film-maker, playwright and poet, and I have a sense of his ghost here. He's the person who's not sitting in the chair by the window, not in the studio at the back, its windows filled like those of a bookshop with his work, not wearing the decorations framed on the wall. I claim my foreigner's licence not to care; I'm here for Vilborg.) Moving around this Hansel-and-Gretel house poses problems for someone who needs a stick to walk, but they're problems Vilborg solved long ago, albeit in ways alarming to the beholder. She swings a little down the stairs, backs through narrow doorways. The paint on the walls shows where things used to stand. Old wiring loops across the ceilings, taking light to the right places for reading. The furniture shows where people's heads have rested and legs stretched out, and books crowd walls and sideboards and cupboards. It's probably the oldest decor I've seen in Iceland, and it makes me homesick, not exactly for our house but for the clutter of households of books and pictures in grimy frames and mis-matched plates acquired or inherited three at a time and chairs that no-one in living memory has chosen to buy.

We return to the sitting room and settle down, me on the sofa and Vilborg in an armchair, surrounded by books. Coffee and biscuits, and there are footsteps on the stairs. My grandson, says Vilborg. He's studying for his exams. At the university.

He comes in, takes a cup. I'm here to visit Vilborg, I say. Oh, he says, are you a poet? No, I say apologetically, only a novelist.

My son is in America, Vilborg explains. He used to run the genome project here in Reykjavík but then they cut the funding and now he is in Berkeley, California. (The Icelandic Human Genome Project lives in the black glass building, curved and shiny as a lake in the dark, that overshadows Alvar Aalto's Nordic House on the marsh in front of the university. They have the DNA of every Icelander and are thus able to conduct research impossible in countries with more sensitivity to issues of privacy and data protection.) So my grandson is living here with me while he takes his examinations.

I am confused by the grandson's name; he was introduced under one name but is referred to as someone quite different.

Ah yes, says Vilborg, our names are not easy for foreigners. No, I tell her. Your nicknaming makes it impossible to know whose essay I'm marking. Someone I've known for six months as 'Disa' turns out to be 'Hrafnhildur Auður' in writing. The bloke whose essays say 'Steingrimur' has always been called what sounds like 'Tinni' in my hearing. (Later, I learn that this is because it's the custom to name babies at around six months. Naturally, you have to call them something in the meantime, and equally naturally, what you call them in the meantime tends to stick. Babies, in my experience, get called some pretty daft things in the first six months, even when they have perfectly serviceable names registered at birth.)

Vilborg laughs. It's good when Vilborg laughs.

'My son was called Goggur! Everyone calls him that.'

'He's named after a cat, isn't he?' asks Goggur's son, as if he hasn't heard the story dozens of times before.

'He was like a cat,' agrees Vilborg. 'He was born two months too early and he was just like a little cat. Or a chicken. It's a very common name for a rooster, you know, Goggur.'

Are there common names for roosters in English?

'But there was a cat,' Goggur's son reminds her. 'A special cat that survived an avalanche.'

'He was just like a wild animal,' says Vilborg. 'He used to roam from one house to another and then he went up into the rocks and he was living there and we were all afraid of it.'

Her English is clear, slightly careful, the kind of thing one might have learnt from the BBC in the 1950s, but the plosive consonants carry Icelandic weight. *Uppp*. *Ittt*. You could write a musical score for her sentences.

'When Goggur was a kitten, there came an avalanche on the house. The people left in time and the house was carried away, leaving just a corner of the wall with a window, and there sat the kitten. And because of that, even when he was coming down from the mountain and stealing food, nobody wanted to kill Goggur. He was a giant. Somehow, he was holy. Once, my brothers had been hunting – everybody went hunting then, in Seyðisfjörður – for birds for our suppers. You have to wait before you take the feathers off, so they left the birds outside and came in for coffee. And when they came out, the birds were all spoiled and the biggest one was gone, because Goggur had been! And my brother said I'll take the gun and shoot that bastard but he never did, no-one did, because it was holy, that tomcat. I think the last time he was seen he was twenty years old. More coffee?'

'Tell me more,' I say greedily. 'Tell me what it was like. No-one's been able to tell me about those years.'

So she does. I go back to her house two more times, leaving on each occasion full of stories, sated with an eye-witness account of Iceland through the second half of the twentieth century. Vilborg's memories stretch from childhood on a small-holding in pre-war Seyðisfjörður to staying with Aria Ben Gurion in Israel in the 1970s and with a women's group in Palestine ten years later. She refers to a friend in Prague, a professor who disliked cooking and lived in a flat so small that even the oven was full of books, to a distinguished lawyer, an elderly Polish Jewish refugee, who befriended her and took her out to dinner when she was a poor student in Edinburgh in the 1950s. Vilborg talks in arcs, swooping to Israel, finishing the story about childcare on the kibbutz and reminding herself of the time her little brother nearly died in the care of the village doctor, going off to find a photo of the doctor's now deserted house and explaining why so many coastal villages were abandoned when Route 1 came through and the coastal supply ships stopped coming, remembering the international guests of the Icelandic writers' union, of which she was the chair for many years.

'You are, of course, a member,' she says. 'But then surely I would have met you earlier?'

I know I should have tried to join. I know of other Anglophone writers who have done so and found the camaraderie, advice on tax breaks and access to residential writers' retreats greatly beneficial. I have envied these writers. 'No,' I admit, 'I didn't think they'd want me.'

I don't think Vilborg recognises this, the sore conviction of my own inadequacy, bruised again by the experience of being foreign. She's looking back on opportunities taken, adventures welcomed, a life, I think, enviably lived. She begins with her childhood in the late 1930s.

'When I was seven it was my duty to drive the cows to the field. There was a boy of my age in the village and we were the only two who were seven, so when the spring came and it was time for the cows to go out we took turns, me one week and him the next, all through the summer. It wasn't really very far, perhaps half an hour, but it seems long to a child. It was pleasant in fine weather, but I had to pass many stones and rocks where there were hidden people, and I was afraid of the Devil. It was a village where everyone who could afford a cow kept one, because they needed the milk. When there was no milk in the cow, there was no milk in the house. There were sheep, too. My father had thirty sheep, but we had no horse. There were very few horses because the ground was too steep for them, but we all had boats, we learnt to row just as we learnt to walk because that was how we always travelled. When I first went to Reykjavík I went on the boat and it took a whole week, because the boat stopped everywhere, for post and supplies, three or four hours in each village and this was splendid. But then they stopped that and put all the transport on cars and trucks, and in the villages with no roads, where they needed the boats, or where they needed at least two or three ships in the winter when the roads were blocked, the people just couldn't live there when the boats stopped. There are just empty houses now, big, beautiful houses, because people had money when the boats came and they built good houses. Our house stood in the homefield, and we had to walk a very narrow path to the gate, because the grass was very precious and you had to save it. And at the gate there was water under the grass, you know, so it was muddy and boggy? We used to run over it in a row, and I was afraid that if my foot went in, a hand would grab me and pull me down, because you know there is a nursery rhyme that is not nice at all: "There was a child in a valley, who fell into a hole. And the monster beneath held his feet and pulled him down."'

Icelandic children's culture seems full of these charming ditties. When you put these habits beside Pétur's stories about going to the barn to share the cows' sewage arrangements, nervous children have a dilemma. Maybe the stories replace the discipline to which everyone swears that Icelandic children are not subject. No-one tells you off, but the dark and the fields are full of waiting, hiding creatures who are out to get you.

'And when I was driving the cows, I had to pass many stones. The first stone, we children were sure that if you put your ear to it you could hear someone spinning. Everyone had a spinning wheel then, my mother and my grandmother, because we all made our own clothes at home from the wool of our own sheep. So we thought there was a fairy woman sitting there under the stone, spinning and spinning, sitting day and night spinning, and when we were all together we would go and listen to the stone. And of course it wasn't far from the sea. We were hearing the sea! But we thought it was the hidden woman spinning and spinning, and I was afraid of it. And further along from that stone was a huge rock, called *Festusteinn*, and I was afraid to pass it even in the mornings, in the sunshine. This big stone was used to fasten the ships that came. We had no quay in those days, so when ships were lying in the inlet they were made fast to this stone. There were hidden people and elves among those rocks, and people said that the *Festusteinn* was their church, because it was so big, and I never dared even to look in that direction. But next to it was another stone which we liked very much. It was all in steps, shaped in steps, and we called it *Trappasteinn*. We children used to go there in the spring and each child had a place on the steps to make cakes of mud, and there was a competition to make the nicest mud cakes. And I went on, and when I had nearly come to the place where I could leave the cows and go home, there was a big flat stone beside the road and it was called *Gaujusteinn*. Gauja was the name of the woman who lived in the house above that stone, which was called *Foss*, which means waterfall, because there were falls in the river there. And Gauja used to go to shop in the big village at the end of the fjord. It was a very nice place, one of the nicest places in Iceland, the most cultured town in the whole country, and the telephone came there first and everything came there first. They had trees everywhere.'

The connection between the 'most cultured town' and its trees isn't as arbitrary as it sounds. There is a national argument about trees in Iceland. The island was forested when the settlers arrived, but has been bare since medieval Icelanders

chopped all the trees down. There is a reforestation programme, regarded by some traditionalists as a bourgeois plan
to make Iceland look European, put forward by intellectuals
who have spent too much time *i útlöndum* and don't value
their own country any more. Forest seems un-Icelandic to
people whose parents, grandparents and great-grandparents
down to the twentieth generation have known the naked con-
tours of mountain and plain. Trees are indeed, albeit falsely,
associated with being cosmopolitan.

'So Gauja went all the way there to shop, and when she
came back with her parcels she would be tired and she would
sit a while on her stone and her name was Gauja so we called
it *Gaujusteinn*, and I would sit there a few minutes myself. My
uncle lived up in the rocks and they had twelve children. And
the boy who looked after the cows when it wasn't my turn, he
was one of twelve as well. And I am one of twelve. There's
nobody living there now. It's just grass.'

I can't – wouldn't – interrupt Vilborg. It would be like
climbing onto the stage to ask an actor to repeat a word you
didn't catch. Later, I ask Pétur about the name 'Goya', which
I haven't heard before. Gauja, he says, the nickname for
Guðríður and other Guð-prefixed women's names. Of course.

'Once when I was driving the cows along there, I saw a
woman mowing the grass, a woman in a blue frock with a
white apron and very big arms, red from the sun. And she was
mowing the grass and the women never did that, because it
was men's work. I had never seen that woman before. I
thought she was a giant woman, a *skessa*, we say, because we
believed that in the old days. Icelandic trolls are very big, not
small like the Danish ones. Our trolls are huge, as you know.
And when I saw that she was there, just by the rock, I was so

afraid that I closed my eyes, and hoped she would be gone, but when I opened them she was still there. But I had to keep driving the cows, and so I came to the field and she was still there, mowing, and she didn't disappear at all and I was so frightened. When I came home I sat in the middle of the kitchen floor and cried. My mother didn't know what had happened so I told her and she said, "Oh, but this is Bjargey, and she is a woman who lives with another woman and does a man's work." Because you see there were these homosexuals in my village and nobody bothered about it in those times. There was Margrét, who was – what do you call it, not a doctor, she was rubbing people – massage, and she lived in a very nice house with Bjargey, just the two of them. And Bjargey always did the man's work, but I was sure she was a *huldukona*!

We knew that there were *huldufólk*, because once my aunt came to stay with us, when she needed to see the doctor in my town. My mother made coffee and she said, "Oh, something awful happened!" My mother had a *brauðskeri*.'

Vilborg smiles, as if she's offering something she knows I want, but I'm not sure what it is. She shuffles forwards and begins to stand up.

'Come upstairs and I will show you what it is, and then I will tell you a *brauðskerasaga* and you will understand.'

Brauðskeri. Brauð is bread. A story about bread? An awful story about bread? Vilborg puts her coffee down – she has been fitting coffee and chocolate biscuits around her storytelling. I wait while she gets her hands onto the arms of her chair and levers herself upright. We go down the narrow hall and she swings herself up the tight little staircase. She takes me into her bedroom. The bed is made and there are books everywhere, colonising the dressing table and the chair by the bed, creeping along the skirting boards. They are mostly hardbacks, as many in English as in Icelandic. The collected works of D. H. Lawrence lean on each other by the bed. A monograph on Frida Kahlo keeps *Jude the Obscure* and *The Woman in White* apart.

'Here!' says Vilborg, removing a volume of poetry in Danish, something by Philip Roth and *Mrs Dalloway* from what looks at first like a small iron bookshelf, the sort of thing I have on my desk at home to hold the books I'm working on. 'Look, it's very nice.' She removes some more books. 'My mother used to make very good, big rye bread. Everything was baked at home.'

Vilborg holds up the *brauðskeri* but it's heavy, built like an old German sewing machine. It's a kind of guillotine, with a shelf that would hold a loaf the size of George Eliot's complete works in hardback. '*Brauðskeri* is its name, the bread-cutter, and you see it's quite a thing! So now I will tell you the story.'

I help her put the books back and we go downstairs again.

'My mother used to keep her *brauðskeri* in the pantry, which had a window that opened onto the hillside. The window was small, half the size of that one, narrow as windows were in those days.' The windows in this house are nineteenth-century, urban, Danish-influenced and probably not, really, ideal for the climate, since they must originally have had the same kind of draughty glazing that makes our Canterbury house so cold. 'You could open a small part of it, but because the house was built into the slope, the window was just in the ground, and therefore if it was open, a chicken would fly into it, and so there was wire mesh over it. So you couldn't put your hand through, and this apparatus, this *brauðskeri*, was too big to pass through. And my mother wanted to cut some bread, and the *brauðskeri* wasn't there. Nobody had done anything with it, but it wasn't there, and it wasn't on the table, and it was not anywhere. And who should steal it? No-one knew particularly where it was, and anyone who did not own such a nice thing would own a knife. And my mother's sister was what was called *skyggn*, she could see things that other people could not see, and she said to my mother, "Don't worry, it comes back. I met a woman who lives in the rock in the next field, and she was holding it, she put her apron over it when she saw me, and she will give it back." And the next day it was back in its place! And they believed it, my mother believed it, though what it is, I don't know. Sometimes you don't see things, and next time you look they are there, so all this about things disappearing does happen, it does! They were telling the truth as they saw it. They believed in ghosts also, the grown-ups did, and of course we had only candle-light and lanterns, we had very nice lanterns, and you had to put them all out at night. I often think about it; we would go to the doorstep and see if they were putting out the lights in this house or that, and of course you are not allowed to leave the light on when you go to sleep. That's how my uncle died. He forgot to put the lantern out and the house burnt down and he died. That did happen, you had to be careful with lanterns and candles.'

'We were of course quite many in each bed. The little boys had a bed, I was sleeping with my sister and my grandmother was in the room also, and she kept the light. So when she said goodnight and put the light out, everyone had to sleep. But I put a book under my pillow and when the moon came out, I did read it, although it was forbidden. The moon shone in the window, right at me, because we didn't have curtains up there. There were curtains for the dining room and for my parents' bedroom and for the kitchen window, my mother was very handy with her needle and she made everything. This village, you know, there is not a house there now. Everything, it's all away. All gone.'

Vilborg offers me another biscuit, a slice of green pepper. I wasn't expecting her to say that, although I know many of the coastal villages are now deserted, cut off by the roads instead of connected by the boats, the people sucked out to Reykjavík as if caught in a vortex. Listening to Vilborg is like reading, and I was seeing the page on her pillow by moonlight, hearing the sighs and rustles after her grandmother had blown out the lantern, imagining her mother with a lapful of heavy curtain material and the needle gleaming by firelight. It's all away.

'People believed in their dreams, too, and they would tell fortunes in a coffee cup.' She picks up her cup, half-full of cold coffee. 'You drink the coffee three times.' She swallows what's left in three gulps. 'You turn it three times.' She swirls the dregs around the cup. 'You turn it over, like that, and let it dry. And then you read it. They were always doing that, at home. My mother was very keen on it, telling the cups. The neighbours did so. It was very common when I was a child.'

It must be another not-very-old Icelandic tradition. Surely people in the villages didn't regularly have coffee until not long before Vilborg's childhood? I think about the Atlantic journeys of early twentieth-century coffee beans.

'Did you believe it?' I ask.

'My mother liked to do it. She knew everybody, and she knew what was going on beneath the surface, but she thought she saw it in the cups. She didn't see the *huldukonur*, only her sister saw those, but she saw ghosts and such beings and she had dreams. My great-grandfather was also like that, it runs in families. People used to come and tell her what they needed to tell, and when there was trouble in a house it was my mother who would be called. She was always there if something bad was happening. Because life was hard, you know. By the time I was fifteen, three of my brothers and three of my sisters were dead. My sisters were fifteen and twenty and twenty-four, and they died within six months of tuberculosis. Two of my brothers died very young. One was two years old, it was the year I was born, 1930, he was ill and there was a doctor there but no medicines, nothing to help. And the other was in his first year and there was a bug that was going around and it affected his lungs. The doctor wasn't sure, he didn't know. My brother just got very ill and they didn't – they didn't do anything.'

Vilborg's voice breaks for the first time, although she's talked to me by now about her dead husband and her abandoned village and Iceland's betrayal of Jewish refugees and her son's emigration to California and the financial collapse of her country (though I'm beginning to understand that Icelanders older than I am have seen more than one previous collapse and resurrection). Vilborg's pleasure in life, her appetite for new people and new stories and new journeys, isn't because she has nothing to cry about.

'And then my brother Jóhann drowned in 1946. There were twenty – twenty young sailors that day.' She breaks off, swallows. 'We lost so many men.' We wait. I can say nothing for her loss, thirty years before I was born. It would feel like an insult to pat her hand. 'That was the ninth of February nineteen-hundred-and-forty-six.' She says February with both 'r's, as even Pétur with his perfect diction does not, and speaks the date as if standing at the cenotaph.

'There came bad weather, and in this weather twenty young sailors — there were three boats and five men in each and another boat, twenty young sailors. And on his boat, Jóhann was twenty-one, it was nearly his birthday, and there was another of twenty-two and three of nineteen. It was like that. Last year is the first year in the history of Iceland that we don't lose anybody at sea. Jóhann was not a fisherman, not at sea. He worked on the land, and my mother had made him promise that he wouldn't go to sea, because he was named after my uncle who drowned and we have a tradition in Iceland that you don't name a child for someone who dies like that. But one man who was meant to be on the boat got drunk and broke his leg, and they were going to sea very early in the morning. At first my brother refused, but they somehow forced him, and he made them swear not to tell my mother. They were in Hafnarfjörður, you see, at the winter fishing. They promised they wouldn't tell my mother he had been to sea, but then he didn't come back. And it was a hard thing to lose him.'

Vilborg passes me a small book from the table at her side. Old leather binding, the size of my palm. Inside, pasted to black pages, are sepia photographs. Her parents, born in 1886 and 1895. The mother of the first Jóhann, born in 1860. Then there are pictures of the village, hard to understand in soft brown and a quarter the size of a postcard.

'Did you climb these mountains?' I ask. I'm wondering if the only way out was by sea, if the mountains felt like a wall.

She pours coffee for me. 'No. Because I was only ten when the soldiers came. And then the fjord was locked, it was a fortress, and the girls were not allowed to wander about when the soldiers were there.'

'Why not?' I ask. National security or a fear of what foreign soldiers might do to Icelandic little girls?

'Well, because they were up in the mountains as well. Going round about and spying after the Germans or whatever. I always felt very safe, though. Because my village was locked, they locked it, and you had to show a passport given by the army if you wanted to come in. It was because from my village you could see right across the firth, whereas in town the mountains block the view, you can see only a little piece of sky. They put gates at the road, and a barrier and a guard standing there day and night, and a barrier across the fjord and a ship guarding day and night, and there were mines in the water, because all the ships coming from Murmansk and going to America and back would use our fjord as a refuge, and the submarines would see them coming and try to sink them. And they put big guns up in front of the church. There was no shelter for the Icelanders when the aeroplanes came, only for the soldiers. Down on the road by the gate there was a flag-pole, and of course we knew when they flew a yellow flag there were planes nearby. And when the planes came they would shoot from the big gun by the church, first three times three and then they were shooting everywhere. They would shoot and shoot so the planes couldn't come down, and three times they shot a plane. The inhabitants of Seyðisfjörður were only a thousand people then, and the British army brought over two thousand. And then came these convoys from Russia and America, and huge ships that a plane could land on as well. So you can imagine how it was then. But I was very secure. The navy officers lived in our house and if I wanted to go anywhere, they sent men to escort me.'

'They lived in your house?'

'They came on a huge ship and they took every house, they took the school. It was a cold springtime, rainy, and when there is much rain there can come a landslide. There was a place in between the villages where there were no buildings because there had been a big avalanche, the year before my mother was born, 1895, and over twenty people died. And first the soldiers came and put up their tents and a big wind came and blew away the tents and all their things and they were running about. They had been sleeping when the storm began and we children thought it was funny to see them running around so. And they did repair the tents and the other things, those that hadn't blown out to sea, and they wanted to build their barracks there, under the mountain where there were no buildings because it wasn't safe. They were told that they weren't allowed to build there but they said it was all right, their buildings are shaped like polytunnels and the landslide will pass over, and they put all their tents there again. And so the policeman and the magistrate and everyone went there and told them they had to move, they did not allow any man to stay because it is dangerous. And the landslide came that night and all the things, the big guns and so on, went down into the sea, and if the men had stayed they would have been killed. So then they knocked on the doors and they said, "Is there a room your family doesn't need? We will have it." And they were in my grandparents' house, because there were no children there and my grandfather had been dead a long time, and there was a lounge and an office, the two biggest, smartest rooms in the house, and they had their own special door for coming and going, and of course they paid rent. They were nice. But the officers got the houses while the men lived in barracks. The Icelanders got much work from them, making their buildings and so on, selling them fish. There had been a crisis and lack of work, but then came the British rule.'

'So people were pleased?'

Vilborg looks at the photos in her lap, pictures of young British soldiers smiling wartime smiles in front of turf and rocks. The journals I read recounted lots of bird-watching in between moving equipment around and keeping an eye on the sky for other traffic.

'When I used to go fetch the cows for milking, late in the afternoon when it was falling dark, they would turn their light on for me. They had a station where they could light up the whole firth, floodlights, and also these small lights – spot-lights – and when I was coming in the darkness all along the road I would have a light spot all the way. Because they knew I was a little girl and it was a long way for me.'

I want to see something very English in this story, in the blatant use of official resources for purposes of private chivalry.

'Everyone talked about how girls would go and make love with the British soldiers but it wasn't so. The youngest in the army were only sixteen years. There was one who was just a boy, and we used to play a ball game. I don't know if you have it in England, but we children thought it a very pleasant game. He wanted to play with us, and we didn't want to have him play, so he sat down on a stone and wept. He was not a big soldier! But they were nice men.'

'Did people like having the British here?'

It's a disingenuous question. I know that, by and large, with notable exceptions, Icelanders reckoned it better to be occupied by the Allies than the Nazis, but I also know that the wartime occupation figures in the Icelandic cultural imagination as the catalyst for changes which are now working themselves out in the shape of the *kreppa*. Europe's wars were Iceland's boom-times, when the price commanded by lamb, wool and fish on European markets rose and went on rising.

'Well, of course in 1941 the Americans came, so the British were not in Seyðisfjörður very long. The day the Americans came it was very nice weather, and we were all standing look-ing out at the huge ship, like those tourist ships that come.' Vilborg gestures down the hill, towards the harbour where one of the first big cruise ships of the season is blocking down-town's view of Esja. 'It came to deliver two thousand Americans and take away two thousand British, and there was a lot of moving around. And I was standing on the concrete steps of our house and I could see because it was on the hill-side, our house. Many things were happening. The British were going, and there was a row of cars going down the road, and the soldiers took off their guns and put them away when they went in the cars. They had been saying goodbye, giving small gifts and toys they had made for the children. And then I saw a plane coming. The sky was blue. And the plane came. Of course when they were arriving they would have planes with them, so I thought it was just an American plane. And then it came low and first there came a huge bomb in the sea and then a second and then the third, and that one came down in the middle of the road, just opposite where I was on the fjord, and I could see it as it came down and there was brown where it hit the road. There was nobody at the big gun, nobody. It was just the moment between the British and Americans, just these three minutes. And then the soldiers ran out and they started to shoot and they shot and shot and the plane got away. They never got that plane, never. There were three little boys who were playing there at the coast, where the bombs came, and all

of them were hurt and one of them lost his leg. This was awful.
And then the Americans came and took over from the British,
and this was very different. There were Canadians as well, and
also a group of Norwegians, and everyone sent their girls
away if they could.'

I still don't understand why exactly Icelandic parents
needed to keep their daughters away from the soldiers, nor
why North Americans were more of a risk than the British.
Did they fear seduction or rape, their girls' betrayal of national
identity or the savagery of foreign men? But before I can frame
a question Vilborg has swept on.

'I was sent to school in the village my mother came from,
and there were only five soldiers there. The house where I
lived was above the bank and the bank manager's son got stuck
in Germany at the beginning of the war, he was an engineer
and he had to stay on in Germany all through the war. And of
course the Icelanders used to sail to Bremerhaven and Rostock
and they liked these places, and just after the war, when I was
fifteen and there came this nice weather at the end of the war,
then there came a German trawler and they called out to us,
they didn't come in, they called, "Are we allowed to come in?"
Something needed to be mended, and they were not allowed
to go to Norway, and not allowed to go to the Faroe Islands,
and they asked, "Are we allowed to come?" Everyone heard
that a trawler from Bremerhaven had come in, all the fishermen there, and everyone heard that the Germans were not
fighting any more, they were back at sea. And everyone went
to the quay and, oh, this was a rickety-rack ship, all in disor-
der, and full of youngsters, fine youngsters. And the women
put on huge pots of meat soup and fed those men, and the
men took the trawler and started to mend what needed to be

mended so they could fish. And before they went off they all had a marvellous meal and new clothes and everyone stood to watch as they went off, because they were back, back at sea from Bremerhaven.'

The Nazis liked Iceland, or at least liked the idea of Iceland, an island of pure Nordic genes where Wagner's gods hung out.

'So the Germans felt more like friends than the Americans?'

'Icelanders had always liked the Germans. And it was very painful when they went on being like that. But we didn't have any Jews, we didn't know anything about the Jews, there weren't any Jews in Iceland. There were many in Denmark and King Christian the Tenth did everything he could to save the Jews when the Germans came.' Vilborg puts her cup down and sits forward, almost takes my hand. 'But, you, you are not British!'

And it's back, something I haven't thought about since I was an undergraduate. I am British. I have a British passport (and an American one, tucked away at the back of my sock-drawer, because when I was born my parents thought it was a good idea for a child with my parentage to have an escape route from Europe). I was born in Glasgow, grew up in Manchester, spent ten years in Oxford and five in Canterbury. These months in Iceland are the longest time I've spent outside the UK, although when I was a teenager I had a German friend and used to spend summers in Germany and people there, older people, sometimes told me I wasn't British. Then they tried to apologise for the Holocaust, usually while we were all in the outdoor pool between the gardens in suburban Düsseldorf for an early morning swim, and I felt doubly fraud-ulent; not only had my father's family left Europe early in the

1930s, but I'm not Jewish even by the lights of people who see Britishness and Jewishness as mutually exclusive. Judaism passes down the maternal line. As a student, I used to flirt with the idea of conversion, but more for the appeal of joining the club of over-achieving outsiders that was the student Jewish Society than because of any particular spiritual yearning.

'My father's Jewish,' I say.

Vilborg laughs. 'I did notice this. I noticed it as soon as I saw you. I am a Protestant and I was of course a communist, a Protestant communist, but I've been to Israel and I do like the Jews, wherever I've been I've had Jewish friends.'

'I'm not really Jewish,' I point out. 'My mother's not Jewish. And my father doesn't practise. He eats bacon.'

'But you need to have some customs,' she reasons.

'We went to church more often, actually. Christmas and Easter.'

'Synagogue?' she asks hopefully.

'No,' I say firmly. 'Church.'

'I think it's the same God. Allah, Jahweh. Have you been often in Israel?'

'Once. For two days. I didn't like it.'

Then Vilborg tells me about her own trips to the Middle East, weeks spent touring kibbutzim and then on the other side, working with Palestinian writers. She remembers seeing children with tuberculosis in refugee camps, and reminds herself of her dead sisters. 'We – I am part of a time when there was much tuberculosis in Iceland. We are the last ones. You see, my sisters, they were beautiful young women and they died all three of them in 1941. In some families all the young people died of tuberculosis. Now it's gone. It's all away now.'

She's getting tired, I'm almost overwhelmed by stories. I

have the same feeling as when I swim to the surface after hours in a novel, a change of element. We part affectionately, and I walk back into town towards the bus, thinking about Vilborg and about listening. Iceland has an oral culture much closer to the surface than in most of Europe. The sagas were told for centuries before they were written down. Impromptu poetry-making is an important part of after-dinner speeches and sometimes political protest; at formal dinners there is often an open mic where people compete to translate limericks from one language to another without losing the rhyme or scansion. Icelanders buy more books per capita than anywhere else in the world. Literary historians tend to see the written word replacing the spoken, books as an evolution of storytelling, but maybe in Iceland narrative is important in either form. Maybe, it occurs to me as I cross the harbour, where the sunlit slopes of Esja hang like a curtain behind the first of the year's cruise ships, I shouldn't turn Vilborg's stories into writing.

11

The Hidden People

Pétur stops by my office for a chat. I planted some of the bulbs brought from home here, in an ice-cream tub that I've kept on the window-sill, turning it assiduously as the buds lean and harken to the pale sun. They bloomed, at last, narcissi like balled tissue paper and miniature daffodils a hesitant shade of yellow, and for a week my office with its bare walls and wipe-down lino floor breathed flowers as well as orange-peel and central heating. But the heavy heads have sickened, the petals are browning and fruit-flies have been issuing from the compost for the last few days. I don't feel able to throw them away. It would be worse than ungrateful, perhaps hubristic, when it's minus four outside and they have done what they are meant to do at home despite air travel, fluorescent light and the ice-cream tub over the radiator. Guerilla planting may be indicated, but at these temperatures I suspect it would be the same as throwing away and anyway I don't have a trowel. So there they sit. Pétur sits beside them and talks. The flies flicker around his hair and after a bit he notices. Oh, you have flies! he cries, as if I have orchids or bottles of rare wine. It's too cold for flies in Iceland most of the time. I know, I apologise, I need to get rid of the bulbs now the flowers have died. No, he says, how can you say that? Little sparks of life in the air? I see a solution. I stand up and present him with the ice-cream tub. He goes off, cackling, and when I stop by his office later he leans into his screen, his wild hair encircled by a halo of fruit flies. I think he is one of the most likeable people I have ever met.

At the end of April, it's still cold. Window weather, says Mæja, meeting me stamping my feet and blowing into my gloves by the radiator in the lobby. Pretty to look at, too cold to go out. We've had a week of window weather, a bowl of blue sky upturned over the island, the glacier at Snæfellsnes flirting over the horizon at sunrise and sunset, sunshine in the air and on the mountains and amber in the streams that are not frozen. Winter is over, you think. You look out of your office window and think it is a shame and a sin to be inside on a day like this, after all that dark and snow and rain. Birds sing and rustle in the still-bare bushes, but there are buds of green pushing through, bright on their twigs like a child's first teeth, a few catkins on the more sheltered willows and an abundance of light now, fourteen hours in which it would be possible to read outside. If it were possible to survive standing still outside for long enough to grasp a paragraph.

Ten weeks till we go home, says Anthony at breakfast. Max and I meet each other's gaze, spoons arrested mid-air. Ten weeks? Three months, I say. Almost three months. Anthony shrugs. He's counted. I shake it off, not wanting to think about the end, not wanting to lose the last three months to a count-down, but it's time to make an effort. Get out and go somewhere. We can't go home having spent eleven months in Reykjavík. Anthony wants to go to Geysir and I say it's too far, the weather isn't dependable and who wants to drive for five hours with two children in the car just to see one geyser? We'll never see it if we don't, he says. Later in the year, I say, when, for example, the sea isn't frozen. The roads are dry, he says. Here they are, I say, you don't know what it's like over the mountain. What about Borgarnes? There's a museum there, inside, and we haven't been that way at all, out to the north. We should see what's round the other side of Esja. I look in the Red Book, the Icelandic road atlas, bible of all that we are not going to do. There's a hiking trail through some alpine forest, says Anthony, reading over my shoulder. You like trees. We can assemble the hot cross buns in the morning and go in the afternoon, forest walk and on to the museum and back in time for supper.

Even Tobias likes the forest walk, scampering goat-like up the lower slopes of Esja. There is sunlight through pine trees, some shelter from the wind, leaping streams frozen in action, icicles growing out of the moss like sea anemones, and just occasionally, in a sheltered spot, perhaps the ghost of the smell of fir, an intimation of what it might be like here in summer when it will smell of earth and trees and growing. But the afternoon is passing; we get back in the car and go on, following signs to The North. The sky over the sea turns grey, and then the horizon is swallowed by dark cloud. Snow begins to whirl over the mountains, and then to settle on the wind-screen-wipers. We exchange glances. There's no point moving to Iceland and being scared by a bit of snow. I can't see the car in front any more, and then I can't see the road. Damn it, I say. Let's just go back to the flat. Window weather. It's not charming, or wimpish, but a state of mind in which a fairly serious hope, that winter is over, that life is returning, is lost. It's the antithesis of Easter.

Then the volcano blows again. It's not a 'tourist eruption' any more, and Iceland is back on the front page. At first I think we can't see it at all, but after a couple of days I notice that, even on a clear day, there's always a cloud in the same place on the eastern horizon. From higher up, from Pétur's office or from one of my teaching rooms, I can see that it's a triangular cloud, the apex pointing below Reykjavík's horizon. At first we keep checking the news, as if it's a major disaster that might in some way unfold, might produce a story. It has the thrill of an international outrage without the vulgarity of suffering held up for mass consumption. Then we realise that our friend won't be able to come from London at the weekend. If it continues past then, I won't be able to go to Singapore for my job interview, and if it continues past then – When is it going to stop? I ask Anthony, who is refreshing the BBC website. It went on for two years last time, he says. They can't close European airspace for two years, I protest. He shrugs. They can if the planes can't stay up. I look over his shoulder at the map, showing the ash making its way south and east across the Atlantic and spreading out towards central Europe. Post comes that way, I think. There are at least two parcels on their way to me now, Spanish chocolate from a friend who runs a Catalan food stall in Canterbury and the US edition of my novel. Our tenant has just forwarded our voting cards for the election. No post. Perhaps we should look at ferry tickets home, says Anthony, and I say, nonsense, they'll have sorted something out by then. But earlier I was trying, and failing, to impress on Max that there is no way of controlling a volcano. Of course, Anthony adds as I disappear with some chocolate and a DVD, we'd have to go round by Akureyri to get to the ferry anyway, drive three-quarters of the way round the island, what with the road being broken by the volcano. Except that at the moment, that section is also closed by ash. There's no way out.

We get used to it. Visitors from England, who have been waiting until spring to visit us, cancel. Our friend Henri, who has been in Somalia for most of the time we've been in Iceland, gets as far as Heathrow and stays there, valiantly, for most of the day. Anthony can't visit his father in hospital, my parents are contentedly stuck on the Amalfi Coast. After long discussion of dates, I have, at last, booked flights to Singapore for a job interview in six days' time. We know someone who has missed his child's birth while trying to get back from Beijing by train, and someone else who couldn't get to her own wedding. The internet is humming with stories of people's rage, resourcefulness and dismay. That's when I approach the volcano again. It feels like going into the eye of the storm, the crater full of curses and howls of outrage from airports around the globe. I'm going there to meet a woman who talks to elves.

Icelanders believe in elves. Maybe. Some of them. When deciding where to build roads, the Department of Transport consults mediums who speak to the hidden people. Many people, especially in the countryside, salute the guardian spirits of particular stones and waterfalls as they drive along. Tourist information magnifies this aspect of Icelandic life until you could be forgiven for imagining a nation that reverences animated garden gnomes frolicking across the lava. The tourist shops downtown do a good line in elf-tat, plaster figurines with toadstool houses or, at the up-market end, handmade dwarves made of undyed felt from Icelandic wool. Hafnarfjörður Tourist Board produces a map of the municipality – the settlement with the highest elf-density in Iceland – showing where elves' houses and playgrounds are scattered between the industrial estates and apartment blocks. Icelanders' ideas about tourists can be as embarrassing as tourists' ideas about Icelanders, and it's so obvious to me that none of my friends and students here believe any such thing that at first I don't ask about elves. But I do like ghost stories. The sagas have some memorable ones, so I ask around for the modern equivalents. Pétur says, oh, but you must go see Þórunn. Messíana knows her. (Messíana knows everyone.) We'll put you in touch. It turns out that Þórunn lives in Kópavogur, the next suburb in from Garðabær, but, says Pétur, I should go see her in her mountain house. Yes, Messíana agrees, then she can show you the elves. Þórunn showed Messíana the elves, but Messíana couldn't see anything. Although she had fun.

I postpone the trip. I find the idea of talking to someone about elves embarrassing, and I'm still scared of driving on the unsurfaced roads outside the city, but one day after Easter Pétur tells me that Þórunn will be available to see me at her summer house on Saturday. He e-mails me a map. It's a long way, much further out of the city than I've been before, and half the roads are gravel tracks. It's also rather near Eyjafjallajökull.

I drive out of the city. I couldn't eat breakfast, and can feel my heart banging as I join the freeway. It takes me a while to work out what the problem is. It's not the driving, not on a bright Saturday with the children safely at home. It's the solitude. I haven't driven anywhere alone since we left England and it feels somehow unsafe, as if, through impulse or mishap, I might drive off the map and not come back. An obese Range Rover roars up behind, and drives along so close that I can't see the number plate in the rear-view mirror. There is an empty overtaking lane but Icelanders try to push you along before resorting to that. I can hear his engine. I follow Hulda Kristín's advice: turn the radio up, ease off the accelerator and stop looking in the mirror. He can't get any closer so there is little point in watching, and as we come up to the hill above Hveragerði I lose interest anyway. I can see the volcano. I'm up among the hilltops here, and can see out across the sea to the Westman Islands and far inland over the mountains towards the glacier. The sky is baby-blue, the kind of blue that dupes foreigners into leaving their hats at home, but over in the eastern quadrant there's what looks at first like an odd cloudscape. But it's too well-defined, its energy too obviously coming from below: grey cloud boiling up far into the sky and sweeping across the eastern horizon in a storm of what might, from here, be particularly dark rain blowing across the sea. It reminds me of the cooling towers and factories we used to pass in the Wirral when going to Wales, when I could see a certain beauty in the movement of smoke and chemical pollutants across the pale skies and grey waves of the Irish Sea. Route 1 winds down the mountainside into Hveragerði. I carry on and find myself beyond our known world.

I leave the main road. The birch scrub beside the road is still leafless, skeletal, and where there is grass it is dry and dead.

But the sun gets high in the sky now, and colours glow in the land, red volcanic soil, brown twigs rising from hay-coloured sedge, patches of bright snow in the hollows and black rock etched onto the grass. Dark grey cliffs lean over the road, and all the time the volcano is steaming and seething in the mirror. I lost the classical music station in Hveragerði and I haven't seen another vehicle since I turned off the tarmac road. I drive on, upwards, checking the map as I go. There's a 'Site of Interest' round the next bend, a place associated with supernatural beings, so I pull off and get out. I climb the col to find a family of Italian tourists photographing each other in front of a volcanic crater lined with red earth like the silk inside a Victorian top hat, and full of still, black water. No wind ripples the surface, no insect lands, no fish rises. One of the Italians is scrambling down to that dark pool, from which it is clear that a spectral hand, or perhaps tentacle, will reach to pull him down. The Volvo is waiting – I see the point of Volvos now – and I scurry back to it.

Just as I'm beginning to listen to my anxiety about being lost – though I still have a mobile phone signal, and actually there are quite a lot of summer houses scattered over these hillsides – I come to the two giant golf-balls I was told to look out for. I turn down the dust track between them, the car wallowing in loose gravel, and right and then left (the boiling volcano switching from one wing-mirror to the other), and there it is: a wooden chalet with a wraparound verandah looking out over the lava field to Eyjafjallajökull. Þórunn comes to welcome me, a small woman in her sixties with dark blonde hair in a rough bob and oversized, plastic-rimmed glasses. She's wearing a mid-calf length skirt and a cream sweater. Nothing about her speaks of the supernatural; you wouldn't give her a second glance on a bus. Come in, she says. Did you have a good journey?

We go up the wooden steps and in through the glass-paned front door, and I am swamped by envy. This little house has bright windows all around, looking over stunted trees and lava towards the mountains. The main room has a kitchen area, a fridge-freezer and an array of knives, seats arranged around a low table where a laptop waits, a big television in the background. There are two smaller rooms, one of which is almost filled by a double bed draped in an intricate patch-work quilt. The other is darkened, with a sofa-bed pushed against the wall. There is a small bathroom by the front door. Birch trees grow around the verandah and boulders slouch comfortably among the hillocks outside. It's a cross between *Little House on the Prairie* and *A Room of One's Own* and as such it seems, briefly, to define everything I've ever wanted in life. I exclaim over it and Þórunn says, yes, she loves it here, when she comes here she can do whatever she likes, whenever she likes. When she arrives she likes to go to bed for a few hours, after the drive, and then if she is bright in the night, well, she can write and eat and go walking then. When she gets back onto 'city time', she knows it might be time to go home. People say she must find it lonely, but she's never alone. I look out of the window and think about what I could write if I could come here alone for days at a time. Maybe we should buy a summer house, I think, and come back to Iceland every year. Maybe we should come here and listen to the wind and the birdsong, although I know that the children's fighting would drown out all but the strongest Icelandic wind and that none of us could sustain much interest in birdsong. Unless elves do good childcare.

I ask what she meant when she said she is never alone.

'Well, there are seven kinds of beings around here. We're talking about hidden people or elves, but to me there's a difference between them. They all look human, all have human form. But the elves are more fun, and colourful, and different sizes. The hidden people are more like the working class, very down-to-earth, just thinking about their livestock and how to get food, and they're always wearing very simple clothes, no colours, just brown and grey and white. I want to tell you about the woman who is just out there by the table.'

Þórunn gestures, and I gaze at the space she's pointing to. I can see my own reflection, out there under the tree, and I can see the table on the verandah, and the wind stirring the rowan trees, and the ash cloud rising into the blue sky.

'She's from the hidden people, and she lives in the lava field with her family. I used to go and visit her, but about three years ago she started to come and see me, just for a visit. And there are tree elves that I can see out there, small tree elves, and the flower elves, which are even smaller' – Þórunn holds her hand about a foot above the coffee table – 'but usually elves are very delicate creatures, with a very fine bone structure. Well, beings, not creatures. And they're in the trees and flowers and in the rocks. Not exactly in, because when I'm looking at the hidden people I'm not seeing the world the way you would if you took a photo of it. Where they live here, it's a golf course, but I'm seeing it the way it was before the golf course was built. I've seen them building their houses in the trees and rocks, especially when the young elves are starting their marriages. Well, their relationships – I'm not sure they do get married. Starting their families.'

I do not ask about elf sex.

'All the elves are starting to show again now. All but three types are hidden all winter.'

I sip my coffee. 'Where do they go in the winter?'

Þórunn shrugs, glances outside, as if there is someone listening. 'I'm thinking maybe it's that I don't see them, maybe because of the light. Because – I saw a therapist once, I was worried that I am not normal, and he said that most people see only five per cent of what there is to see, but people like me, born this way, we can see from fifteen up to twenty-five per cent. But there is still seventy-five we cannot see. So I've been thinking I don't see them in the winter, but I can still feel them very strongly on my skin. We know that dogs hear what we don't.'

There are lots of legends, across the North Atlantic, about animals seeing beings invisible to most people, horses refusing to pass a murder site and dogs that run to the door when the master's ghost comes calling. I've felt things on my skin too, usually in darkness, on stairs and in long passages. I don't much want to believe in them.

'And small children,' I add, remembering that Max used to be able to hear bats.

'And small children. I just love them. Up to about six years old, you can just see that they can see and hear everything, just by watching them and talking to them, not feeding them a line. It's such a beautiful time. Because they really know everything, until we start trying to teach them. That's when they forget. It's very sad.'

Tobias's current favourite game is rounding up imaginary spiders and chasing them out of the flat. Sometimes he opens the front door to check if there are any on the landing, once or twice he's been woken by them in the night. Tobias's spiders are about a foot high and it's quite important to me that they don't exist.

'Wordsworth thought that,' I say briskly, mostly to myself. 'But children learn other things that they need. Reading and writing. So do you hear the elves and the hidden people as well as seeing them?'

She has the patient expression of people who try to explain to me how aeroplanes stay up. 'I cannot hear them with my ears the way I can hear people that have left the earth, but I can communicate with them. Actually, I have been writing down old stories the elves have been telling me, about where the hidden people came from, and how long ago, and why. I don't care if anybody believes it or not because I know what the elves are telling me. Although not all of the elves are psychic. From the family down there, there are only two beings that are psychic for the whole community. But I can communicate with different kinds of elves. Once, I was walking in the mountains in the winter, with four other people. I met three types of elves, first an old man and a woman – she said, "What do you want?" – and then a younger mother with a crying baby. I wanted some way of showing my companions that there was more life there than met the eye. So I asked this old man, this small old man, if he could do something to let my friends see that he really was there. And there was a pine tree, a Christmas tree, and lots of snow – you know how it is beautiful. And he reached down, took one of the branches, and shook it so the snow fell down. And I was so happy! Because sometimes I wonder if I'm just imagining things. But luckily, I have had proofs many times. The elves can get physical. When it's about Mother Earth, then they have a bit more control.'

I thought elves could disrupt road-building and move things

around people's kitchens. I thought that was how we knew they were there. 'So they don't have any control over the built environment?'

Þórunn glances around her little house. 'They wouldn't disturb anything here. But when there are eruptions in the land, on the earth, then they can make a difference.'

The ash cloud behind her shoulder is bigger and darker than it was when I came, surging across the bright sky. There are farms round the other side of the mountain that will be uninhabitable for years to come, villages where the children have not set foot outside for weeks. In earlier centuries, there have been eruptions that have depopulated half the island.

'The elves can control volcanic eruptions?'

Þórunn smiles, doesn't look behind her because she knows what I'm thinking. 'No. But they can have a little to say about it. If they would like to stop an eruption progressing, they could do it. Not like taking a tractor or anything like that.' (I think she means that elvish interference with volcanoes is less mechanical than human control of machines, but maybe elves have form for tractor-theft.) 'But they can make it difficult. I never have any trouble with them. I'm often asked to come and talk to them, when people are trying to build something and it's not working. It's always just a lack of communication.'

'So you negotiate?'

'Yes. There's always a way of coming to an understanding. If people aren't selfish.'

'So the elves can stop people building houses?'

'They can make it really difficult. And anyway, people will never be happy in a place where they've torn down the elves' house. Sometimes it's only to give the elves a week to move to a better place, or even sometimes it's enough to move their house, if it's a stone, to move it just a little bit. It's all about talking to them.'

She's an elf consultant, I think. And there are houses where people are unhappy, houses with presences you try not to think about. We moved into one when I was eleven, a house with too many doors in which you couldn't hear what was happening in other rooms. It came with a complicated alarm system that didn't make anyone feel better.

'Can you give me some examples?'

'Well, the most recent one is in Reykjavík. The people had built their house into the ground, because they wanted it to be as natural as possible. But no-one could sleep in the main bedroom and the little girls who lived there were unhappy, and people kept hearing things and sensing things. At first they thought it was ghosts, so they called me. But they'd taken land from a father and a young daughter, and he was angry because he didn't have his home any more. So we agreed that the owners would put a big stone back in the corner of the bathroom, and they wouldn't touch a huge rock in the garden. So the elf man and his little girl had a small corner in the house, and their main home in the garden. And then everyone was happy.'

A kind of elf reservation. 'I'm surprised the elves were happy.'

Þórunn shrugs. 'Well, they were forced to be. They're more understanding than we are. They prefer to build away from us, but we're always moving, and then what are they to do?'

In the human version of this tension over land rights, in Israel and Northern Ireland, for example, they usually resort to explosives.

'So they're always benign? Well-disposed?'

'If they're approached with goodwill. I've never in my sixty years come across a bad being. I've never seen any demons or bad elves. Not when I haven't understood why they're behaving like that. Usually it's because something has been done to them.'

'What about ghosts?' The ghosts are what I'm really interested in. I know there are powerful Icelandic ghost stories but no-one will tell them to me. Even Pétur and Vilborg respond with courteous distaste. They are not nice, I'm told firmly, and I haven't yet been here long enough to know how to get people to talk to a foreigner about things that aren't nice.

Þórunn doesn't want to tell me about ghosts either. 'I don't like the word ghosts. My guides have a word for people who have passed over in the last two hundred years. There's always someone around but they're not doing much, just watching over. They're not very different from when they were alive, asking why you painted the wall a colour they don't like. If there's some event, a wedding or christening, they're always very excited. But I've never seen a bad person who's gone over. I've seen them frustrated – I was at a funeral for a young man, and he was there in the church by the coffin where they always stand, and usually one or two with them. He was very angry and he had to be taken away. He was young, and he was very drunk when he fell and wrecked his head, and he was angry. But usually when they are buried they go and say goodbye to their nearest and dearest. And that's very interesting for me. Maybe a widow was being very brave, but when her husband comes and touches her shoulder, then she breaks down. And also I can see it with the children. And that's what people don't understand. They say, "Oh, it was when I heard this song, then I just broke down." But that's not the reason. It's the final goodbye. Maybe I just don't want to see anything bad. I love to go out here in the winter at night, just to have the complete darkness surround me. It has never even entered my mind that there could be anything to harm me out there.'

'That sounds comforting,' I say. I am trying to imagine Þórunn's world.

'It is comforting. And for me, it's normal and I feel safe. People say they saw a big black shadow or they felt cold. Well, I feel people who have passed, and if they drowned or froze I can feel their cold. But it's just part of life. Maybe because I was born that way.'

Þórunn has seen the hidden people all her life, played with them as a child. I turn my question around.

'When did you realise that other people couldn't see them?'

She laughs. 'It's very strange, but I was thirty-five years old. I was working in a bar, and there was a young man who often came there. And after he'd had three or four vodka tonics, another guy would come in and lean over him, nudging into him. I couldn't hear what they were saying but it was clearly, "Go on, have another, just a little one." I knew this beautiful young man and he couldn't handle his liquor. It went on for months, and one day I said to my boss, "I'm going to say something to that guy. He's no friend to Siggi, getting him to drink so much." And my boss said, "Sorry, which guy?" And I said, "Come on, the guy hanging over his shoulder." And my boss said, "What do you mean? There's no-one there." So I just—' Þórunn zips her mouth. 'Some people do say that other beings drink through them, and it's not exactly like that, but sometimes alcoholics who have passed over, they can see the aura of drinkers getting less protective. And even if the beings or the dead people can't drink themselves they can enjoy the – the drunkenness. You know?' She babbles in a deep, slurred voice. It's not quite uncanny – any woman with a trained voice could probably do it – but it sounds male, drunk, and not like Þórunn.

The ghosts made him drink, I think, and I'm attended by spirits who tell me to check my e-mail every ten minutes when I'm writing and eat chocolate all afternoon. Why not? Something makes us fail, something uninvited. Hidden.

'So they look so human that you couldn't tell the difference between the guy drinking and the guy telling him to drink?'

'When I looked closely there was a difference. The dead guy was wearing clothes that weren't modern, and the colours weren't as bright. His hair wasn't a specific colour.'

These are Icelandic beings, then. They live in rocks around town, dance attendance on men who get drunk alone in bars. People don't see elves in Canterbury, say, or Verona or Chicago. Has Þórunn ever seen them outside Iceland?

She brightens up. She used to be married, and her husband was a keen golfer. She went with him to Hawaii and there were the elves, more lightly dressed than the Icelandic ones but just the same. The Swedish ones, though, in the forest, were slimmer than Icelandic elves, and the Italian beings were more like angels. Maybe, I suggest, it's because Iceland and Hawaii are both volcanic islands. Þórunn half-closes her eyes, tilts her head. She's hearing something.

'I just asked my guide, and he's telling me –' She pauses, like someone waiting to translate. 'He's telling me that both Iceland and Hawaii have connections to the middle of the earth, where there is a floating, something floating like lava . . .

It's like the hidden people are connected to the lava, but not every kind of lava. Just this kind.'

So there are different kinds of hidden people connected to different geologies?

Þórunn attends to her guide, and then looks at me again. I don't know if the guide, who seemed to be standing at her left shoulder, is still present. I don't believe in any of this, I remind myself, but I'm looking at the space beside her and fear strokes my neck and ruffles my hair. 'I was too curious once when I met a being I had never seen before on a mountaintop. It's the only time I have been harmed – well, not harmed, but the only time it didn't do me good. I gave them access to me for about two years and it made me sick, it drained me. I just got sicker and sicker, and then I stopped communicating with them.'

It doesn't sound as if it's all about peace and love.

'So there are some beings with whom it's dangerous to communicate?' I ask.

'Well, love and nourishing, that's my thing. But there was no love from them, it was all calculated. I was so eager, so curious, and I just didn't notice that they didn't have a heart. But they weren't evil, not demons or anything like that.'

But they weren't, I think, particularly friendly.

'So are these ancient beings? Were they here before people?'

Þórunn smiles slowly. She tells me a story that 'the old men' told her, that there were hidden beings in Norway, 'two or maybe three thousand years before Iceland was settled'. The people in Norway then were given to evil, greedy, almost as materialistic as we are now, thuggish. (I'm not sure if these are human or hidden people.) There were four families of hidden people who survived a particularly violent raid (can humans then kill hidden people?), and one good man among the Norwegian villains helped them and their livestock to escape in four shells. The shells drifted out to sea and came at last to shore in the north, south, east and west of Iceland, and the families multiplied, divided into slaves and landowners, and populated the earth. And then, a thousand years later, the people arrived from Norway and Britain.

Þórunn talks for a while about how she knows this, about the old man in 1950s clothes who told her these 'beautiful facts'. But I don't need convincing; we've known this story from Genesis and before. It's a settlement legend, as if the hidden people are the indigenous inhabitants missing from more conventional accounts of Icelandic history, in which the island remains uninhabited until the medieval Norse coloniza-tion of the ninth century. There is a version of national history in which Iceland was an egalitarian democracy from the moment in 872 when the first settler Ingólfur Árnarson cast his house-pillars from his boat as a kind of augury and saw them come to rest on the shore where his statue now stands in Reykjavík. Revisionist histories have proved the presence of Celtic slaves who were not equal to their Nordic masters, but there's still a popular idea that Icelanders have never oppressed anyone, that Iceland is a guiltless nation. From what Þórunn is saying, it seems that in the absence of an oppressed aboriginal population it is necessary to invent one. The hidden people were here before we were, they know how to live in harmony with Mother Earth, and instead of honouring their wisdom we steal their land to make golf courses. The hidden people bear the sins of the world, although unlike Christ they can also per-sonify what we like least about ourselves. I see the appeal. And I'm hungry; Þórunn invited me for noon, which is after lunch for many Icelanders, and we've been talking for over an hour.

I look around. The house feels peaceful to me, scattered with handmade objects, formed around its owner's sense of the necessary. 'Finally,' I ask, 'tell me what you can see now that is invisible to me.'

Þórunn looks around, smiles at someone who must be either sitting with us at the table or just outside the window. 'Well, she is out there, and she's very, very curious.'

I strain to see. I would like to catch the suspicion of a glimpse, at least an intimation of something. I see wooden decking on the verandah, rowan trees. And the volcano. 'Where your reflection is?' I ask.

Þórunn nods enthusiastically. 'It's good you said reflection. Sometimes it's just like that, like a reflection, or even just a shadow, and other times I see her the way I see you now.' She stands up and crosses to the other window. There are birch trees, a pine dark against the watercolour greens of Icelandic spring, and the Volvo waiting for me on the gravel track. 'They're just waking up out there. There's a tree-elf, here, he's always the first to show himself in the spring, and a beautiful little being here in the Christmas tree.'

She turns back into the house, holds out her hand as if to a toddler coming out of the second bedroom. 'And I have this little one here, a house-elf. His name is Oli. He's very playful, sometimes he's taking things from me. He's shy now, I don't know why. He's been playing in my bedroom.' She smiles at Oli, who is smaller than Tobias. 'I love this little guy, I wouldn't be without him.'

As I move to put my shoes on, Þórunn says, now you drive carefully, get safely back to your boys. Thanks, I say, I will. I dislike it when people say 'drive carefully', calling into being the possibility of accidents, of twisted metal and bloodied windscreens. Goodbye, I say, and thank you again, thank you for so much time on this lovely day. She follows me to the door. You go safely now, she says, take care on our Icelandic roads, drive safely. I walk over the stones across the turf to the metal gate. There are chimes hanging from the trees, and fibreglass toy houses under them. Is there a throng of unseen beings watching me go? I manage not to glance back to see what frisks behind me. I get in the car and close the door quickly, as if I could stop it getting in, coming home with me. But once I set off, I'm fine. It's easier driving on gravel than I thought; I don't need to creep along as I did on the way in. It's like steering a boat down the waves: you know how it's going to slide, when to pull round before it goes too far. I can do this. I speed up, begin to sing to myself, the kind of thing that privately-educated British women sing when alone. And did those feet in ancient time, walk upon England's— and there's a Hummer coming over the brow of the hill in front, going too fast and far over onto my side of the road, and now that I look down my own speedometer's showing nearly a hundred. It's not really a near-death experience. I slow down, pull over, and he passes with at least ten centimetres to spare, the kind of thing that happens several times on any Icelandic journey. And still, I find, I haven't learnt my lesson. All the way back to Route 1, the needle creeps up, and the Volvo swoops over the hills, as if there's an imp in the passenger seat saying, go on, you can do it, you're not scared. It's a bright day, a good road. See if you can take that corner at ninety. Wheee!

12

A Small Farm Under a Crag

At the end of term, I take a group of students from my writing class to the National Museum. Most of them, they confess, have never been there, even though it's on campus and offers free admission on Wednesdays. Even with your kids? I ask, because although I lived in Oxford for eight years without going to the Ashmolean from one season to the next, once Max could walk we went every week. And to the Pitt Rivers Museum and the Natural History Museum, not because I imagined that a toddler would learn from the exhibits but because it was something to do, somewhere to go, a change from the flat and the playground and feeding the ducks. I still don't know what Icelandic families do. Oh no, the students say, we wouldn't take children to a museum.

We've been writing about objects, and about the way objects have stories. The curators here don't like visitors to use pens and paper, or even laptops, and while I negotiate with the woman on the desk I think about the groups of primary school children with clipboards who roost on the floor of every museum in London. At last I prevail, and I ask each student to

238

find one object and write about it, first a still-life exercise in description and then an account of the object's journey. I wander with them at first. Some exclaim over the national dress costumes, remembering their grandmothers wearing such outfits on feast-days, looking forward to their own graduation ceremony when those who have them will wear the black woollen floor-length skirt, embroidered white lace petticoats, bodice and head-dress passed down the generations. One woman has already become fascinated by a carved chair from a seventeenth-century farmhouse, its arms worn by the hands of the woman for whom it was made, and two of the men settle beside the axe and bloodstained block used at the last execution in Iceland in the late nineteenth century. Someone else stands in the replica turf hut, his head bent to fit under the ceiling. He could, if he tried, reach the beds that line the walls on both sides at once. Despite the flicker of the synthetic 'fire', it's too dark to write in there. Whole families used to spend the winter in those houses.

I wander off to visit the object that called to me last time I came, a Chinese porcelain tea-bowl that was found in the eighteenth-century layer at Skálholt in the north. Skálholt is a cluster of buildings that was once the episcopal centre of Iceland, the dwelling of bishops and site of an important church, but by the eighteenth century it was a school serving the elite families of the area, the big farmers and landowners. The tea-bowl is broken, and you can see the point of impact on the side, where the fragments get smaller, like an eggshell newly knocked against the bowl. Some smaller pieces are still missing, leaving jagged holes. It is a sandy, reddish brown on the outside, glazed white on the inside with blue flowers, maybe some kind of blossom on a stem, painted where it would waver under milkless tea. There is no blossom in Iceland. Fashionable across Europe in the C18, the label says, but with no explanation of how or why this particular piece crossed the North Atlantic at the end of its journey from China. It was made for export, mass-produced, but still, of course, hand-painted; transfer-printing came later. These flowers were painted quickly, on some kind of assembly line. I have little sense of who and where in China was making this stuff, but some hand cupped that bowl, dipped a brush and shaped a stalk, a few blooms, put it down and picked up another. And then the bowl made its way across to the nearest port, and over the sea, almost certainly to England, and then back to sea, to Iceland, to the see of Skálholt, where it was used (probably) and dropped (certainly) and lay in the ground until 2002. There's no reason, I remind myself, why eighteenth-century Icelanders shouldn't have had porcelain and tea just as in the drawing rooms of Regency London, and the same layer held broken Dutch clay pipes, jet rosary beads and signet rings, making it clear that Icelanders had plenty of imported goods. But none of them, I think, are things that you would lose lightly, or without remembering, and being upset. Someone must have sworn, and prodded the bruise of his or her clumsiness in the night.

In the next case, from the floor of the first printing house in Iceland, less than a century after Gutenberg, there is what the label calls a 'knitted sock'. It looks more like a slipper than a modern sock, boat-shaped, heavy enough to hold its rounded shape three hundred years later in a glass case. It is worn through at the heel. Not where modern socks wear out, where the top of the shoe rubs, but under the heel, where the foot falls first and heaviest. The stitches are tiny, dense; it must have been knitted on very small needles, and the wool is thick enough that this would have been difficult. I remember the easy, swimming motion of Icelandic knitters, and think that this was harder work than that. The sock is a grubby beige now, darker around the sole, dark with sweat three centuries old. When it was made it was a creamy brown, oatmeal. Everything, then, was made for someone, for and by a particular person. The sock is smaller than my outstretched hand, about Max's size.

Back in the classroom, I ask the students what they thought of the museum. It made me proud, says Arni, because I was thinking about these museums in Europe, the Louvre and especially the British Museum, and most of the exhibits don't come from those countries. European museums are full of stuff stolen from other countries. Ours is simpler, we don't have the Roman statues or the Egyptian scrolls or whatever, but we made it all ourselves. There is no stealing. Yes, says Hrafnhildur, at first I was a little ashamed. I was remembering the big museum I saw in New York and thinking that we have nothing so important, but that is because we are a small nation and we have never had any colonies or empire and we have not wiped out anyone who was here before us. I was looking, she says, at this carved door from the thirteenth century, from a church. She holds up a postcard. It is — she pauses at a new word — Romanesque. I do not know what that means, but it is like the European carving at that time, and it was done here in Iceland, look, with a knight, and a falcon, and a dragon. A French story, told in an Icelandic way by an Icelandic crafts-man, because even then we knew what was happening in Europe but we did things our own way. Everyone nods and murmurs agreement. Yes, says Rosa, I liked the carvings from the eighteenth-century church. If you think of St Paul's in London or of course the churches of Venice from this time, these are nothing, they are the scribbles of a young child. But they are not made to intimidate. They are to please, not to make you feel small, and these were buildings to hold perhaps four or five families from the valley when they could come together. No great nobleman paid and no great artist was commissioned, and in a way I am proud of this.

I like the way they've come up with a post-colonial reading of great museums, but I notice again that the first reaction is shame or pride, fear of losing face in the eyes of the world and then pride in independence and simplicity. I've sometimes looked at the Victoria and Albert and the British Museum and thought that they are nothing but heaps of loot, but I don't feel enough ownership to be ashamed. My national identity seems to me accidental, a source of neither pleasure nor pain. Everyone must have one. I associate the kind of national feeling which seems normal for Icelanders with earlier ages in Britain. None of the English people I know would hear 'unpatriotic' as an insult.

I still have not had my job interview in Singapore. I explain to the professor across the world the difficulties of leaving Iceland at the moment, that the ash blows either over Iceland, so I can't get to a European hub to fly to South East Asia, or over Europe, so that I can get to London but not from London to Singapore. Anthony and I spend several evenings trying to piece together flights the long way round, Reykjavík – New York – San Francisco – Tokyo – Singapore. And back. We also spend quite a lot of time reading the blogs of expats in Singapore, trying to imagine ourselves in a world without seasons, on a campus planted to provide shade and cool, eating spicy street food and fresh mangos and ice cream. There are, we gather, excellent international schools. I wander Reykjavík, enlisting incredulous shop-assistants in my search for affordable interview clothes in which I might look employable in temperatures twenty-five degrees higher than the Iceland summer average. Meanwhile, I am also called for interview in Cornwall. My students, and some of our Icelandic friends, tell us to go for Singapore. Keep going, follow the money, raid foreign shores. I know what Pétur would say. He doesn't approve of money.

I don't ask his advice. Instead, over waffles, I recount my trip to see Þórunn. I don't believe it, I say, I didn't change my mind. You are not saying she is making it all up, surely, says Messíana. You know these things are important to many people here. No, I say, of course not, I never doubted that she is in good faith, that she has the experiences she describes. And I was, I admit, a bit spooked by the end, alone with the seer and her spirits in that strange landscape. But there must be rational explanations. Pétur and Messíana look at each other. I do agree with you, says Pétur, but one night when Þórunn came to dinner she began speaking in a strange voice and held forth about many things, political and economic things, about which she knows nothing at all, using words that couldn't be in her usual vocabulary. And then she fell silent, and then became herself again and cried a little. It was odd, very odd. Messíana shrugs. It must be a cultural difference, she says. You two did not understand each other. You should go see Brynja.

Messíana has a friend who made an elf-map of Brynja's farm out to the north-west, beyond Borgarnes. In her studio overlooking the fjord, Messíana shows me postcards based on the map. They show humanoid couples, coloured in bright pencil crayon, superimposed on photographs of a lava field with cliffs behind it. Some of the couples are squat with bulbous faces vaguely reminiscent of medieval squalor, others are elongated like cartoon characters stretched out and about to ping back into shape. Most of these beings stand in front of dwellings rather smaller than their inhabitants, which are canopied with blue and red rainbows. You might find her more familiar than Þórunn, says Messíana.

On the appointed day, Kathy and Alec have come from the Netherlands for a few days. Many friends promised to visit, but most of those who got as far as booking tickets have been thwarted by the volcano, which allows take-off and landing from London when the wind is in the west *or* from Reykjavík when the wind is in the east. Every couple of weeks a north wind lets the post through, although too late for our postal voting cards and a crucial birthday present. We are disenfranchised by the volcano. But in the middle of May Kathy and Alec have got through, at least one way, and are happy to come elf-hunting.

I pick them up from their hotel on an industrial estate behind Route 1, the only one that had vacancies with so many tourists stranded in Iceland. Alec volunteers to map-read. It's not summer, not even spring by European standards. There's low cloud over the city, with only the lower slopes of Esja visible. The squeak of the windscreen wipers is the day's metronome. It's the end of rush hour, I say, and the traffic is still a bit crazy. SUVs weave across the lanes, three people drive bumper to bumper at eighty kilometres per hour, horns blaring and lights flashing in the aftermath of an altercation. We have about 100 metres before our entry lane becomes an exit lane and we get funnelled back into suburbia. I accelerate hard into a gap between two jeeps that doesn't exist as I start to pull out but does, just about, before we get siphoned off to the south. Bloody hell, says Kathy. It's roughly what would happen if you let Italian drivers loose on American freeways, observes Alec. Worse, I say, worse. Think Greeks on the M25. Driving tanks in heavy rain. I spend too much time trying to find metaphors that will convey the awfulness of Icelandic driving and am pleased to have a willing audience. (I do not tell them that a few days ago, driving home alone, I found myself thinking that I'd better indicate at the approaching intersection because it's not a place where anyone would expect me to make a left turn. And then realised that I'd driven across the city while thinking about my book and not noticed anyone's driving. I fear I may lose my UK licence before we get home from Gatwick.) We leave the city via a slalom race over gravel tracks around roadworks, and all the extra lanes peel off into malls, industrial estates, supermarkets and the outer suburbs that trickle towards Esja, until Route 1 is dual track and the car behind is a Golf in no particular hurry to overtake. The windscreen wipers creak, and we crane up at the mountain. There's a lovely walk up through those trees, I tell them. Maybe on the way back, if the rain clears. We round Esja and the city is gone. The rearview mirror holds sky and sea, and a mountain, dark with rain, fills the windscreen. There's some kind of factory at the far end of the fjord, a complex of white tanks and tubes extending spidery legs across the turf. Follow signs for the tunnel, says Alec. The tunnel under Hvalfjörður, which is nearly six kilometres long and one of the deepest in the world. There have been no disasters that I've heard of, but I can't help feeling that tunnels under the sea are the sort of thing best left to the land-locked Swiss, say, or the Germans, people with an eye for risk assessment. We go down. And down and down, until after a while I can't tell if we're going down or up. The orange lights in the walls swoop. Down, says Kathy. Up, says Alec, definitely up, and we embark on a futile argument that takes my mind off the distance between the fire extinguishers and the near-certainty that there's no escape route. They've just cut the number of fire engines and firefighters at the airport, because there's never been an accident, and I dare say there's never been a pile-up in the tunnel either.

(A few weeks later, the *Iceland Review* reports that the Hvalfjörður tunnel has been found in the annual inspection of tunnels to be the most dangerous in Europe, requiring urgent remedial action to meet basic standards. I read the EuroTAP report. The lighting is too weak, the inclines too steep, there is no automatic fire alarm system, the one hydrant in the middle of the tunnel is inadequate for fire-fighting, the escape routes are not marked by lighting and the ventilation system would ensure that the whole tunnel filled with smoke in a fire. I begin to have more faith in my judgements about Icelanders and risk.)

A paler light appears in the distance, but when we come out the rain has closed in. Without the fog, you'd be able to see over to the glacier there, I tell them, right across to Snæfellsnes that way. There are white farmhouses stretching gravel tracks towards the road, and corrugated iron barns low under the cloud. Horses stand beside stone walls, as if waiting for the rain to stop, and then flurries of snow come scrambling off the mountainside and buffet the car. In Leiden, Kathy and Alec have been cycling to the beach with a picnic.

The town of Borgarnes appears at last in the bottom left of the windscreen, crouching under a black mountain and muffled by cloud. Route 1 goes along a causeway across a kilometre or two of sea to get to Borgarnes; it's not a town that you could reach at all without a vehicle. Or perhaps, in good weather and with a good crew, a boat. Gosh, says Kathy, as we set off across the dark waves, which is what we said to each other a lot fifteen years ago, when we'd look out of the bus and see water on both sides. Let's stop for coffee, I say, because with only a few weeks left to go I'm beginning to feel more adventurous about spending money on coffee when there's a perfectly good kettle at home.

Borgarnes is another town built for cars. It has two clusters of shops around car parks: a couple of banks and petrol stations, a video rental place, two small supermarkets and a shop (closed) with mannequins in the window wearing women's fashions of the late 1960s. Streets peter out up the mountainside, as if the houses have slid slowly from the top until inertia overcame them on the shore. I drive through the town, which is doing a good impression of having suffered a poison gas attack in the night, to the Settlement Museum, which tells the story of the first people to arrive in Iceland. I park at the tip of the town's peninsula, and we force the car doors open against the wind and huddle under the boot struggling with zips and scarves that flail in our hands.

There's a path down to the sea so we take it, and it leads round the headland and then winds up the hill towards a sculpture positioned and presented like a war memorial, looking out over the fjord, across the causeway to the scree-covered slopes on the other side. It stands on a black marble plinth, behind loops of knee-high chain, and we prepare to be reverential. A shipwreck, perhaps. The loss of half the settlement's men. A landslide slicing the roofs off houses in the middle of the night. We approach, rain mottling all of our glasses. It looks like a flying snail, says Alec. Maybe one landed here, suggests Kathy, one dark and stormy night. Perhaps that's how the elves got here, I add, and then we start making fun of the sign explaining that we are standing on the very spot where someone in *Egill's Saga* threw a rock at somebody. The Flying Snail is there to commemorate the throwing. We've had fifteen years' practice at making each other laugh, but I'm over-reacting; there are tears running down my cheeks and I feel a flicker of concern for my pelvic floor. It's not that funny, says Alec, and he's right, but I realise it's a long time since I laughed so much. Maybe since we left England (in fact, since Guy visited six months ago and we bought the car). I feel as if I'm not allowed to find things funny here, because the least the foreigner can do is to take everything seriously, nod earnestly over Icelandic history, and I know I'm behaving badly, crying with hilarity over the Icelandic reverence for the sagas and the way the tourist board assumes that the rest of the world is just waiting to find out Egill Skallagrímsson's nurse's gnomic utterance when her charge was dropped on his head one winter's day a thousand years ago. We take pictures of each other in silly poses until our hands are too cold to control the camera. I'm freezing, says Kathy, can we go get a coffee? Not easily, it turns out, because although it's mid-morning the waitress has just laid the tables for a Norwegian bus tour that will be stopping here for lunch and she doesn't want us messing it up, so we take our drinks out onto the stairs and compare and contrast the rudeness of waitresses in Russia, Germany and France. We're acting like tourists, like bad tourists, and it makes me feel good.

We drive on, the windscreen wipers marking time. We're the only people going this way, winding through wide valleys with white, red-roofed farmhouses scattered along the rivers. The fields are a lifeless shade of yellow-green, grasses bowed by wind and rain. We pass barns, their red roofs darkened by rain, and horses hanging their heads in resignation. Two lines from Auden's 'Journey to Iceland' murmur at the back of my mind: 'A narrow bridge over a torrent,/ a small farm under a crag.' I can't remember the rest of the poem, or why it suddenly matters now. On. There are summer houses, and I can't imagine why anyone would want to spend their summer surrounded by agricultural land with Borgarnes as the only source of amusement. I can't, anyway, imagine how people pass the time, weeks and weeks of summer, in Icelandic summer houses, although many remote hillsides and valleys are sprinkled with wooden huts. There is an enduring distrust of the city here, despite the almost complete urban drift of the population over the last twenty years, a widespread instinct that real life is in the countryside that now has very few permanent inhabitants. Are we nearly there yet, I ask Alec. We have to pass the university, he says, the university of Bifröst, and after a while it appears on the hillside ahead, a set of low white buildings raked across the slope like a barracks or a prison. Imagine going to university there, I say. Like the tower block in Garðabær, the university has a Soviet air, as if a few blocks of downtown Minsk had appeared on an Icelandic mountainside. There's no-one moving around, no cars, and we sweep past it and on, at last, to Hraunsnef, where two wooden watchtowers, like something out of a low-budget Dungeons and Dragons film, guard the track. I turn between them. There's a new building to the left, with a patio and rain pouring off a striped awning over a barbecue, and a house that looks deserted on the right, lace curtains hanging askew and cracks across the pebble-dash walls. A Labrador comes bounding from the older building. Alec distracts it while I sidle out of the car, keeping Kathy between me and the dog, and after we've walked around the old house Brynja comes out of the new one. I understand immediately what Messíana meant about Brynja being more familiar than Þórunn; she's dressed, like us, in jeans and a coat, but there's something about her brisk walk and her smile that feels uncomplicated, as if, despite the elves, she's just a busy woman working like the rest of us. The dog rushes, but Brynja catches it and makes it go away somewhere. She ushers us into the bar, which is so clean that our wet coats and shoes are an insult. The tablecloths hang in ninety degree folds, with second tablecloths making exact margins. The white-tiled floor shows no sign of having ever been touched, and there is a straight row of Icelandic chocolates across a white plate. Rain runs down the windows, and piped music plays. There are carpentry noises off; Brynja's husband is hurrying to get the noisy work done during the day while the guests are out. Out where, I wonder, and doing what?

Brynja and her husband moved here from Reykjavík in 2004, she tells us. She used to be an occupational therapist and he was a car-salesman, working all hours, never home. They used to go on holiday and fantasise about running a hotel, and then one day they decided to do it. They offered on a place in Akureyri, near the ski-slopes, but then the vendor found a hot spring on the land and put the price up. They were upset about that, had had their future all set up. Then they looked to the east of Reykjavík, out past Hveragerði, where there are a lot of hotels, but then there was the earthquake and they were a bit worried about all the volcanoes round there, and then they found this place, just along from the university which gets a lot of visitors, and it's close to the city and not particularly close to any volcanic activity. So they bought it, and moved, and that's when they started to hear that there were a lot of elves on the property.

'And at first we were like, yeah, there's lots of elves everywhere. And then what happened was that my husband's mind kept turning to these beings while he was working out there.' She gestures up the hill, where we saw some low outbuildings. 'His mind kept thinking about these things. And he thought he should do something about it, so he came in and told me, "Please call Erla. Ask her to come and tell us what we should do about this." You know Erla?' Brynja asks.

I nod. I haven't met Erla, but everyone I've been asking about elves has mentioned her. Erla is the national elf expert, now abroad.

'I asked Erla and she came at the end of August that year, and she told us that these gnomes who live round here are really after the publicity, they want the world to know about them, and that's why my husband had such strong thoughts of them while he was working up there. And we thought that could be the beginning of something big. So my aunt helped us, we started to make a map of the property with drawings of all the elves and other creatures on it, so that people can get some sense of what Erla is seeing around here. And these postcards come from that map.'

Brynja fans out eight large postcards on the table, the ones Messíana showed me. 'We've put up signs, out in the field, to guide people around where these beings are.' She hands me a card showing the elongated elves, almost as tall as the mountain behind the house. 'A lot of people tell us that the elves in the mountain here are royal, but they don't always look very royal because they are so tall, up to a hundred metres tall.'

Alec, who has not heard adults talking about elves before, is entirely composed. 'So your aunt drew these based on what Erla described? She didn't see the elves herself?'

Brynja nods. 'Yes. Erla describes it, my aunt draws it, and then Erla gives her approval. Or not! Some of them took a very long time. It can be very difficult, like the hair on these ones.' She shows us a card where the elves' hair stands out around their heads, reaching across the hillside. 'In some versions it just looked like messy hair, but it's a mixture of light and sound waves, and they can receive sound with their hair, so if you go out here and sing to them, they'll sing back. And their houses look like towers, but they give out tones too. Erla came here in the winter once, and she said that she travelled with them in her dream. She said that all the colours get misty in the wintertime and she doesn't see them so well, so they're mostly alive in the summer, but she went to visit them inside their house in the mountain. They have big halls, and they make music all the time, and she said they were doing something like working, enjoying making things. They had great windows that opened, and she said she could see right through to the other side of the mountain and it was beautiful. And we could just see it in our minds when she told us. So those Erla calls the Longlegs, but these ones here are really small, maybe only twenty centimetres or so. And

Jóhann, my husband, he says I have one of these with me all the time.'

'So he sees them?' I ask. The hall in the mountain reminds me of *The Lord of the Rings*, though the Icelandic palace came first. Tolkien was an Oxford professor of Old Norse.

'No. But he gets a sense of them.' She picks up another card, one showing something that looks like a giant hedgehog standing on its hind legs and holding a broom. This, she says, is Hraunsnef's hermit. We must have driven past his house, a rock sticking out from the hillside where the road bends. The hermit is the family's protector, and Erla has told them that it's important to greet him as you pass. When Brynja started to wave as she passed the rock, Erla told her that the hermit began to clean and sweep his house, as if expecting visitors. One day, a man from the Highways Agency called at the house, hoping to arrange to buy the land on either side of Route 1 to lay pipes and cables. The sale would have included the hermit's rock, and the Agency was planning to move it because at the moment the rock is exactly where a car coming off the road on the bend would hit it. Brynja and Jóhann said no, and explained about the hermit. They protected their protector. The man from the Highways Agency understood. He asked for the hermit's postcard, and carries it in his wallet.

Alec, who works on European cultural history, though so far as I know with more of an interest in technology than elves, leans forward. 'What does he protect you from?' he asks. 'From weather? Or something else?'

Brynja pauses. 'I don't think there's any one kind of protection. It's just what's in his remit. Not bad weather, because we certainly get that, but this is more about emotional – no, not emotional – I don't know.'

'Maybe security?' Alec suggests.

Brynja shakes her head. 'No. More from bad influences and things like that. Bad thoughts.' She shows us another card, where the beings are on human scale and of human form. 'These are typical elves. Guardians. They look like Vikings, and they've been here since the time of the Vikings. This is their hill. When we came here it was covered in long, wild grass, so my husband wanted to cut it. But they tried many times, and every time the tractor got near the top of the hill, the belt that keeps the motor running would break. At last he went down and sat on the hill and talked about what he wanted to do and why. And after that, it was amazing, the tractor just went on. They were protecting their sacred place, not exactly a temple, but where they gave sacrifices to the gods.' I've seen museums that have evidence of some fairly comprehensive pre-Christian Viking sacrifices, though not in Iceland. 'She's not seeing blood, or anything like that.' Brynja adds. 'There's no killing, just harvest symbols. Erla said that these two guards are moving closer and closer to the road, watching people coming and going, so we built those big watchtowers for them. So now they're checking out people who come here, and I think they'll protect us from anyone who shouldn't be here.'

There's an established relationship between elves and roads. Route 1 is a recent arrival, at least in the hidden people's timescale, and yet clearly a focus of elvish (elven? elfin?) interest. Maybe because it constitutes the only major change in land-use in a lot of places, since many of the farms are on sites where there's been a dwelling of some kind for centuries, or maybe because routes and pathways hold ancient appeal. And I suppose we know much less about what elves might be doing away from the beaten track.

A Small Farm Under a Crag

They had an 'incident' once, Brynja tells us, when a group of men tried to leave without paying, claiming that since they hadn't slept they shouldn't pay. There had been too many of them in one room anyway. Brynja was alone in the hotel that night and had no way of stopping them from going, but when the men had loaded their car and were about to set off, they found that one of the tyres was punctured. 'So I stood there and watched while they unloaded everything and got the spare wheel, and that one was flat as well. So they couldn't get away without our help. But by that time Jóhann was back, and when they asked him for our pump he reminded them that they hadn't paid us. And then they said, "OK, what do we owe you?" So then we lent them the pump and they left, and we never saw them again. But I think we had help from the elves: you don't leave here until you've paid up!'

There are more cards, more elves. Some who perhaps fly a little, others who have appeared in Brynja's and her daughter's dreams. There is, Brynja says, a lost book in the Bible that tells how God came to visit Eve after she had left Eden, giving notice so that she could wash and dress the children. But Eve had many children, and when God arrived, some were still grubby. She hid the unwashed children behind the house, and in punishment God hid them from human sight.

Brynja has a story to match Vilborg's *brauðskerasaga*. One night, when the hotel was full with a tour group and Brynja had two girls helping her in the kitchen, they were drizzling the plates with balsamic syrup. One bottle ran out, and Brynja sent a girl to the store-room for more. The girl came back and said it wasn't there, so Brynja, who had just bought a new multi-pack, went to look for herself. She'd put the bottles on the shelf that morning, and they had gone. Mid-service, they garnished the remaining dinners with chocolate syrup. (Alec and I, who have co-authored a book about chocolate and get mildly competitive about cooking, don't look at each other.) When all the guests had gone to bed, Brynja and the girls went to check the store-room again, and there were the bottles, back in place. I want to ask if the elves had used any of the syrup, but I'm struggling not to sound incredulous and there's a more important question, one that seems rude to ask but impossible to avoid.

'Have you ever seen them? Any of them? Yourself?'

'No,' says Brynja. 'No, I can't say I have.' She rallies. 'But I think we get their help when we're doing the right thing, and we struggle when we're not. It's just Nature, you know? When we moved here, I had such a strong sense of Nature, that we're not alone in this world, that there's something we can't ever conquer. Like the volcano. And you have to show respect, that's all it's about, showing your respect for Mother Nature. Even if it's just by getting permission.'

We are all nodding and murmuring agreement. Most of the Icelanders I know are rather enjoying their volcano, flattered to find Iceland on the front page of British newspapers again. There are jokes about mis-hearing what is still called, even in headlines, the Icesave Thing, and returning ash instead of cash, jokes that are not quite jokes about showing the world what happens if you mess with Iceland, as if Eyjafjallajökull is enacting the will of the Icelandic people not only by erupting but by erupting 30,000 feet into a south-east wind, as if the land speaks with the people's voice. The volcano is erupting to avenge the financial crisis, although Icelanders who depend on income from tourism –

an increasing number, and increasingly important to an economy in desperate need of foreign currency – are watching the
flight schedules and feeling sick. Brynja, for all her acceptance
of Mother Nature's omnipotence, is among them.

'We have to know how to live with Nature here,' she says.
'We have to learn respect. You notice, even with the volcano
and all this ash, nobody's died.'

'Nobody even seems frightened,' I point out. I've been fascinated by the absence of the apocalypse here. We've been
told to keep young children inside if ash is visible in the air and
that a group of medical researchers is taking this opportunity
to investigate the long-term effects of ash-inhalation, which is
not currently believed to cause more than passing symptoms.
The English headlines, read online, are much more panicky
than any in Iceland, fearing ash drifting over the North
Atlantic, causing lung problems and possibly affecting crops
and groundwater. In Iceland, air-freight isn't arriving from
Europe as regularly as usual, but since few Icelanders can
afford to buy air-freighted produce anyway, that's not having
much affect on food supplies. The swine flu epidemic, which
reached Iceland just after Christmas, has similarly led to pre-
dictions of the new Black Death in the UK and been greeted
with mild concern for the vulnerable in Iceland. Icelanders
don't do panic.

'Nobody panicked because this happens here every four or
five years. It just doesn't usually close down international airspace, that's all. But we're getting the calls now: "I'm
panicking, I'm afraid, I want to cancel my booking for August
because I've heard about the volcano. Maybe next year." And
I'm like, yeah, OK, but next year you're going to be even
more afraid because Katla's gonna go.'

Katla's the big volcano. One of the big volcanoes. Big volcanoes are serious; the Laki eruptions in the late eighteenth century killed seventy-five per cent of Icelandic livestock and twenty per cent of the human population in the resulting famine. Katla has erupted roughly every eighty years since records began, and is now ten years overdue and rumbling. Every previous eruption of Eyjafjallajökull, which comes from the same underground source as Katla, has been followed by Katla within two years. We've all been given notice. I haven't met an Icelander who's much troubled by the prospect.

'Honestly, I think if we hadn't read about it because of the air traffic being disrupted, we wouldn't have known anything about this volcano here. Nothing looks different. But I had a family from Lebanon – *Lebanon* – who stayed with us at Christmas last year send me a card: "Our thoughts and prayers are with you." Er – thanks!'

'I suppose it's awful for the farmers, though,' I add. There are some farms too close to the volcano.

'Yeah, well,' says Brynja, gathering her coat. 'If you take a farm in the path of an active volcano, you kind of know what's going to happen. It's *when*, not *if*. Shall we take a walk?'

We go out into the rain. A lorry sweeps along Route 1, past the wooden watchtowers, with a sail of spray behind it. Low cloud hangs in front of the hill above the house. Brynja points out the hermit's rock, a truck-sized boulder at the bend in the road, and we promise to wave as we leave. We walk down the field, stepping from tussock to tussock, towards the guardians' hillock. 'It looks like a barrow,' Alec remarks. 'Some kind of artificial mound.' A burial mound, I think. Unexcavated. There are several on the Orkney Islands where you open a trapdoor provided by Scottish Heritage and climb down a ladder to see where the bodies of people subject to ancient and alien ritual lay for centuries. There were often animals there as well, horses and eagles beheaded to accompany a powerful man into the next world. On a bright day, with a square of blue sky in the doorway, it feels like a daring rather than foolhardy thing to do.

'The road's been cut into the end,' I point out, and we go down to look. Maybe the road-builders disturbed bone and silver.

'It is right at the edge of the flood plain,' says Kathy the archaeologist. 'The land's getting bumpier anyway.'

'You mean it's natural?' I ask.

'Could be. Look, there are more hillocks at this level.'

Brynja stops at the sign showing the guardians with their blue and purple glow obscuring the road. Another lorry passes, and a jeep going the other way. Especially on a wet day, you can hear each vehicle approaching, coming up the hill from the university, and fading away to the north. It's a restless place, I think, the side of the road. The Road, the one road. I can see why the hermit would come out and watch passing traffic, and why you might want watchtowers at your gate. Brynja conducts us back up the hill, over the rough yellow grass towards the dark cliffs, which reach into the low cloud. Rain splatters my hood and glasses. She tells us that they run team-building exercises here out of season. Her husband tells the corporate groups the stories she's just told us, and then leads them through competitions and outdoor activities. She looks back over her shoulder, rain on her pink cheeks. 'And he tells them they're old games from Viking times, but really he makes them up!'

'Because the Viking raiders did lots of team-building,' I mutter to Alec.

But I can imagine that this would work. The bankers are called Viking Raiders in Icelandic. There is a tincture of pride in Icelandic shame ('we do better self-loathing than anywhere else in the world'), and I'm sure that business leaders enjoy finding a Viking rationale for their endeavours.

'Here,' says Brynja, standing still. 'Here, you can feel the energy here. Stand with your feet apart and breathe deeply, feel the energy coming up from the land.'

Alec stands square, drops his shoulders, closes his eyes and inhales the cold, damp afternoon. Kathy and I smile. British, self-conscious, the girls who spent five weeks travelling without talking to anyone at all.

'The cliffs are full of energy and light too,' says Brynja. 'And do you see this bright line here?' The grass in the field is last year's, poking into my trousers needle-sharp, the colour of old hay, but there's a diagonal line of green running up from the road. A ley-line, perhaps, or the elves' path to the stream. Brynja grins. 'It's where the hot water pipe comes up from the mains.'

I don't know how to respond. Brynja's teasing our credulity, but she does also, I think, believe that there's something out here. I don't want to laugh at the hidden people, on much the same principle as I wouldn't curse St Francis or summon the spirits of the decapitated eagles in Orkney's Neolithic tombs, because it seems unsafe as well as offensive, but I'm not sure if Brynja is amused or impressed by her disappearing balsamic syrup, or maybe both. Brynja takes us past the playground, where there's a sunken trampoline and a set of swings for the dwarves and the children to share, and pauses to greet the pigs, which she can't think of eating, and the hens. Icelandic Settlement Hens, descendants of those brought by the original Viking Raiders a thousand years ago. Settlement Hens look ordinary to the uninitiated, but they're valued both as emblems of Icelandic difference and because they cope well with the climate. There are some rocks where a new family of elves have just taken up residence, and then we come to the rock where you can hear the tall elves' song. Sit on it, Brynja instructs us, and join in with the vibrations from the mountain, sing back to them. A raven flaps out of the cloud, rain patters. Alec takes a seat but I can't sit on a hillside and sing to elves in a cliff. I can't, in the same way that I can't pretend to be a bear at toddler music group, even if it means sitting stiffly while all the other mums growl on all fours. One note or a song? asks Alec. Just relax and enjoy it, Brynja tells him approvingly. Let it all go. Alec intones a low note. Ommm. Alec's a trained singer, and the note goes on a long time. He takes another breath. Ommm. Longer and lower than you would think possible, an American historian sitting in a knitted hat on a wet rock in Iceland, waiting for tall elves with electric signals in their hair to sing a duet with him.

Later, I find the poem. It's the one that's famous because Auden wrote, in pen, on paper, 'each poet has a name for the sea.' Christopher Isherwood wrote back, admiring the line, 'each port has a name for the sea', and Auden decided the mistake was better than the original. I'd remembered it, vaguely, as yet another saga-worship poem in the tradition of William Morris, but reading it again properly, with the landscape outside Borgarnes in mind, I see that it's doing something different, and darker:

Here let the citizen, then, find natural marvels,
a horse-shoe ravine, an issue of steam from a cleft

in the rock, and rocks, and waterfalls brushing
the rocks, and among the rocks birds;

the student of prose and conduct places to visit,
the site of a church where a bishop was put in a bag,
the bath of the great historian, the fort where
an outlaw dreaded the dark,

remember the doomed man thrown by his horse and
  crying
Beautiful is the hillside. I will not go,
the old woman confessing *He that I loved the*
best, to him I was worst.

I recognise my own distrust of Icelandic tourism, of the collector's desire to tick off geysers and volcanoes and midnight sun on some kind of Lonely Planet checklist, totting up experiences like any other commodity. There must be a better reason to travel, a better way of travelling, than the hoarding of sights your friends haven't seen. I'm also, I find, resistant to the lens of the 'student of prose and conduct' who finds 'places to visit' because of historical events. I don't want to see the bath of the great historian. I don't want to know that the great historian had a bath. I want to sense the long-dead outlaw's dread of the dark, not to be told about it in an interpretation centre. I want, I suppose, an unmediated Iceland, even though I know there's no such thing. I read on:

A narrow bridge over a torrent,
a small farm under a crag

are natural settings for the jealousies of a province:
a weak vow of fidelity is made at a cairn,
within the indigenous figure on horseback
on the bridle-path down by the lake

his blood moves also by furtive and crooked inches,
asks all our questions: *Where is the homage? When*
shall justice be done? Who is against me?
Why am I always alone?

Our time has no favourite suburb, no local features
are those of the young for whom all wish to care;
its promise is only a promise, the fabulous
country impartially far.

Tears fall in all the rivers: again some driver
pulls on his gloves and in a blinding snowstorm starts
upon a fatal journey, again some writer
runs howling to his art.

These aren't William Morris's sagas. For Morris, the sagas hymn the lives idealised by many late-Victorians, presenting a wilderness society shaped by the fights of heroes, a world where Nordic men are Nordic men known by their swords and no-one else matters much. Auden's doing something different here. The voices could speak from any time, but the last verse puts its hand on my arm. Auden wrote his *Letters from Iceland* in the year he calls 'the eighteenth of our western peace', 1936. He encountered Goering's brother in a hotel in the north, and eavesdropped on German tourists talking approvingly about the blondness of Icelandic children. Auden himself was only seven in 1914, but of a generation of writers for whom fighting had no glamour. 'Again some writer/ runs howling to his art': the sagas are an inadequate response to a culture of hurt and betrayal. I think again about Brynja's affection for her 'guardians', about the enduring sense of dark presences in the Icelandic landscape. The thefts of balsamic syrup and bread-slicers are easy to mock, but these stories are ways of domesticating fear. What is outside is dangerous. Yule Lads, hidden people, molten lava, boiling quicksand, blizzards pouring black cloud across a blue sky, aurora sweeping the mountainside like searchlights. The doomed man thrown by his horse and refusing to go into exile, refusing to become an outlaw in the wilderness. Elves seem synthetic to me now, embarrassing, but somewhere behind the electric hair and painted rainbows of Brynja's story there's a very old instinct about this landscape.

13

In Search of the *Kreppa*

By late May, the air is full of the chatter of birds, especially noticeable late at night. There is sunset on my late-night walks again, and it's hard to remember to go to bed. Start a book or film last thing in the evening, and by the time you've finished it is daylight again. The grass, which has been yellow and dead since early September, is green again. There is still snow on the top of Esja. Anthony comes back from the school run. Is it warm enough to go out without a cardigan? I ask. He wrinkles his nose. No, he says, not quite, not yet. We both know that I am not asking if it's warm enough to go out in indoor clothes. (Even in July, you take a coat.) I'm hoping one layer will do, a coat without a woollen cardigan underneath. And it won't.

I still haven't found the *kreppa*. I still feel like a poor person here, the only one who can't afford a cup of coffee, who brings sandwiches to work and mends her children's clothes. It's normal for the UK, I tell friends who observe us rationing use of our pay-as-you-go phones, walking to save the petrol, turning the heating down. But it doesn't seem to be normal for

Iceland, even with the papers full of tales of financial ruin and woe. Unemployment is up, to nearly ten per cent, houses are being repossessed, small businesses are in trouble. Some schools have started giving the children free porridge when they arrive, in the belief that their parents can't afford to feed them. I read about poverty, but I can't see it. My students are facing the three-month vacation which is not covered by their subsistence loans because Icelandic students and even school-children have always had summer jobs, helping with the harvest until recently and now in a state-funded programme maintaining community gardens and litter-picking, things that need doing only during the summer because for the other nine months of the year Icelanders don't spend time outside. And working in tourism, where they are much in demand because they are multilingual. But this year, all those jobs have been taken by people who have lost their real jobs. The students can't get unemployment benefit because they're students, and so have no means of support. There are rumours of people torching their own cars because they can't afford the loan repayments any more, substantiated by both of the Icelandic insurance companies who have begun to treat all fires as suspicious. Most of the migrant labourers whose work fuelled the building boom have gone home, causing a signifi-cant drop in Iceland's tiny population, and there is also a steep rise in the number of young Icelandic families leaving, mostly for Norway. I don't doubt the existence of the *kreppa*. I'm probably not seeing it because I don't know where to look, maybe because I don't know how to read what I can see, but in any case I would like to find it. We have less than a month left; I'm running out of time.

There was an article in the *Iceland Review* a few weeks ago, reporting that 'the charity Fjölskylduhjálp Íslands (Icelandic Family Aid), which distributes food packages to those who cannot afford groceries, has begun prioritising native Icelanders above Icelandic residents of foreign origin.' MPs, including the Minister for Social Affairs, have expressed their revulsion. I would like to know more: this sounds like an unusually explicit articulation of Icelandic racism, coupled with a more concrete *kreppa* story than most. Food packages? In Iceland? I poke around on the internet and discover that my favourite Icelandic bloggers have already tried to investigate this story and been told that the charity does not speak to foreigners ('foreigners' in this case including 'Icelanders who blog in foreign languages'), which seems to confirm the director's xenophobia, but also constitutes a dead end as far as I'm concerned. Given my customary inability to make unusual requests of Icelanders because I feel stupid and foreign and as if I have no right to be making a nuisance of myself, I cannot possibly phone a woman who does not speak English and is known to avoid foreigners in order to prove a perfectly reliable report. Stalemate.

Then I mention my interest in this story to Einar, who is taking a couple of my classes, writing a polished prose in his fourth language. Einar is a photographer, who left Iceland at twenty to train in Copenhagen, and then made a freelance career in Amsterdam. He planned to stay in Amsterdam, he says. He had an apartment and was gradually moving all his stuff to the Netherlands, an extra suitcase every time he came home. His career was going well. And then one day everything changed. That was it. It was time to come home. Why, I ask him, how did you know? He shrugs. He just did. Nothing happened, it was just time to go home. He sold what he couldn't carry and returned to Reykjavík, where he still takes photographs, some of which become postcards and calendars for tourists, and is taking a second BA in English. He's also a jazz musician. Sometimes the trombone comes to class too, and I like having it there, lolling at the back, as I like having another student's new baby, who sleeps through discussions of Wordsworth in a way Wordsworth would have enjoyed. Einar knows everyone, has photographed everything. I'll talk to the manager, he says. Leave it to me.

I haven't yet learnt the extent of Einar's powers and am therefore surprised when he calls me a few days later to say that he has arranged for us to visit Fjölskylduhjálp Íslands' headquarters next Wednesday, when the week's food parcels are being distributed, and furthermore that the director has instructed everyone to show me everything and answer all my questions without reserve. How did you do that, I ask, and Einar shrugs and smiles, blue-eyed. I just asked her, he says.

Einar comes with me, to translate Icelandic and to translate Icelanders. He collects me from work in his car and drives, more like a Dutch person than an Icelander, across town. I understand, now, why there is sometimes a huddle of people on the embankment above the dual carriageway when I pass on the bus home. They're waiting for food parcels. Usually Icelanders don't queue, don't stand around in groups. Even at bus stops, people position themselves as far apart as possible, one behind the shelter, one a few metres along the road, another the other way, as if they've all been dropped from a height. When the bus comes, everyone saunters towards it, not acknowledging either each other or the fact that the bus driver has the power in this situation, and boards in order of arrival at the doors. I've never seen people congregating outside, not even teenagers on summer evenings.

There is a queue already when we arrive, although the doors won't open for nearly an hour. Einar finds Ásgerður Jona, the director, and introduces us. You are welcome, she says, looking me in the eye. Come. Ásgerður Jona takes us into a large room like a village hall, with a lino floor and high windows. Tables are arranged in a U-shape at the end opposite the doors, and there are people, mostly young people in jeans and boots like those worn by my students, taking food out of large cardboard boxes and arranging it on the tables. There are crates piled as high as my head. There is milk, bags of sliced bread, bags of potatoes, boxes of eggs, *skyr*, yoghurt, buttermilk. The basics of the Icelandic diet. Some frozen chickens, and then oddments; a few packs of sliced mushrooms, something in a sachet claiming to be 'guacamole mix'. Behind the counter at the end of the tables are some mini Easter eggs, children's toothpaste and baby-shampoo. Ásgerður Jona calls for silence and tells everyone that they are to speak freely to me. Then she takes us into a back room, crowded with more crates and boxes, where other people are sitting around a table drinking coffee and sharing home-made cake, and says it again. Einar and I wander around, chatting to busy people. Almost everyone speaks English. The charity has to buy the food, so several of the volunteers spend most of the week trying to source the cheapest bulk deals. The number of people coming has risen steadily for a couple of years; last year, it was a busy week in which they gave out 200 parcels. Now, especially at the end of the month, it's usually over 400. The numbers are small, I think, 400 households in a city of around 200,000 people, but if these are people who can't afford to eat and need to be given potatoes, then something has indeed gone badly wrong. The needy get benefits, but the benefits aren't enough to live on, not by the time people have paid their foreign currency mortgages and car loans. About half of them can't work because of disability. Fjölskylduhjálp aims to give each family about half of their weekly food. There's nothing fresh, I murmur to Einar, no fruit or vegetables. They probably can't store them, he says. Onions, I think, apples. Easier to store than milk. I'm distracted by the kinds of food available, by what it says about the Icelandic idea of necessities, how different it might be in China or Nigeria or France. For Icelanders, the answer seems to be dairy produce and potatoes.

We meet the man who manages the logistics of distribution. He takes us over to his computer and shows us his spreadsheet. There are social security numbers, names, numbers of adults and children in each household. Data protection, I think, identity theft! But no-one in Iceland worries much about data protection. You have to give your social security number, your *kennitala*, to the vendors of electrical goods to validate basic consumer rights. (The *kennitala* incorporates your date of birth and also gives access to tax records, held in real time and online using information supplied by the bank, the Icelandic version of the DVLA, the insurance company, the Ministry of Immigration and your employer.) Bank tellers often request my PIN. Students hand in assessments blazoned not only with their names but with their *kennitala*. CVs, I will discover, routinely state not only age but marital status and number and age of children. You can't be anonymous in Iceland anyway, says Matthew, when I complain about this state of affairs. There's no point pretending people don't know who you are, and who you're married to, and who you slept with when you were in high school and how your degree was classified and why you crashed your car. But identity theft would be impossible for the same reasons. No, I think, impersonation might be difficult but the theft of someone's official identity would be rather easy.

'We give cards to the regulars,' the man explains. 'People present themselves at the desks where the computers are, we print out a list of what they can have and then they are given it at the tables.'

'In what state are the people who come here?' I ask. 'Are they really starving?'

'Several people I know have been hungry for quite a while before coming here. Months. It's been changing a little because of all the media coverage of this place. People are a little less ashamed. But no-one wants to be seen here.'

'Are you carrying them through a short-term crisis, or are they dependent on you for a long time?'

He begins to unpack cheese. 'Quite a lot of the Icelanders who come here are disabled, so that's not going to change. Most of the foreigners are unemployed, and that's not going to change either. Unless they go home.'

'Migrant workers probably wouldn't be here if there were jobs at home,' I point out. This is not the moment to argue that for some of the 'foreigners', this is home.

He shrugs. 'OK. So that's not a short-term problem either. And we've no steady income, it's just donations. We're a charity with no state support. And food prices are going up, and there are more and more people coming here. We're running out of money. We'll probably be closed by December.'

'Do the supermarkets give you anything?' Einar asks. 'Do you have to buy it all?'

The man explains about food distribution chains, in which supermarkets have to return unsold produce to the supplier. But the supermarkets give them whatever discounts they can. 'It's a lot of work, chasing these bulk buys and special deals, and there's only one person here full-time, everyone else just volunteers two or three days a week.'

'How far do people come?' I ask. 'I noticed on your database, there are people from outside the city.' From towns over a hundred kilometres away.

'Yes, from all over. We've been giving people who come from more than fifty kilometres away one-and-a-half times the usual amount.'

'Doesn't the petrol to get here cost more than the food would?' I wonder, knowing the prices of both.

'Yes, the price of gas is ridiculous now.'

The question I always ask in Iceland, and one that clearly doesn't make sense in some way I don't understand: 'What about people who don't have cars? Or can't afford the petrol?'

'Exactly. The poor things are going by the buses!'

Taking the bus here seems to be the last word in shame and deprivation, an equivalent to burning the furniture to keep warm, and yet the buses are cleaner, more frequent and more punctual than in European cities where catching a bus is perfectly normal behaviour for salaried adults.

'I take the bus,' I say firmly. 'But fifty kilometres away there isn't a bus.' There's no public transport outside Reykjavík and Akureyri, Iceland's 'second city' in the north.

'That's true.' He opens a new box of cheese.

'So they just sit there in the villages and starve?'

'Yep.'

'How many people are we talking about? Have you any

idea how many people are starving and can't get to the free food?'

'Nope.'

Einar and I look at each other.

'So there could be hundreds of families all over Iceland who have no money and no food and no way of getting either?'

'Yup.'

It's only later that I think this isn't really very likely. It's hard enough to keep a secret in Reykjavík, and must be almost impossible in the smaller communities. People would know if a neighbour were starving, and if they knew they would do something about it, however strong the sense of shame. I think. Probably.

Einar and I wander outside, towards the queue. I put my gloves on. If it's too cold to stand around here in May, what is it like in December?

'Shall we talk to them?' Einar asks.

I feel my insides knotting with shyness. We should, of course. It's what we came for. I'd make a terrible journalist.

Einar approaches a couple, explains that I'm a visiting academic and am interested in the effect of the *kreppa* on ordinary people. 'No,' they say. 'No, thank you.'

He tries someone else, a woman in her mid-twenties with teased hair, heavy make-up, and a three-year-old without a coat who keeps wandering off and scrambling up the embankment separating Fjölskylduhjálp's yard from the dual carriageway. 'Well,' she says. 'I'm an unemployed single mother of two. There's no more to say.' She pulls up her hood and turns away. Her friend shouts at the child, the first time I've heard someone yell at a child in Iceland.

Ashamed of our curiosity – and cold – we go into the

clothes store, where they sell donated clothes for token sums, which are used to subsidise the food parcels. 'We used to give the clothes away,' the woman there confides, 'but teenagers were coming and taking the best items just for fun.' It's as if Icelanders don't know how to do this, second-hand stuff, as if they lack a blueprint for poverty. Which is bizarre, considering the stories I've heard from Vilborg and Pétur and a few others with long memories. It's as if there's been a collective forgetting, as if Icelandic poverty were as shameful as French wartime collaboration or the British concentration camps of the Boer War. A woman comes in and begins to rummage through the children's clothes which I've been trying not to regard with a covetous eye, although there's a pair of trousers that would fit Max, who has outgrown almost everything, and a coat that would be good on Tobias. I noticed this woman earlier, because she's wearing a skirt I admire and has blonde plaits wound Heidi-style around her head. She looks as if she's popped out of one of the downtown art galleries, or come straight on from a launch party. She looks like the kind of person I can talk to. She pulls out a pair of waterproof trousers to fit a boy smaller than Max and taller than Tobias. She's not making eye contact, angling away from us. Einar goes up to her, explains again why we're here. The woman looks at me with loathing, spits something at Einar in Icelandic which makes him redden, look away and stride out of the building. I follow.

'What did she say?' I ask, worried that I've caused offence.

'She said it's bad enough having to come here without talking to us about it,' says Einar, avoiding my gaze. 'Did you see what she was doing?'

'Buying trousers?' I hazard.

'The poor woman,' says Einar, recovering himself. 'She was ashamed. Imagine the shame, buying her little boy's clothes here.'

'But I buy second-hand clothes for my kids,' I protest. 'I always have. Everyone does. It's obvious, kids outgrow things before they wear out. What are you meant to do, throw things away just because your child has grown?'

I remember the queues outside twice-yearly NCT jumble sales in Canterbury, the way academics and lawyers and architects assemble outside the church hall before it opens on a Saturday morning to buy other people's second-hand Boden. I remember a few treasured garments worn by both children, a pair of red-and-white striped OshKosh dungarees and a Petit Bateau Breton top, which came from the British Heart Foundation and went back to Oxfam six years later. Is it pretentious, I wonder, is there something odd about the English middle-class pleasure in thrift? We could all afford new Petit Bateau, and probably buy it for ourselves, but somehow it's better to clothe children on the cheap. Is there cultural capital in the rejection of consumer imperatives?

'You do?' asks Einar. 'Really? You buy things from charity shops?'

I shrug. 'Yes. Why not? Especially things like waterproof trousers, they don't get much wear before they're outgrown.'

'Oh, you're right,' he says. 'Of course, you're right. There's no reason. But people don't do that here. Nobody buys their children's clothes from the Red Cross. They'd be so ashamed. Things get passed around families, but no-one would buy a stranger's cast-offs.'

'But why?' I ask.

There isn't an answer. I wasn't expecting one.

We go back out, towards the queue, which has got longer, curving round the building into the car park, and doesn't seem to have moved much. 'Shall I try again?' asks Einar. I dither, remembering the blonde woman's expression. Einar's photographic projects have included sequences of images of homeless women and hospice patients in the Netherlands, but he's finding this uncomfortable, going up to his own people in his own city and asking them to give me their shameful tales. I watch him square his shoulders to approach a couple standing with their arms wrapped around each other, perhaps because their padded coats are flimsy and threadbare. They are both in their fifties, she with dyed hair, make-up, handbag and jewellery that even I can see are cheap imitations of the Russian mafia bride look that prevails among mothers at the International School, he with a two-day shadow and smoker's skin in a cracked fake-leather jacket and baseball cap. She used to own a business, she tells Einar, until she had an accident and couldn't work. He used to earn too, not a lot but enough, until he got sick. They try to keep their spirits up, but there are debts left from the business and yes, if they didn't come here they would be starving. Before they came here they were hungry most days. They've looked into taking some courses – English, maybe, or Computer Studies (the two tickets out, I think) – but you had to pay and they can't. No, they don't see things changing any time soon, but you have to have hope, don't you, or you'd really have nothing left. Einar rests his hand on the woman's arm and thanks them, but round the corner, out of sight, his body stiffens. This isn't Iceland, he says; this isn't my country. We thought we were the best country in the world and everyone was happy. There's no such place, I tell him. The poor are always with us.

Without discussing it, we leave the queue and go back to the store-room to talk to the staff. Round the back, one man is chucking cardboard boxes to another, who is breaking them up for recycling. I manage not to ask for one for the kids, who played for months with our removal cartons. It's still cold but the sun has come out, and over the roar of traffic on the ring road I can hear the little planes leaving for Greenland. Right, I think, ask the real question.

'I noticed when you showed me the names,' I begin. 'There are lots of foreigners, aren't there?'

He breaks a box over his knee. He's wearing scuffed jeans and a T-shirt with a bomber jacket open over it. 'Yup.'

'Do you notice differences in the way they relate to the charity?'

'Yeah.'

Another box. We're watching him work.

'Tell me about it.'

He throws the box onto the heap.

'Most of the foreigners that come are from Poland and the Baltic countries, where they are obviously used to establishments like these, so they consider it their right to come here and get whatever they want. They're really aggressive, they won't say thank you.' He breaks another box. 'It's frustrating when you're trying to do something like this. Everyone here is a volunteer, and they won't even say thank you when they walk out the door. They argue with us, they're pissed off when they think they don't get enough food. Sometimes when we're getting close to closing time we run out of something and the foreigners come and argue with us, basically just being very boring.'

I shift my feet. He breaks another box.

'Why is that, do you think?'

'No idea. Must be a cultural difference.'

'Do they have a different approach to queuing?' asks Einar, dangerously.

'Yes they do. We've been trying different approaches. At the beginning, we just got people to line up outside and then one of us came out and distributed tickets with numbers on them, and then they could leave and come back in an hour or whenever their number would be called.' Because, I think, the shame of simply waiting your turn is even greater than the shame of needing a food parcel. Because in Iceland it's not decent to expect people to wait in line. 'But after a couple of weeks we found that one guy from Poland was turning up at the front, and the line would form behind him, but just before we handed out the tickets a whole bunch of foreigners would come and join the man at the front, fifty people or more. So the person who'd been second in the queue until then would be number sixty or whatever. So we gave up that system. I tried a few different versions, but the one we've got now seems to be working.'

'Just one queue for everyone?' I suggest.

'Yep. Just one queue. You show up, you wait your turn, and you walk straight through. It works much better. I tried to divide the queue between the computers, so people could register quicker, but the foreigners just ignore me, go where they want, walk right over my toes.'

'Is that because they don't understand the system?' I'm wondering how many people's toes I've walked right over in the last ten months.

'I don't know. They can see that I'm directing the lines and they completely ignore it. It's so dumb.'

'Well, it's your system,' I say.

'Yes.' He chucks the last box. 'No matter how dumb they are, it's my rules.'

Einar and I sit in his car. He's staring out of the window, keys still in his hand. I'm shocked by his shock, struggling to understand why Iceland should imagine itself exempt from the economic inequality that characterises every other capitalist society. We all knew, I thought, we all accepted a deal, that there is poverty for some and wealth for others.

'Not in Iceland,' says Einar, his gaze still locked on the sky over Perlan. 'Not in my country. I had never imagined, it had never crossed my mind, that there were hungry families in Iceland. Not people needing help from strangers.'

I remember all the hungry families in Halldór Laxness's fiction, and the pride taken in a sparse diet by later writers. Hunger seems as foreign to Einar as excess was to his grandparents' generation. Young Icelanders keep telling me that there's no class system in Iceland, that inequality is a foreign phenomenon, but the fact of many of my students' alienation from poverty seems to prove Icelandic social inequality. I remember a colleague in Sociology telling me that not only is there a difference between the middle class and the poor, but the difference is so great that the existence of the poor is news to some of the middle class. Einar starts his car. 'I did not know,' he says. 'That is the worst thing. I did not know.'

Maybe, I think. Or maybe the worst thing is that I've known about poverty all my life and I'm not shocked.

14

Knitting and Shame

Teaching is over for the year. My students drift away, many into jobs (although there aren't meant to be any jobs), some abroad to seek their fortunes or find themselves. My colleagues are reaching the lower floors of their towers of marking, and the piles of books to read over the summer are growing on their desks. There are plane tickets in the shared printer at the end of the corridor, people going to libraries in Paris and Copenhagen and conferences in the USA. Our tickets, our one-way tickets, were booked last month, and these final weeks seem to blur into each other. The nights are brief again now, each day blending with the next, and the sea flickers under the sun, the light in the sky electric, too bright, after winter's candle-light glow. I flutter around Reykjavík, trying to make the most of it, restless as a bird not quite ready to migrate. I talk to an archaeologist who worked on the Skálholt dig and to an expert in eighteenth-century northern European ceramics. I invite new people to dinner, as if there's any point in making friends now, as if I can concentrate our aborted Icelandic future and take it home with me.

Knitting and Shame

I have been unable to get to Singapore, although I packed and went as far as Keflavík airport twice to find my flights cancelled because of the volcano. I have, however, reached Cornwall, albeit by a circuitous route, and I have been offered that post. My prospective new employer in Cornwall, reasonably enough, won't wait for the volcano to subside so I can visit Singapore before making a decision and so, in the end, Eyjafjallajökull decides for us. I like Cornwall. The job will suit me well, and there are good schools. The imagined smell of flowers heavy with tropical rain, the imagined suddenness of tropical nightfall, the imagined taste of chilli with fresh lime and coriander, drifts in my mind like the perfume of someone who has left, a future that won't happen.

I've meant to find out more about Icelandic knitting all year. Icelanders knit everywhere. On buses, in restaurants, during meetings, in class. In the first week of term, several students came into the classroom, put down their cups of coffee, took off their coats, hats and scarves and pulled out laptops, power cables, poetry anthologies, knitting needles and wool. I didn't, I decided, mind. (Not that I would have dared, then, to say if I did.) I can crochet while watching a film. Women in Shetland and St Kilda used to knit, often rather complicated patterns involving several colours, while walking miles with toddlers over rough ground to milk the cows. Icelandic undergraduates, it turned out, can knit while drinking coffee, taking notes on their Apple Macs and making enlightening contributions to discussion of *Lyrical Ballads*. I watched the pieces grow from week to week, comforted, somehow, by the progress of socks and matinee jackets as we worked our way through from Gray's 'Elegy Written in a Country Churchyard' towards *The*

Prelude, as if the knitting were a manifestation of accumulating knowledge. Colleagues knit in meetings, which seems a far more constructive use of time than the doodles produced in the English equivalents. I wonder if anyone would say anything if I tried it in committees at home, instead of drawing borders of trees and wonky geometrical patterns around the minutes. A couple of cafés have a kind of free-range knitting, left in baskets for anyone to continue, although the results aren't as exciting as you'd hope. Every Icelandic girl, the students tell me, has to make at least one Icelandic sweater. It's a rite of passage, a step on the road to full Icelandic status.

Icelanders also wear their knitting. The people on the streets of Reykjavík wearing handmade Icelandic sweaters are not tourists. When it's possible to go out without wearing a coat (it's never sensible, never Icelandic, to go out without *carrying* a coat), you can see that the next layer down is an Icelandic sweater. My mother had a phase of making them when I was a child, and I remember the multiple balls of wool and the special needles, connected to each other by a plastic filament so you don't make rows but just keep going round and round, following her around like a loyal pet. The finished jumpers had intricate patterns in soft shades of grey and purple – no chemical dyes in my childhood – and they kept us warm on the hills, although it could be hard to move our arms and I still shudder at the memory of the wool against my neck. Icelandic wool is as thick as a pencil but so soft you can easily pull it apart, still smelling of sheep and coming out almost waterproof if you knit it tightly. The high-end yarn shop on Laugavegur offers the odd Danish or even Japanese import for specialist tastes, but in general it is un-Icelandic to use foreign wool and all the supermarkets – which have a knitting aisle after the loo paper and washing-up liquid – carry the standard range of three kinds of Icelandic yarn.

I'm not a knitter. I like the idea. I can make a square, or at least a quadrant, but the arcane language of knitting patterns, the need to be forever counting things, puts me off. I flick through my mother's and my friends' patterns, admiring the pictures, and occasionally get as far as buying wool, once or twice beginning to knit until I come to instructions I don't understand. I will never be able to carry out an instruction to 'Sl 1, k2, k2tog, k to last 5 sts, ssk, k3.'

Instead, I crochet. (I suspect crochet may be un-Icelandic.) My friend Kathryn, who can make gloves and skirts and fitted sweaters so fine you think they would drift towards the ground if you dropped them, gave me as a parting gift a box of cards detailing increasingly complicated lace stitches. Of course you can do it, she said, and she was right. Given a long winter's evening and the box set of *Mad Men* which she also pressed into my hands, I can. I've learnt to do Blackberry Puff Stitch and Double Shell Stitch. Crochet is mostly holes, and therefore cheap on wool. I find that the finest Icelandic wool, *loðband Einband*, which feels like something you might use to snare rabbits, is fine enough to show off my precision and wiry enough to hold its shape. I graduate to Picot Double Fan Stitch, and embark on a shawl in dark grey. You could use the resulting mesh to catch large, angry fish or restrain lemmings, but it has an Edwardian intricacy and is eventually received with convincing pleasure by Kathy.

Early in May, when I've tracked down some traitorous Danish mercerised cotton and begun on a scarf I might wear myself, my student Mark comes to see me. He's taking my Food and Literature class as part of his MA, one of a group of teachers from *Menntaskóli* who are now required to have an MA and therefore relieved of teaching to attend the university part-time. Icelanders tend to translate *Menntaskóli* as 'high school' but that misrepresents it; *Menntaskóli* is a college for sixteen- to twenty-year-olds which prepares people for university, further vocational training or employment. Mark, who is Canadian, here because he married an Icelander, teaches English. He stopped coming to class half-way through term, e-mailing to explain that he and his wife had a new son and he was taking some time to learn fatherhood. He's kept up, and handed in a memoir about his childhood diet that makes me want to chat, for the unprofessional reason that his parents seem to have taken the 1970s denial of sugar and passion for wholegrains even further than mine. While I'm left feeling deprived by any meal that doesn't include dessert, he is distressed by the idea of boiling rather than steaming vegetables.

Mark's response to 'how are you?' is a jolting reminder of why not to have kids. He's tired. Very tired. Maybe not as tired as his wife, with whom he has argued. There have been no meals for some time. None of the things he normally does, likes doing, are possible, and he cannot imagine how he will ever be able to do them again. I try to explain that life will become possible, bearable, even pleasurable again, albeit on new terms. I remind him that parents do write books, climb mountains and take long-haul flights. Maybe, he says, red-eyed, hollow. It's not the kind of thing you can tell people, so instead I admire his sweater, which is a particularly fine example of the craft, in shades of green that aren't part of the usual Icelandic palette.

His face changes. Really, he says, you like knitting? I explain about me and knitting, and he explains about his sweater. Yes, he knitted it himself but he also worsted the wool. His wife Sigrún María has a spinning wheel. They live out in Mosfellsbær – the last settlement out towards Esja on Route 1 – in a, well, a sort of cabin, really. He rebuilt it himself out of an old summer house. Sigrún María spins and weaves and they both knit, and they're growing vegetables and working on the fruit and thinking of hens next year, Settlement Hens. He's making a henhouse with lumber from the dump. They don't have central heating, relying instead on a wood-burning stove.

He glances up at me, gauging the real extent of my enthusiasm, and then goes on. He and Sigrún María got much of their furniture from the dump, too. I didn't know you could, I say, and recount our attempts to find unwanted furniture, the way we thought we'd be able to pick it up second-hand or free and found that that market doesn't exist here, certainly not for foreigners. No, he agrees, it's crazy. Every time he goes to the dump he sees useful and valuable things thrown away: garden furniture, sideboards, tables and chairs, a cement mixer he thought he could use. Televisions and computers. So after a couple of times he asked the guys there if he could take some of it. It was only going to landfill. They said no. He asked why not. They glanced at each other – crazy foreigner! Because, they explained slowly, someone's thrown it out. It's someone else's trash. Mark didn't mind. No, they said. No way. Imagine if you take it and someone sees that you're using their trash! Imagine it!

Mark imagined, and was untroubled. He could see some prime building timber and a set of garden chairs. What if I just take it, he asked, what would you do? You can't, they told him. Mark pulled out his phone and offered it to them. OK, he said, if there's a law against taking other people's trash, call the police and get that law enforced. Otherwise, I'm taking that wood and those chairs.

They didn't call the police. He took what he wanted, and since then he's been back, until their house is furnished with other people's trash. But when he recounted this experience in the staff-room at *Menntaskóli*, most people couldn't see his point, and one of his colleagues said the idea of taking things from the dump disgusted her. When she'd bought a new sideboard, she'd smashed up the old one before throwing it out. Why? Mark asked. Because I wanted it gone, obviously, she said. I don't want someone else using it when I've decided it's trash.

Mark and I marvel at his story, both of us having grown up with furniture from auctions and junk shops, pulled out of skips or passed on by elderly relatives, and continued these methods in independence, both of us liking the past lives of the things we live with. The Icelandic horror at the idea of the second-hand seems to be partly to do with the impossibility of anonymity here, the fear of 'strangers'. The risk is one of disclosure, that the person who classified the object as 'trash' might see the same object reclassified by someone else, though it seems that it would be the new owner who should feel ashamed. Maybe, it occurs to me, this is why second-hand clothes are so terrible, because the anonymity of charitable giving might be broken, you might recognise your child's outgrown coat on someone else and thus have to acknowledge some kind of hierarchy. One of the most widely held beliefs among Icelanders is that there is no hierarchy here. I remember Gunnar Karlsson, one of the first people to whom Pétur referred me when I started asking about the old days. Gunnar is a historian in his seventies who grew up on a remote farm and went on to take his PhD at University

College London in the 1960s. In his view the Icelandic conviction of absolute social equality was partly responsible for the crisis. 'In Iceland, everyone compares him or herself with everyone else. No-one thinks, I am a common person and this car or this telephone or this computer is for the rich and not for me. I think we have not realised that when the rich in our society get richer, everyone spends more money because we cannot acknowledge a divide between the rich and the ordinary. When we put the children of rich people in the same state-run schools as everyone else, we exert pressure on poorer families to spend beyond their means to keep up. Because they will not tell their children, "We are poor and they are rich."'

I wonder if this idea explains the apparently disproportionate outrage at Mark's and my interest in used clothes and furniture. We are poor and they are rich. Coming from Canada and the UK we find nothing unusual or disruptive in this idea, nothing that affects our self-esteem, but in Iceland such a statement threatens national identity.

You should come to our place, says Mark suddenly. If you'd like to. I don't invite Icelanders much. We like the way we live but sometimes I'm ashamed. Most of our friends live in houses with so much plastic and glass and chrome, and we know people who are horrified by our place, but you–

I'd like to come, I tell him. It sounds like a nice place to live.

It takes us a few weeks, with his new son and my repeatedly postponed trip to Singapore, but late in May we manage it. I meet Mark at Álafoss wool mill, which he says I will like. 'Foss' means 'waterfall'; it's an early twentieth-century building on the river, where Icelandic wool was first processed industrially. The river is fed by hot springs and warm enough that they used to wash the wool in it as well as using its energy to power the carding and spinning machines. There's still one central yarn factory processing almost all Icelandic wool into one of four weights, but it has moved and the mill is now a shop and a kind of tourist attraction, although only tourists with a passion for knitting or old knitting machinery are likely to be much excited by it. Mark lingers over the hardcore stuff, the sort of wool you have to twist with your fingers as you knit, while I flutter around the Danish imports. There are big buttons and toggles made of horn and bone, and stripy wooden knitting needles. Mark shows me around the rest of the store, part shop and part museum. There are handmade sweaters knitted in soft colours according to traditional patterns, and cheaper, machine-knit ones in bright shades. There are sealskin slippers and silver fox fur hats, and sheepskin gloves which I would want if we were staying for another winter. The original knitting machines, looking like the wartime telegraph equipment at Dover Castle, are out back, facing over the river towards the green slopes of Esja. They date from the 1890s, still, Mark remarks casually, a couple of generations older than the Icelandic sweater.

What? I didn't think Icelandic sweaters went back to the sagas, though only because the research for my most recent novel involved some investigation of the early history of knitting, but I thought they were at least pre-industrial. Nope, says Mark, they're not even part of the invention of national tradition in the late nineteenth century. Post-war.

Oh, I say, and then inadvertently administer a return shock. You mean it's a twentieth-century version of Walter Scott and kilts?

Knitting and Shame

We stand there, me holding more balls of stripy sock wool than I can quite control, and discuss nationhood and myth-making among the mittens. Icelanders, says Mark, generalising grandiloquently as foreigners do, believe the whole lot. They think revisionist history is a form of treachery. Well, I say, that's kind of the point.

We get in the Volvo and Mark directs me to his house. We're driving along gravel roads and I'm equally worried about making a fool of myself by driving idiotically slowly or skidding off the road, but when I remember to look around I can see exactly why he chose to live here. The track runs between a steep rocky hillside and the lake, which is ruffling in the wind and dotted with birds. More birds flicker around the cliffs up the hill. There are stands of spruce trees and a couple of wooden cabins. No street lights, no traffic. We jolt and lurch over the gravel. Here, he says, park here. You can't get a car up to the house. We get out. I hear wind, lapping water, the chatter of birds. The air smells of trees and turf. Max and I heard a new bird while walking in Heiðmörk at the weekend, something with a curlew's beak and fast-beating wings that ascends until you can hardly see it and then drops in swoops, once each swoop calling a piccolo phrase that doesn't sound avian at all. *Hrossagaukur*, said Einar. A kind of snipe, Pétur glosses. There are two above us, waltzing in three dimensions, their clear notes echoing off the cliff. We walk up a steep track, through a painted wooden gate and under tall spruce trees into a garden neat as Mr McGregor's. There are vegetable beds, edged with turf, terraced up the hill in semi-circles, a pear tree in a greenhouse, some flow-ering trees that aren't coping with the wind, a sheltered area for sitting, and at the top, under the trees and looking out over the lake, Mark's latest work in progress, a study for Sigrún María who is working on a PhD and needs a room of her own. Sigrún María texts from the house; she's trying to get the baby to sleep and would rather we didn't come in until he's down. So we go into her study. It's perfect: away from the house, with a view of trees and hills and water, and the inside made of perfectly jointed wood, double-glazed against the climate. Envy nibbles my fingers.

The study seems to be more of a spinning-shed at the moment. There are bags of raw wool and baskets of spun hanks. There's a wooden spinning wheel, not the ancient artefact I'd been expecting but newly made of birch, with rounded treadles that invite touch. It reminds me of the heavy wooden toys we left at home, the garage and the push-along caterpillar with the same pale curves. Mark offers me some yarn to feel, dark and shiny. It's cool and soft to the touch. Dog hair, he says.

I recoil. I wouldn't voluntarily touch a dog unless it was attacking my children. Even dog-owners think dog hair is dirty, don't they? I remember Mark's colleague talking about 'trash' and take the dog yarn into my hand. Sigrún must have washed it, anyway. Sigrún asked her friend to collect it when he combed his dog, Mark explains. Here, this one's goat hair.

It's coarser than the dog hair, though both of them would knit into the silkiest clothes. There are skeins of unworsted wool too – carded roving, Mark says – and he shows me how to worst as you knit, twisting the strands as you wind them round the needles. Sigrún María texts again; the baby is asleep and we can go in.

Mark has another flurry of worry as we cross the garden. He hopes I won't think it's poor and makeshift. He's always

anxious about bringing people back here. My kids, I remind
him, play with cardboard boxes. We've been using garden
chairs as dining chairs all year; we're all sleeping on air-
mattresses on the floor. We go in, through a long lobby
designed to keep warmth in and muddy boots out. It's all
wood inside, warm and comforting as an old sweater. People,
I realise, aren't meant to live in concrete, they're meant to live
like this. There are plaited rag-rugs on the floors, not trodden
into grey anonymity because no-one wears shoes in Icelandic
houses, and books, books in Icelandic and English and Danish,
jostling each other off floor-to-ceiling shelves. Steely ligh
floods through the windows, which face over the lake.
There's a kitchen area, with wooden shelves and counters,
and armchairs gathered around a wood-burning stove.

Sigrún María comes through one of the doors leading off to
the bedrooms. She has short honey hair, blue eyes, high cheekbones, carries herself like someone riding the waves and
watching the horizon. I thank her for letting me visit, tell her
I won't mind at all if she wants to go rest while the baby
sleeps. No, she says, just at the moment she needs adult company even more than she needs sleep. Mark makes tea, and we
all sit down by the fire and talk about knitting, while outside
the spruce branches sway and the wind moves across the lake
like a magnet over iron filings. I curl up in my chair, which is
covered by a blanket, and warm my hands on my mug. Well,
Sigrún María is saying, when I used to work as a crime
reporter—

I sit up. A crime reporter? In Iceland? 'I thought there was
hardly any crime,' I blurt.

'We have about the same rates of violent and sexual crime
against women as you do in the UK,' she says. 'Domestic

violence is endemic, just like in the UK, and a quarter of women report sexual assault in anonymous surveys.'

I stop myself dropping my tea.

'Well,' she says. 'OK. Actually all the Nordic countries report fairly high rates, though we're the highest. It's partly that there are fewer taboos about reporting sexual violence here than in the UK, for example.' Sigrún María also has nursing qualifications, and spent a few years working in London hospitals. One year, there was a rapist who preyed particularly on nurses in uniform making their way to and from the Tube during the night. 'A lot of our police force is female and there's no bullying of women who've been attacked. It's not clear if Icelandic women report a higher proportion of rape or suffer more rapes. Of course there are reasons why you'd get higher reported rates that might not mean a higher incidence.' There surely are. I've discussed this with my friends at home. None of us, a completely unrepresentative sample of middle-class working mothers in their thirties, would report rape in the UK. Sigrún María pours more tea, picks up her knitting. 'But anonymous surveys and police records together suggest that our rates are pretty high, especially domestic violence. Basically, Icelandic men damage Icelandic women, especially at home and especially when they're drunk. Which is rather a lot.'

'But it's meant to be the most egalitarian society in the world,' I protest. 'You know, lesbian prime minister, almost full employment among mothers, shared nine-month parental leave, a majority of women at university –' Only at undergraduate level, I remember, not among lecturers and most certainly not among professors; I have not yet seen a portrait of a woman among the dozens displayed around the university.

'Some people say that's partly why. That Icelandic men find it very hard living in a feminist society and take it out on their partners behind closed doors.'

We look at each other, not knowing where to start with this idea. I remember reading about a survey showing that Icelandic men do less housework than the men of any other northern European nation (though still more than the Portuguese and Italians; the further south you go, the greater the sexual inequality – blame the Pope), and various friends complaining that their partners won't entertain the idea that people with penises can clean bathrooms. Anecdote, and easy enough to find English women sharing the same complaints, but I don't know any thirty-something professional men in England who deny the principle of equality, whatever happens in practice.

'Also, of course, there are drunken fights among men. A lot of those. And recently we've had a spate of drug-dealers having someone beat up the families of people who owe them money.'

I remember Hulda Kristín telling me back in August that Iceland had no drug problem until immigration rose in the boom years.

'I never read about it,' I say weakly. 'None of it. And people keep telling me how safe it is here.'

'It is,' says Mark. 'Compare it to London, or Vancouver. It is. But we have crime like everywhere else.'

Not in the English-language media. Yesterday Pétur told me that, at the same time as a violent molester of children had been given a five year prison sentence, a group of young people who entered the parliament building – which every Icelander has the right to do – during the demonstrations, has been told to expect seven years in prison. The headlines in the English language *Iceland Review* and on the English pages of *Morgunblaðið* were about a cycle-to-work scheme and Eyjafjallajökull's most recent contribution to international airspace. I don't think there's any conspiracy; these sites are meant for and used by tourists, who want Iceland to be green and geologically interesting and have little interest in the workings of the judicial system. The crime rate is another thing, an important thing, I've missed by being foreign and in particular by not making enough effort to learn Icelandic.

'I still find it easier being a woman here than in the UK,' says Sigrún María. 'I found it really upsetting the way men would open doors and hold my chair. I was like, "Get off, stop it!"'

I think about this.

'It was really intrusive,' she says. 'As if I wasn't just like them. Manipulative.'

'It's just training,' I tell her. 'My husband could no more go through a door first than I could start eating before everyone's sitting down, or take the last piece of something.'

'Icelanders don't have that either,' Mark points out.

Mark makes comparisons with violence and alcoholism in British Columbia, where he taught in a Native American village before coming to Iceland, and then I notice exactly how Sigrún María is knitting. It's completely different from the English way. Her fingers are doing something I've never seen before, and the whole dance of yarn and needles and hands is unfamiliar. And much faster. Maybe if I could knit like that . . .

'Show me,' I demand.

'Oh, this is how we do it,' she says. 'I've seen the British way. It's weird.'

But then the baby wakes up, and we all stop what we're doing and admire him, because he's that kind of child, until he reminds me of my own admirable kids. Time to go.

Mark's directions were plain enough, and all I need to do is go down the valley until I come to the sea and then turn left to follow Route 1 along the coast back into the city, but somehow I get lost. I find myself on a tarmac road, with markings down the middle, punctuated by mini-roundabouts every few hundred metres. Up and down hill, with rocky turf on both sides. At the tops of the hills, I can see the sea straight ahead, so I keep going. There are street lights but no traffic, no pavements, as if the road was built just for me. I glimpse Route 1 over to the west and take the next turn towards it. There are houses ahead, but when I come to them − after a couple more mini-roundabouts − I see that they are unfinished. There are walls and roofs, and in most cases windows, but some are no more than foundations with steel rods sprouting into the sky, and none are inhabited. I slow down, peer down side streets. It's a whole suburb, abandoned as if the bomb had fallen one night after the builders and plumbers and electricians had gone home. It reminds me of Heimaey, of Clearance villages in Scotland, entombed settlements, stories cut short, a broken history, and as I keep going, guessing my way out, it begins to be alarming. What if I never get out of here, what if I keep coming to more roundabouts and making more wrong deci-sions and driving through more of this aborted town? I come to a crossroads, with a traffic light and a pedestrian crossing. The light is at red. I check the mirror, want to reach out and lock the doors, as if fearing an elvish car-jacking. I am English; I stop, and am relieved when there is no beeping.

No invisible hand has pressed the button, and as I breast the next hill I can see a slip-road onto Route 1.

Next day, I start checking my facts. Checking my assumptions. Statistics are a blunt tool, especially when dealing with a population as small as Iceland's, and especially in inexpert hands, but it takes me only a couple of hours on the websites of the United Nations, the World Health Organization and Statistics Iceland to find numbers seeming to suggest that Iceland is much more like the UK in quantifiable ways than I, and most of my friends here, believed. Iceland's murder rate between 2003 and 2008 averages just under 1 per 100,000 against England's 1.4 (and the United States' 5.6: http://www.unodc.org/unodc/en/data-and-analysis/homicide.html). There are 1,068.2 burglaries per 100,000 English and Welsh people, and 865.7 per 100,000 Icelanders, which suggests that the basis for Icelanders' tendency to go out leaving the windows open and the British interest in discussing when it's OK to shoot a burglar is not statistical. Denmark reports 1,715 over the same period and France a mere 480.6: England and Iceland are both near the European average for the incidence of most kinds of crime, including sexual assaults and crimes against children. I feel safer in Iceland than I do in England (except on the roads), and I feel that my children and my possessions are safer in Iceland than in England (except on the roads). All the Icelanders I know feel safer in Iceland than they do anywhere else, and most will say that Iceland is a safer country than any other. The differences are real, but not, for the most part, quantitative.

I keep exploring, though I'm no longer sure that I want to know what I'm learning. Maybe I'm about to find that

Icelandic roads are safer than those at home and that Brits own more cars. I am relieved to find that according to the World Health Organization, Iceland reported 10 road deaths per 100,000 people in 2006, the latest year for which statistics are available, compared to the UK's 5.4. Iceland beats both Serbia and Italy at killing people on the roads, a particularly impressive feat given the new age and large size of cars in Iceland (http://apps.who.int/ghodata/?vid=51310). And Icelanders own 645 cars per 1,000 inhabitants against the UK's 457, a smaller difference than living in university towns in the UK and the wealthiest suburb in Reykjavík had led me to expect. I go on playing with numbers, comparing the pay gap between men and women in the UK and in Iceland (about the same, despite the highly subsidised childcare; perhaps early child-bearing makes a difference, after all), the percentage of household income spent on vegetables, life expectancy, dental health, number of televisions per capita . . . The next week, I talk to the director of the rape crisis centre, who confirms that Icelandic women are subject to levels of violence similar to those in the rest of Europe, and to the Minister for Social Affairs, who describes levels of poverty and deprivation similar to those at home. The stories told by numbers and research are quite different from the stories we tell ourselves and each other. This is not to say that either is wrong.

I go back to the yarn shops, pretending to myself that I might make an Icelandic sweater. Everyone does, says my student Anna. I made two when I was a teenager. Do you still knit? I ask her. I want her to prove my ideas about the way Icelandic women don't conform to Euro-American norms and say yes, but she shakes her head. Not really. Not any more. She's still, of course, a member of her sewing circle, the same ten women meeting every few weeks at someone's house since they were all in primary school, but they don't really sew. I have a wave of envy. Women keep mentioning their sewing circles, and these meetings were background events in some of the Icelandic films I watched over the winter. A couple of the creative writing students have turned in stories in which women returning from abroad don't fit into their sewing circles any more. Sewing circles seem to be established in adolescence and continue until death, although some are inter-generational and therefore, presumably, infinite. Many women are members of more than one, which is probably part of the answer to my question about what Icelanders do in winter. Yes, confirms Anna, it is lovely. We're all doing different things now – a doctor, a banker, a teacher, a shop-worker, and most of us have spent time living abroad – but we still get together and it's still the same. Don't you still have friends from school? Anyway, if you're interested in knitting you should go talk to Ragga. She's the goddess of Icelandic knitting.

So I go talk to Ragga. Ragga works in the *Hugmyndahús* down on the harbour. The University of Reykjavík, which is mostly a business school, runs the *Hugmyndahús* in collaboration with the Icelandic Academy of Arts. The *Hugmyndahús*, the 'House of Ideas', is a real house, an old fish-processing unit that was a shop selling the sort of furniture that only bankers could afford during the boom years. The furniture shop went bust when the bankers fled Iceland in 2009, and now people who are trying to set up new creative businesses in Iceland can apply for free workspaces in what used to be the showroom and talk through their plans with experts from the university. There's a café where anyone can go and sit with a laptop for as long as she likes without any pressure to buy coffee or move on. I've known about it since the summer and thought that I ought to have used the café as a place to write, especially on the days when I found myself arguing with Max over who got to use the car parked outside the flat as a reading-room. I was too shy.

But now I'm braver, and today I'm going there to meet the Goddess of Icelandic Knitting. Her website makes me want to knit full-time until I can do cabling and intarsia and Japanese shaping and speak in the language of knitting patterns. The day's so warm that I walk across town with my coat open. The space around Tjörnin is full of terns, flickering snow-white against blue sky. Daffodils rustle under the low trees in the gardens of the old wooden houses, and tourists are beginning to shamble around the city centre. I bump into one of last term's students and stop for a chat, which means that for once I'm almost running late. I hurry down a side street and come out across the road from the old herring-processing plant, white in the sun and tall behind the rat-race of cars, navy sea and grass-green mountain sunbathing behind it. The new opera house, the one Iceland can't afford to finish and can't afford not to finish, is taking on its final shape, glass fish-scales glinting on its stepped sides. I cross the car park, and notice that I got here without thinking about it, that not only did I not look up directions on the internet nor carry a map, but neither did I look for street names and lefts and rights, didn't have to imagine a bird's eye on my progress.

I go in. The space is so big, so white that the doorway seems to contract behind me, and the café to one side is like Playmobil, its tables waiting to be rearranged by giant hands. I go over to the bar and ask for Ragga. Round here, says the woman who was sipping coffee and laughing with the waiter. Follow me, it's time I got back to work anyway. We cross the concrete floor, scarred as if the giants have dragged something heavier than Playmobil across it, and round the corner, in front of a glass wall overlooking the harbour where a trawler is coming home, is Ragga. There she is, says the woman, have a good talk. (I didn't apologise for speaking English, I think, I just walked in here as if I had every right and expected people to speak to me in my own language.) Wool has entwined Ragga's laptop and there are knitting books open among the spreadsheets on her desk. Children's jumpers lounge on the chairs and across the bookcase. Ragga is writing, and while she finishes her paragraph I read the itinerary for one of the tours that she's running this summer. I want to go on it, and I want to go to the Loops Nordic Knit Art festival at the Nordic House, which starts the day after we fly home.

We settle on sofas in the café with hot chocolate. Clouds are hurrying over the sea outside and the light has changed, muted as if someone's flicked a switch.

I tell Ragga about the way the students knit in class, the way I've noticed people knitting on buses and in meetings and in the slow moments of political protest. (Why is that worrying me, asks Anthony. *Les tricoteuses*, I reply, and then wish I hadn't when we have to spend the next twenty minutes explaining to Max.) The way even knitting addicts don't knit in public at home.

'It's completely normal!' says Ragga. 'Why wouldn't you knit? You're waiting for a bus or something, use the time. I first heard about this, the way people in Europe and America don't knit, when I read about this KIP, Knit in Public Day. It started in the US. I read a blog by a woman who said she took a sock with her and knitted on the bus and I thought so what?

Everyone knits on the bus, what else would you do? But she says she's some kind of rebellious knitting icon because she knits waiting in line.'

I lick cream off my spoon. 'It's not exactly rebellion. It's not as if knitting's indecent. It's just not done. I don't know why.'

'I wonder how that came to be, how societies came to this. We never stopped. Everyone here has some sort of relationship to knitting, everyone learns how to do it in elementary school. But it seems in the English-speaking world most knitters start *after thirty* or something. It's just so weird.'

When did the English stop knitting? Women in eighteenth- and nineteenth-century novels are forever knitting and sewing, always have their 'work' about them, although Austen and Brontë are both pretty scathing about it, and even Elizabeth Gaskell remarks what a shame it is that rich women are so bored they have to invent unnecessary labour while poor women work so hard outside the home that they don't have time to mend their children's clothes. Most of my friends think my crocheting habit is bizarre.

'What about during the financial boom?' I ask. 'Did people knit just as much?'

'Maybe not quite so much. I think it was around 2007, 2008, suddenly there were knitting cafés starting up, and then it escalated as the economy faltered. I published a knitting book in December 2008 and that was the beginning of a flood of new knitting books here. I'd been living in Sweden and I moved back in 2008 and started a group in the yarn store — you know, on Laugavegur? — and then there were groups popping up everywhere, hundreds of them, meeting two or three times a month, and now I'm sure you'll find one in every little town on the island. Before, back in the old days, say

2006, 2005, there was this tradition of the sewing circles, but they weren't really about sewing or any kind of crafting, just gossip and coffee and cake, just to get out of your home and leave the dishes and the kids behind, but now they're really going strong and people are really making things. I don't think many women now would go out without something to do. This has just become part of women's culture in Iceland.'

'Women's culture,' I say.

'Well, there are men who knit, of course. And sew. My uncle, for example, he's had a sewing circle for twenty years with his male friends and they do sew. They've done it all these years.'

I tell her about an exhibition about lighthouse-keepers that I saw at the Maritime Museum in Falmouth. Lighthouse-keepers knitted, impossibly complicated Fair Isle, the kind of thing you might do if you found yourself in solitary confinement for a couple of months with only knitting needles and yarn.

'Of course,' says Ragga. 'That makes sense. My great-grandfather knitted. He was a fisherman, and when the sea was too rough to go out, he and my great-grandmother just sat and knitted, socks and sweaters, until the storm passed. My grandfather remembered going to sleep and hearing the click, click of the needles. There's a lot of knitting on that side of the family. My grandmother died in Hofsós, and we've kept her house just as it was. I was there in February to record my DVD about knitting, and it was so much fun just to be in her house again. We'll return there this summer, looking at knitting and the locale, following the wool from sheep to sweater on one farm.'

I long to watch this, suddenly, although my parents keep sheep and my mother not only knits but used to wash, card and spin the wool she picked off hedges and barbed-wire fences. I know perfectly well where wool comes from, and anyway I don't like to wear it.

'How old is the Icelandic sweater?' I ask, partly to see if Ragga is selling false consciousness.

'It's not very old,' she says immediately. 'It's really become the symbol of Icelandic knitting. We often talk about the three pillars of Icelandic knitting heritage: the sweater, the shawls, and the rose-pattern shoe-inserts. The inserts are a very special part of Icelandic knitting. They are very intricate little designs, complex motifs in interesting colours. In those days people wore sheepskin shoes, and they put these soles into them. It was a craft of women, in the days when people were wearing only grey and brown, homespun colours, everything very dull, and then there were these bright decorations hidden inside their shoes. They were for warmth, really, they had a function. And then there are the shawls.'

I have one of 'the shawls'. I'm wearing it as I write this, on a clear January day in Cornwall. On a similar day in Iceland, a little later in the year, I had a meeting with Katrin, who was writing her MA dissertation on American feminist biker narratives. Katrin is one of those women whose appearance reminds you that Titian wasn't necessarily exaggerating, and she is rushing to finish her dissertation before the birth of her third child, as well as working full-time. Sometimes, she confides, she takes her motorbike out in the early hours of the morning, just for a break, just for an hour away from the kids and the work and the studying and the dishes. Even when you're pregnant? I ask, remembering how hard it got to balance a pedal bike in the last few weeks. She shrugs. Sure, I'm still a person. Anyway, she says, look, I have something for you. She opens her shoulder-bag, which is bulging but light, and hands me a lapful of knitted wool, creamy as porridge and dense and springy as summer turf. I begin to unfurl it, can't tell what it is. I made it a while ago, she says, and it's been waiting in my cupboard for the right person. When you were talking about how cold your house in England gets in winter, I thought you were the person. See, you can wrap it like this, your arms and hands are still free to write but it'll keep you really warm. She helps me drape it, a cloud of wool in my vinyl and concrete office, and I recognise one of those rare objects perfectly designed for a simple purpose. The shawl is stiff enough to hang away from my body, heavy enough for the points to stay crossed over my chest, light enough that I don't feel it on my arms as I type. There, says Katrin, I knew it was for you. It's lovely, I tell her, but I can't accept this, all those hours of work you put in. Of course you can, she says, it's been waiting for you for months.

I stroke the shawl while we talk about feminism and biking – not a combination to which I have previously given thought. As it warms in the radiator's heat, the smell of sheep blooms around me. Tell me, I ask Katrin, tell me how you made it? Oh, it's very easy, she says. They're very traditional, everyone knows how to make them. You just start at the point and increase until it's big enough. Some people like to make fancy borders with lace stitches and colours, but I wanted to keep this one plain.

'I have one,' I tell Ragga. 'But I still don't really understand how they're made. It's as tall as I am, knitting needles don't come that big.'

'You start in the middle, at the back, and increase every other row, and at the edges so it grows both ways. It's a good project for a beginner. In its simplest form, it's just garter stitch. You can decorate it how you like and you can use any kind of yarn, and you end up with something really functional that you actually wear a lot. I use this pattern a lot when I'm converting people – I mean – oh, you know what I mean.'

Yes, I do.

'I think this was also an artistic outlet for women in the old days, because you know people knitted all the time, walking between farms or to get the cows—'

'They did that in Scotland as well,' I interrupt.

'There are stories of people who fell down the cliffs while knitting, and one about a girl who fell into a lava kettle and didn't even drop a stitch.'

Lava kettles are underground bubbles, often taller than a person, formed when the lava was molten and bubbling and now solidified into hollow spheres of smooth rock. People fall into them because the tops are too thin to bear a person's weight, and then can't get out because the hole is out of reach and the convex sides are too smooth to climb. There is no way of finding someone lost underground in a lava field.

'Did she knit her way out?' I ask.

'Yeah,' says Ragga. 'Probably. Of course, they weren't knitting for fun then. Knitted goods were one of our main exports, all made by hand on the farms. I read that one year in the 1800s, there were 30,000 pairs of socks exported. And the population was only about 70,000. Now, of course, you can just go to Europris or Rúmfatalagerinn and buy acrylic made in China, so knitting is for enjoyment, and a way for us to reconnect to our history. You get interested in how did my grandmother do it and how did her grandmother do it, and we're part of the old Iceland again.'

'Healing the nation?' I ask. 'Knitting Iceland back together?' Broken bones knit.

'Yeah. Something like that. And it's just fascinating. It's good for people's self-esteem, especially now people don't make things much, they sit in front of a screen all day. Lots of knitters say they're not creative but they are, even if they follow a pattern they choose the yarn and the colour, make it new and different from anyone else's sock or sweater. And then there's the second step, the activity, and that's a kind of physical mantra, monotonous, repetitive, or of course with a more challenging pattern it can be quite complicated mathematics or like chess: you're thinking ahead three, four, five moves. And then you get the results, and that's where you find your self-confidence.'

'If it works,' I point out, remembering all the times it didn't.

'Well, that can be an exercise in how you view the world too. You learn how to do it better next time.'

Ragga's right. I sometimes think it would be a good writing exercise to get people to knit something complicated and then unravel it, again and again until that yarn is in its best possible form.

'And another big project we're working on is developing our own yarn. We're working with a mill in Belgium at the moment, and our goal is to develop a blend of Icelandic wool and cashmere and alpaca. We'll have the first batch out in November, and then the plan is to move the production to Iceland, but we can't do that yet because there aren't any small mills in this country, just this huge factory, Ístex, which ruins everything. That's why Icelandic wool is so harsh. It's not like that at all if you process it differently.'

'I'd wondered about that,' I say, although on reflection I

haven't wondered enough, have found it merely logical that Icelandic wool would be coarse and wiry to the touch. Because Icelanders are tough, perhaps, too hardy to notice the rasp of wool on skin, or because it somehow stands to reason that Icelandic sheep would have coarser wool than their Scottish cousins.

'It's because there's only one, national, factory and they just blend all the wool from all the farms so it's all the same. And they wash it at too high a temperature, use too much salt, card it really badly. You can get much better results with the same wool, but we're having to go abroad to do it. I'll show you a sample. It's never been done before, and some people say it's wrong, to blend our pure Icelandic wool from Icelandic farms with foreign alpaca. But we're respecting what's good about the Icelandic wool, it's so warm and light, and adding alpaca to make it softer and even better. So we'll have to see how that's seen here, but we're not competing with Ístex, we're not competing on price. We're just saying that our Icelandic wool is a resource we have here and we're not using its potential—'

She breaks off. There is shouting outside and people at the bar exclaiming and pulling each other towards the door.

'Wow! Foreign rain. Do you see that? We don't get that in Iceland, that's European rain. Must be the volcano or something.'

My grandfather would have said it was raining stair-rods, the kind of rain that falls in lines rather than drops. There are bubbles in the puddles in the car park and the sound of small stones against the windows. Two women run in with water streaming down their faces. I am amused by the idea of 'foreign rain', but of course she's right; the rain in Iceland is usually persistent but fine.

'Anyway, so it's all starting now, the tours and the yarn and the webshop. It's going well.'

'It's an interesting time to start a business,' I suggest.

The waiter is giving the women towels.

Ragga laughs. 'Some would say, yes.'

I count back and realise that she gave up her job in the most acute phase of the crisis, the weeks when the news was worse and worse from one hour to the next.

'I've been asking lots of people about the effect of the *kreppa*,' I tell her. 'Most of them say it hasn't actually had a huge effect on their lives.'

'Well, it's limiting. Cheese is horribly expensive and you don't buy ham unless you really need it. We can't afford to travel any more. But I don't think – I mean, provided you have a job, most people are just eating differently and travelling less. I don't know anyone that bought Range Rovers or took huge foreign currency loans for a house, not personally. But of course for some people it's horrible, everything is ruined. It's all comparative, anyway. When I moved back from Sweden, things were weird. Everyone was like, wanting to work in banks, and changing their kitchens all the time, and wanting to live in these new buildings and flying to Europe for the week-end. And a lot of people think it's not bad that these excesses were stopped. Even though it's traumatic and we're hurt and we didn't really want to believe it was happening. It was really shocking to realise that this country, this Iceland which we thought was the best in the world, was really full of corruption. The whole atmosphere was just so strange, there was something about people's attitude, the relentless adoration of the money people, it was surreal, it wasn't my home. We never knew where the money was coming from. We thought the bankers must be so brilliant that the rest of us were too stupid to understand. And of course you don't ask many questions when the money is everywhere. Our money used to come from the fish in the sea but there were no more fish and suddenly there's this new way of doing it. It seized our society, we were in a weird collective state of mind. I have a friend, an Icelander living in Sweden, who felt so bad about it, because she wasn't keeping up with her peers at home, she was renting a small apartment in Stockholm. Her friends here were buying Range Rovers and moving into these huge new houses and putting in new kitchens and automatic lighting and everything, and she wouldn't let them visit her she was so ashamed. Such a waste of energy, all that shame. It was horrible.'

'So you're starting a new business for a new country?'

'People might say it's crazy to start a new business in Iceland in 2009, but if you're going to do it, this is the right kind of business. There's a global movement towards buying something sustainable, traceable, buying quality. And internet shopping is going up. I think these are long-term trends, not passing crazes. So I have very little money at the moment, but I'm optimistic about the future.'

We've finished our drinks. Ragga walks me back to her desk and lets me fondle the prototypes for her new yarns and turn her jumpers inside out to admire the colour-work. I pick up a schedule of this summer's tours and wonder how much Anthony would object if I came back to Iceland for a week or two once we're settled in Cornwall. Maybe I'll have another go at knitting. Maybe I'll buy some more wool and take it home to make an Icelandic shawl.

15

Last Weekend

We have one week left. I still haven't been round the National Gallery and we never made it to Pétur's summer house in Stykkishólmur. Anthony and I have not had an evening out together, barely seen the city after the children's bedtime. We haven't bathed in a natural hot spring. I haven't learnt to knit the Icelandic way. We haven't travelled more than a day's journey from Reykjavík, and our plans to drive all the way around the island have been displaced by the need to go home and move house before a new academic year begins. I'm not ready to leave.

While the children are at school and nursery, Anthony and I spend the day driving out to the depot on the far side of the city to collect our packing boxes, back into the centre to hand over my bike to Ása Björk, whose friend wants to buy it, to Kronan for the last time. We buy dried fish and *flatkökur* to take home, our last Icelandic lamb for the weekend, and poke the sad apples and oranges and think that it is nearly cherry time in Kent now. Without quite meaning to, I add a few more balls of wool to the trolley, although I've already got more than I'll use in the next two years. Good padding for packing, I explain to Anthony, who is not fooled. New wool is literally the substance of things hoped for, the future in material form.

I'm finding it hard to say goodbyes, ducking and weaving, pretending each time I see someone that I'll see her again before we go, that this isn't really goodbye, not yet, although we both know it's nonsense. Our flight leaves (volcano willing) early in the morning, so we're spending the last night at the airport hotel in Keflavík, a refurbished US army barracks a few kilometres from the terminal. Pétur has offered to cook for us and then drive us out there on the last night, closing the circle begun when he drove out there at midnight to collect me when I first came here for my job interview eighteen months ago. We should, then, be saying goodbye to everyone else. But I'm not.

Our friend Guy is due into Keflavík today. He's been trying to return to Iceland throughout the spring, repeatedly thwarted by the volcano. We've been checking the flights online and it seems that his has actually taken off. It's a hot morning, hot enough that Anthony and I have the car windows open and I discard the shawl I wrapped around my shoulders as we left the house. There's a slight haze in front of Esja, which is still there even as we drive towards it, and as we return to the flat the haze thickens to a pale yellow cloud. Esja's been our barometer all year, entirely or partially visible, the snow line higher or lower, smog at the bottom or cloud at the top. This must be a summer version of winter's green smog, I think, and prepare a quick lunch. School ends at 2 p.m., and I want to take Max up into Heiðmörk for a last walk. We've been there so often through the spring in our sweaters and coats and scarves and hats and gloves, sniffing the air under the trees to convince ourselves it smells of greenery, pushing our hoods back to see if it's bearable to expose our ears, that I want to take him again now it's warm, warm enough to stroll and sit down and feel the sun on our backs, and still enough to hear all the birds in the air. By the end of lunch the air is odd, brownish, muted, although the white sun is still strong behind the fog and the heat is almost oppressive. Something's brewing. Best take Tobias's cagoule, I suggest to Anthony, who is off on the nursery run, and I shrug a jacket onto my shoulders before I leave for school.

But by the time the bell rings, the fog is so dense that there's no point going to Heiðmörk, where a lot of the pleasure is being able to see from Esja to the airport and far out to sea as you climb out of the woods. Instead, we drop Max's bags at the flat and head out along the coast path towards Hafnarfjörður, our daily walk but different in every light and season and weather. Weird weather, Max says. Despite the fog, which is so dense we can see it eddying in front of the rocks by the path, there's a warm wind. Usually there's a carnival of children along here after school, swooping on roller-skates and bicycles, kicking balls into the paths of joggers, throwing stones into the sea and bread for the swans, but there are only a few solitary walkers today. I check my watch: if Guy's plane was on time and he had only hand luggage, he could be at the flat soon. We turn back, walking briskly. Max is talking about space travel, but I'm listening to the voice in my mind chuntering about the move, about the need to sell things and pack things and give things away, see people for the real last time, worry about whether the shipping firm's assurance that everything will be all right results from expertise or poor English. The other two are still out when we get back, and I check my phone for messages from Guy to find that Vodafone have disconnected our mobile phones a week early. I'm waiting for calls, from people who might be buying the washing machine and the car seat, not to mention the car, which Ása Björk has had checked by her mechanic. I use the landline to call Ása Björk, who does want the car and whose friend has bought the bicycle. She'll pass on the cash after the weekend; she's about to go to Stykkishólmur now, ash permitting. Ash? I ask. You drive to Stykkishólmur. Yes, she says, haven't you looked out of the window? This horrible thick fog of it? Don't go out, it's really not good for you.

God, but I am stupid. And Anthony and Tobias, who is asthmatic, are out there, walking home from nursery. Max, remembering Pompeii again, pales. Mummy, they'll be dead! he says. His eyes fill. Mummy, quick! Do something, they'll be dying out there. No they won't, I say, look, there's someone walking past. He's not dying. We were out in it, weren't we?

Though I do now have a sore throat. The official line is that there's no evidence that volcanic ash inhalation causes long-term health problems, except in vulnerable people, which includes small children and asthmatics. Would nursery have told Anthony that it was ash and Tobias shouldn't be outside? It's not as if he could have called me if he needed collecting. I leave a message for Guy and bundle Max into the car. He holds his breath until the doors are closed. I close the vents. We cruise the route to nursery, turn round and come back. They're not there. The car is getting hotter and hotter under the brown sun. I try to call again, trying not to hear ambulance sirens. Tobias's inhaler is in the kitchen cupboard. I park, badly, in front of the flat, and rush Max into the lobby. They're back, and Guy's called from the bus stop. Anthony heads out to meet him and I cuddle Tobias and worry.

We all spend the rest of the day in the flat, with the windows closed. It's hot. The children fight. The windows are dimmed, and a fine layer of grit settles on the countertops, on the window-sills, on my keyboard, on the towels and soap in the bathroom, which has no windows or external walls. We've never had the windows closed before, even at minus fifteen in January. No-one in Iceland has the windows closed, not with underfloor heating and triple glazing in every room. The heating is centrally controlled and although we keep it as low as possible, we can't turn it off. It gets hotter. The sun, boring through the fog, won't set until after midnight. Guy builds Lego aeroplanes with Max, helps Tobias construct a wooden train track, talks me through a flap about whether making cookies would be worth having the oven on and making us even hotter. Everyone is coughing. We look out at the cars, under a brown snow which drifts and eddies along the road exactly as white snow did on Guy's last visit. The adults stay up too late, revelling in adult company after so many weeks of nuclear family life, and looking at houses in Cornwall on the internet. Guy's ideas about how we might live after the move are grandiose; he keeps pulling up small-holdings and disintegrating Georgian piles in ex-mining towns, scolding when I offer heritage-painted cottages in seaside villages. We giggle, and it gets later, and dustier, but not dark. We crane at the kitchen window to see the sun, a beige disk, slide slowly behind a brown curtain of ash. The world's gone sepia. At last we go to bed, and I lie there, hot, airless, wondering how the flat is ventilated. When we lived in a newly built, double-glazed flat in England, there were little vents set into the window-frames, but there aren't here. There are three heavy, sealed, double-glazed doors and two flights of stairs between our flat and the outside world, and not a breath of draft around the triple-glazed windows. I remember a wartime story I read to Max last week, in which people trapped in an air-raid shelter were told not to panic because hyperventilating would use up too much oxygen. How long will it be before we can go out again? They can't, can they, have designed a flat with a finite air supply? I must be being ridiculous. It's not a submarine. (But I remember about Icelandic health and safety.) I turn over, tweak the piece of fabric we hang over the roller blind as a kind of curtain. Nothing has changed out there. There's no birdsong.

The ash is still there in the morning, maybe even thicker. The sun's bright but there are no shadows, and we can't see Esja or even across the bay. The balcony is carpeted with brown dust, swirling idly as the wind plays down the street. Guy is worrying on behalf of people who care about the state of the paintwork on their cars, and the temperature in the flat is twenty-six degrees and rising. I start to make waffles, panacea for everything, or at least a distraction for me. Even the mixing bowls in the cupboards are gritty to touch. I've wiped the counters, but every time I put anything down it leaves a paler outline on the white stone. Guy and Anthony are online, their laptops back to back on the table. Government advice, says Anthony, is that dwellers of the city should live in their homes. Guy runs it through different translation software, but the message is clear. Guy has flown from London for the weekend and no-one's going anywhere.

It's twenty-nine degrees and the children are fighting over a book neither of them wants to read. I soak tea towels in cold water, open the windows and try to drape the towels to cover the gaps. More dust comes in. Sweat trickles down my side. The children are chasing each other up and down. Wearily, recalling the techniques for winter weekends – but then at least we could go swimming – Anthony gets out the arts-and-crafts box and I take Tobias into the lobby to ride up and down in the lift. Later, I go out and move the car into the under-ground garage so the children can get in without going outside and we drive to the mall, which is full of parents chasing young children the length of its stone floors and buying noth-ing. The piped music is too loud, constantly interrupted by announcements of sales on cookware and mobile phones. Being in the mall quickly becomes worse than being in the flat. There is, I remind Anthony, the indoor pool in Hafnarfjörður, but neither of us can face it. We are out of courage, out of energy, out of adventure. Time to go home.

By the end of the week, the wind has changed, carrying the ash out to sea, and our seven boxes have been taken away by men in a van who seemed to know what they were doing. My bike is gone. Mæja posted our washing machine's availability on Facebook and a young couple, about to move out of his par-ents' house, came round and bought it. (The taboo on second-hand goods may be shifting after all.) I've cleaned the fridge and Anthony has helped a man with a van manoeuvre it out of the flat so it can be returned to Hulda Kristín's step-father. Pétur comes to disassemble and collect his bookshelves and the Formica table that has been my desk. Hot, now, in the sun flooding through the triple glazing, I pack everything too precious to go in the boxes. There are a lot of precious things and many of them are heavy. Wooden toys, books. More books. Computers. Children's drawings and schoolwork. When I've finished, and lined up the cases in the middle of the bare room, there is still too much left. I call my students and they come round, while Anthony and the children are still swimming. The two shop-soiled IKEA wicker armchairs go. Sigrid, who has three kids, takes the elephant rug we bought for Tobias in IKEA, its matching cushion and both children's duvets. I can't, she says, let me at least pay you. You can take them, I say, remembering the house full of objects waiting for us in Canterbury, and needing to be sold so we can move to Cornwall before the new school year begins. And you can't pay, I don't need any more króna and they were always meant to be disposable. I give a pestle and mortar which have always been too small, so the spices ping out when you try to grind them, to another student. She drops it while loading her car; oh well, she says, it wasn't meant to be. It was a wedding present. Mads accepts our duplicate copies of *Peter Rabbit* and *Jemima Puddleduck*, 1970s editions with odd colours and mismatches between text and pictures, because he enjoyed the week on children's books in my food and literature course. Mads and Mæja are among the people I'll miss most, and he's a bibliophile, so that's all right, I tell myself. Part of the circulation of objects. It is all right, but I think my dead grandparents gave me one of those when I was a toddler. Katrin takes a piece of batik that I bought when I first went to university to cover my bed, which lay in a drawer in Canterbury for years before I brought it here with the intention of abandoning it at the end. I love the blue, she says. I loved it too, I reply. Enjoy it. I give away the cutlery my grandmother stole from aeroplanes in the 1980s, which no-one has been able to dispose of because it's perfectly serviceable although everyone in the family now has proper sets. One of the students cannot remember metal cutlery on aeroplanes. No, I tell him, it wasn't a more innocent age, only one whose terrors did not include cutlery at 36,000 feet. (But I keep the four-pronged fork and serrated knife from El-Al, all the same.) Even the cheap plastic mixing bowls we've used all year are somehow hard to leave. I give it away, all of it. I send our things out to begin Icelandic lives. Mæja arrives to help me clean, Mæja who despite her expertise in linguistics likes to go down on her knees and scrub. We work together. Come and see us, I say. Come to Cornwall.

Everyone has gone, Anthony and the children already at Pétur's house, which we will leave for the airport after supper, Mæja back to the flat full of grace and books and a grand piano, the students back to their summer jobs in restaurants and hotels and offices. I wander round the flat for the last time, though I know really that there's nothing left. I go out onto the balcony, which still has traces of dust around the edges, and run my finger along the window-sills, which have been washed by Mæja and are therefore clean. Esja is alpine-bright, the patch of snow on the summit glistening against a sky so blue you can tell it's black at the top, the pine trees massed on the lower slopes. The church at Kópavogur bathes in sun on the headland, the spire of Hallgrímskirkja rising behind it. The waves in the bay are lazy, and I can hear children playing on the artificial beach at the end of the road. Some of them will be swimming. There isn't time for the last walk on the lava field that I'd been planning, but I let the door close behind me for the last time and walk down to the shore, where it does, at last, smell of growing turf and rotting seaweed. The goslings have been hatching this week, seizing the short weeks of summer, and they stagger peeping and pecking at clouds of flies. It's not quite midsummer yet, and they have a few weeks to grow their wings before Iceland tilts away from the sun and the nights begin to lengthen, telling them to leave. I'm not ready to go either.

16

Beautiful is the Hillside

But we do leave. We go home and move the length of the country, from the eastern to the western corner of the British triangle, and start again.

England looks different now. I understand for the first time what Americans mean when they say that everything is so small here. The landscape seems miniaturised, intricate as embroidery. The richness of trees and hedges and canals and bridges and shops and pavements is too much, requires faster reactions and shorter sight than come naturally now. Shops are the size of sitting rooms, town gardens the size of bathrooms, and half the sky seems to have gone away. The colours are too bright, vulgar as Technicolour after black and white. The news seems parochial. I forget to lock the car doors, but take Tobias's woolly hat in my bag every time we go to the park, all summer. Now three, he can swing himself high on the big swings, and I try to explain to my friends why I'm not trying to stop him climbing to the top of the big slide and jumping off the big climbing frame. I don't say that I have learnt that children don't usually fall, and also that they learn only by falling.

He forgets the Icelandic songs, and, during a summer spent in shorts and T-shirts, how to do up a zip. He forgets how to swim.

Iceland stops seeming real to me after the move. Tobias tries to speak Icelandic at his new Cornish nursery, but gives up within a week and by Christmas cannot remember his first handful of nouns, losing the language as fast as he found it. I put postcards of snowy mountains and the Northern Lights and Reykjavík on my office wall, but they are only postcards and when I tell people that we spent last year in Iceland I feel as if I am lying. In my mind, I follow the cycle of the year in Iceland: the departure of the birds, the lengthening nights, the week when you stop hoping that it will be warmer today. And then the first snow, the first aurora, the day you start thinking about lunch before sunrise, the day the waves are contained under ice. In Cornwall, the roses in our garden are still blooming on Christmas Day and Max and his friend dare each other to swim in the sea at New Year. In Iceland, I know, the snow on the ground is brighter than the sky and on the brightest winter day the shadows stretch away like ghosts. In spring, Pétur sends me pictures of Icelandic students celebrating the end of term with a barbecue that has to be secured in the corner of two buildings and sheltered from horizontal snow with umbrellas, while from my office I can see people sunbathing around the fountain while they revise. Most people, I know, prefer Cornwall to Reykjavík. At the beginning of the summer, these people begin to trickle down the A30, bringing tents and surfboards and bicycles. As soon as the school holidays begin in mid-July, our new hometown is crowded with families coming for the beaches and the coastal walking, admiring the palm trees along the seafront and the cafés where you can eat organic ice cream from the local farm while watching the harbour. That's when we go back to Iceland.

It's raining when we land. The bareness of the landscape between the airport and the outside of the city is startling again: fifty kilometres of lava, a cold desert the colour of tarmac that stretches towards the horizon, where dark mountains loom. The ugliness of the industrial buildings that line the road into Hafnarfjörður is still upsetting, though they are no worse than what you see from most of the M25. The sea below the road seems like a different element from the Cornish coast, although Cornwall has a darkness of its own in winter. It's all the North Atlantic, the Viking and Celtic searoad, but comparing Iceland's sea and Cornwall's is like comparing a cello with a violin, oil painting with watercolour. Every port has a name for the sea. There are flowers in the cracks in the lava, and rowan trees gathering in the hollows. Esja is monochrome in the rain, its top blotted by cloud. Tobias leans on my shoulder, watching out of the bus window, until we come into Hafnarfjörður, when he turns to me as if with a question. We used to come here, I say. Do you remember? There's a swimming pool up there, he says. I fed the ducks on that pond. He sits up now, intent as if the windows are showing a film he can hardly follow. We bought *kleinur* there once, he says, pointing to a bakery. *Kleinur* are cardamom-flavoured doughnuts, and we have not mentioned them, so far as I know, since we left Iceland. There's my old school, says Max, turning away as if from the scene of an accident, not wanting to see that what he has lost is still there. And my Lundaból nursery, Tobias adds, pointing out of the other window. Am I going back there? No, I say, watching as my bike-route to work begins to unfurl along the beach. No, this is just a holiday, remember?

I can see Pétur before the bus pulls into the station, and we're the first ones off. We hug. Tobias remembers him, and remembers his car, and remembers that there was a different child-seat in it last time. He takes us to the university flat where we stayed when we came house-hunting two years ago, and that hasn't changed either. The small planes are still taking off over the hedge, and the northern sea at the end of the road is still reflected in the sky. Pétur takes me to the big Bonus in the industrial park by the harbour, and even the sight of the oil storage tanks and the corrugated iron warehouses in front of Esja lifts my heart.

Bonus has changed. There is coconut milk and wholewheat noodles and agave syrup, and miso powder in sachets and Earl Grey tea, all at prices comparable to those at home. No, Pétur says, things haven't got cheaper, it's just that British prices have risen so much that ours seem normal to you now. And our salaries haven't gone up either. But maybe there's a wider range of food again. You were here at a strange time for Iceland, you know. Look, we've got four kinds of apple now. And Spanish peaches and air-freighted American basil, and look at the cheese! We stand together in the chiller aisle, looking at the cheese. There are perhaps a dozen kinds of Icelandic soft cheese, and several blue cheeses, many of them named after the farms from which they come. Some of these, I remind myself, were available a year ago, but we couldn't afford them then. I choose one, and a leg of Icelandic lamb to celebrate our return, and barley *flatkökur* and a pot of *skyr*, and when we come to the checkout I find that I still can't say the Icelandic words I have in my head, and still can't bear the arrogance of asking people to speak English for me, and still, therefore, mutter and smile as if I had no language at all.

We've been travelling since before dawn and it's ten o'clock by the time the children are fed, washed and settled in bed, but there's a candy-pink light coming out of the west onto the concrete buildings between our flat and the coast. I'm just going out for a minute, I say to Anthony, who is trying to keep his eyes open long enough to brush his teeth and find his pyjamas. You're mad, he says, and I'll probably be asleep when you get back. I know, I say. I slip my shoes on, take my coat, ease the door open and step out. The evening smells of rain and turf, of the wildflowers that are scattered wherever there is grass, making the most of the brief summer. I have to admit that it's cold. If I had gloves, I would put them on. I put my hands in my pockets and walk across campus and down one of the streets lined with big, mid-twentieth-century houses to the sea. This is a wealthy part of town, but there are only a couple of SUVs, and most of the cars parked along the road are European. I pull my hood up. There's no-one else out. I take the path between the gardens that leads via a playground to the shore. There are flowerbeds in some of the gardens, filled with poppies and lupins and daffodils, and children's tricycles scattered on the lawns where they can stay all night. The sea gleams across the road, where the bike track passes a sculpture of fish on the pavement that Tobias has always liked, and when I get there, around eleven, the sun is just slipping below the church on the hill in Seltjarnarnes, and the shoreline and the hills behind Garðabær reflect the sunset. A handful of birds skim the waves, and the lights of Álftanes across the bay are beginning to twinkle over the water. I sit on a rock and watch night coming across the sea.

We have another three days in Reykjavík. We swim, and see friends, and one afternoon I drift around the city centre and buy a few of the things I coveted but couldn't afford on a local salary. Downtown feels different. Vacancy spread like mould along Laugavegur and its side streets during the *kreppa*, and several people mentioned these empty shop-fronts as one of the first and most painful signs of crisis. They are tenanted again now, mostly by designers and craftspeople for whom Laugavegur would have been too expensive during the boom years. There are more Icelanders than tourists in the cafés, which wasn't usually the case last year. The woman running the shop where I buy a new raincoat is comfortable chatting about what's changed in Iceland: yes, she says, people are more relaxed than they were. And more humble, she adds, because we needed this, this correction. Iceland was out of control and we needed a lesson and it's better now.

I wander out and up a side street towards the cathedral. It seems to me today that even the street fashion is more playful than last year. Hulda Kristín and I used to discuss Icelandic women's proclivity for head-to-toe black, whether it was because a black uniform is easy to put together or because of a fear of being seen to be different, or maybe just because winter coats and boots need to match everything and blondes look good in black. The tourists are still wearing climbing gear on Laugavegur as if they think the whole country is a hiking trail, oblivious to Icelanders' mockery, but I see

Icelandic women in bright shoes and tights, layering skirts in shades of sage and terracotta, wearing patterned dresses over leggings, and even men wearing coloured T-shirts with their black jeans. Maybe it's just a seasonal variation, but I remember noticing the black in May 2009 as well as 2010. There are flowers in hanging baskets. I cross the city, heading to Mads and Mæja's new house for lunch. I don't know if the new happiness is mine or Reykjavík's.

We go back to Perlan with Matthew. Perlan is one of the city's landmarks, pleasant although in itself pointless, a collection of disused water-towers, which, with the addition of a large dome, have somehow become an attractive destination. There's an artificial geyser on the hillside just below the dome, and a commanding view of the city from the top. We climb up and the children rush around, peering through the telescopes at each cardinal point as they always did, and the adults stand watching flurries of rain blowing in across the mountains and out over the sea. I circle the dome slowly, greeting the tower block in Garðabær where we almost lived, the church at Kópavogur, the domestic airport and the National Library and the hospital, Esja, the hills where Route 1 climbs out towards Hveragerði, and around it all the sweep of mountains and sky. I look back down into the city. They finished the concert hall! I exclaim. Sure did, says Matthew. I'd love to know what you think, shall we go see it?

The concert hall down on the harbour was conceived at the peak of the economic boom. It was going to be Iceland's Eiffel Tower, Iceland's Statue of Liberty or Leaning Tower or Brandenburg Gate. The former owner and chairman of

Landsbanki, Björgólfur Guðmundsson, took over the project during the boom years, intending to present the nation with a jewel that reconfigured the capital's waterfront. The *kreppa* came when the hall was a hole in the ground and steel rods, a project planned to be spectacular at any cost, and for a few months the building site froze like so many others across the city, arrested at a stage where it seemed equally impossible that it could stop existing and that it could ever be finished. Landsbanki collapsed, the wealth of the Icelandic banks was revealed to be imaginary, and the money needed to finish Harpa turned out not to exist. The assets Landsbanki had funnelled into the project were not theirs to spend; there is British and Dutch Icesave money in those shimmering windows. Some city-dwellers said Harpa should be left unfinished to remind Icelanders of their folly every time they glanced up, others said it was too shameful that foreigners and tourists should see a city branded by its own greed and that it would be better to complete it even if it pushed a bankrupt city further down the spiral of debt, even though amenities much more fundamental to daily life than a new concert hall were closing for lack of funds. After a few weeks, no-one really wanted to talk about it, although given the size and position of the half-built hulk, it was impossible not to think about it. The new government decided, in the end, to go ahead, and the building rose black across Reykjavík's horizon, scribbled with yellow cranes. When we left, the scale of the place was becoming clear, the way it blocked half of Esja from the harbour-front and flashed its fish-scale windows across town. From where I'm standing on Perlan now, it glistens between the city and the sea, towering over the wharves like the cruise liners that sometimes dwarf the Victorian terraces of Falmouth. Do you mean we can just go in? I ask Matthew. Of course, he says, it's a public building. We can go now if you like.

But first the children want to see the geyser, and look for rabbits in the woodland that runs down to the sea. The rabbit colony developed from escaped pets, though I still don't understand how they survive the winter. We wander down the tracks, hoods up against the rain which has been not so much falling as congregating in the air for the last three days, and come out by what I remember as another building site, the new campus for the University of Reykjavík. Háskólinn í Reykjavík is a private institution, specialising in Business and Computer Studies, and for all of the time we lived in Iceland there were rumours (at least in Háskóli Íslands) that Háskólinn í Reykjavík was on the point of bankruptcy, had been born of the economic boom and was dying in the collapse. The new buildings, it was said, would push it over the edge. But apparently not. Háskólinn í Reykjavík, Matthew reminds me, recruits internationally by offering salaries two or three times those paid by the national university, but also keeps academics on short-term contracts and offers none of the benefits of public sector employment (in Iceland, these include highly subsidised holidays in summer houses owned by the union, free adult education classes in anything from knitting to advanced software design, and meal tickets for use in the university café). Most staff at Háskóli Íslands see its competitor's approach to human resources as distasteful, un-Icelandic or perhaps un-Nordic, driven by commerce rather than intellectual value. I see the point, and Háskólinn í Reykjavík has no interest in the unprofitable Humanities anyway, but for a building like this I could probably bring myself to prostitute my talent. It's Sunday afternoon and even HR is closed, but we peer through the windows to see a circular atrium brimming with diluted sunlight, although it's still drizzling outside and the sea gleams no more than creased leather. Stairs lead off this atrium like the warp of a spider's web. All the external walls are glass. We go round to the café on the shore, which I also saw taking shape week by week. It was finished before we left, a granite and glass cube where people richer and less anxious than I was sat sipping coffee and chatting over new laptops. I used to feel like a stray cat looking through a fish-monger's window. We can go in, says Matthew, so we do. Hot chocolates all round. It looks too smart for children, full of couples of a certain age with well-arranged hair, dressed in shades of beige and black. The couples have cream-smeared plates and foamy coffee cups, the end of a Sunday treat. Nonsense, says Matthew, this is Iceland, children rule, and then the waitress brings over pencils and colouring blocks with our drinks, and they do fine. I like it here. There is a single gerbera in a white vase on each black table, and the white walls reflect the sea's glimmer. If we lived here, I too would come with my laptop. We treat Matthew, being at last in a position to return favours, and leave with another ghost laid.

And so to Harpa. Matthew drives into an underground car park lit like a 1980s disco. Coloured lights splatter the walls with pink and green and red, and the zebra crossings are beamed from the ceiling onto the asphalt. We make our way to sliding glass doors with the hall's emblem etched across them, over a black stone floor that shines like still water and

up broad escalators that remind me of the Moscow underground. We ascend, and come out into a space taller than St
Pancras, taller than the British Library, whose floor stretches
from our feet like a frozen lake. One wall is the matt black of
old lava, the other those fish-scales, which turn out to be
hundreds of prisms, each the size of a person, stacked up the
height of many generations. Pale concrete stairs snake up to
the sky, and the stairs are lined with concrete terraces where
there are black sofas and purple stools. We go up, Tobias running ahead, Max daunted by the space, to the very top, where
there's a bar and more seats and you can see out across the
docks to Esja. In the atrium far below, children run and call.
At Harpa's feet, the ground is scarred and steel rods grow out
of puddles and churned mud. That, says Matthew, was meant
to be another underground car park, over which there would
be a plaza with trees and benches and an infinity pool. I guess
it's just going to sit there like that, an eyesore, for the fore-
seeable future. We turn back and look down into Harpa's
depths.

So, says Matthew, what do you think?

I think it's spectacular, I say. I think it's very Icelandic, an
outrageously ambitious project that hasn't been compromised
in the execution. No-one's tried to cut corners or scale things
down. Wherever the money comes from, Icelanders are good
at spending it.

We begin to stroll down the upper slopes. There are
groups of friends chatting on the sofas, a few solitary adults
lounging in the floor-level prisms with books or notebooks or
laptops, families congregated around the tables. People are
using it like an indoor park, like a real public amenity. In the
middle are the concert halls, of all sizes, and some meeting

rooms. It will never pay its way, says Matthew, it's mostly for classical music and the audiences just aren't there on this scale. I might feel differently if these were my taxes, I admit, before remembering that, one way or another, between Icesave and my Icelandic contributions, some twinkle of Harpa's scales does come from my purse. I can't imagine any part of the British public sector ever building anything like this. Maybe it is always easier to love the place that isn't home.

Pétur has lent us his summer house. It's in Stykkishólmur, a village on the northern side of the Snæfellsnes peninsula, behind a chain of mountains that's occasionally visible from Reykjavík on a clear day. We drive the familiar route to Borgarnes, and then branch off from Route 1's circuit, over the hills and down the other side. This area, Pétur says, was one of the first to be settled when the Vikings arrived in Iceland. There are twelfth-century road-works over some of the ravines. I look up the valley at a track winding across the hillside, thinking about a time when people walked these fells every day. As promised by Pétur when we left the damp city, there is sun here, and the shadows of clouds play across the birch scrub. When we stop for a break, the children find the first blueberries ripening on a south-facing slope, and sheep watch as we follow their track down to the river-bank. I think about taking my coat off. Wind rustles through the bushes and ruffles the water where a flotilla of swans rides as though at anchor. Pétur names the mountains for me as we drive: Drápuhlíðarfjall, the 'Poem Slope Mountain', Írafell, the Irish mountain (lots of Celtic settlers round here in the ninth century, Pétur says), Helgafell, the Holy Mountain, where

Guðrun from Laxdæla saga, the woman Auden quotes in his Iceland poem, is buried. *He that I loved the best, to him I was worst.* Those lines, Pétur tells me, are already a quote, from an early Irish poem that must have been known to the saga-makers. He found them one day when researching something else, evidence of Norse and Celtic cultural integration at the beginning of Icelandic history. Max repeats the lines, wondering what they mean, as we pass Guðrun's grave.

Stykkishólmur is visible for miles before we reach the cluster of red-roofed buildings tumbling down the hillside to the harbour, partly because it has a new white church on the prow of its hill, overlooking the dozens of islands dotting the sound between Snæfellsnes and the Westfjords across the water. Pétur's summer house turns out to be as small as he promised. You can stand in the middle and see out of the windows in all four walls. From the outside, the building seems too small to enclose a kitchen, bedroom, sitting area and shower-room, the essence of domesticity. It's not possible to make a mess. No-one could expect any serious cooking. The work of family life is reduced to essentials and everything else must happen outside, overlooked by the mountains and in sight of the sea. Maybe this is the point I've been missing about summer houses. Where do I play, asks Tobias. Max shows him the turf garden outside, with a slope for rolling and a hillock for jumping and some rocks for clambering. On neighbouring plots, children younger than either of them freewheel down the grass on tricycles and stagger over footballs, but the plots are unfenced, big cars lumber by and I know, now, that there's no magic force-field keeping Icelandic children safe from the usual perils. I take my crochet outside and sit, keeping an eye on children and traffic and strangers and asteroids that might fall from the sky, until it's time to make them go inside so I can cook supper. Icelandic children swirl around the gardens and roads, enjoying the kind of neighbourhood play that shaped my childhood. Mine sit at the table and draw while I chop vegetables, continually distracted by the view through all four windows. It feels as if the village, despite being on the sea, is cupped by hills. The harbour is sheltered by a small, conical island, garnished with a lighthouse like the cherry on top of a cake. To one side is the church on its hill, and to the other another hill, topped by a building that reminds me of a paddle-steamer, with a wall of windows curving out over the sea. There are glimpses of sea between the hills, and real mountains appearing over the clouds, higher up the sky than seems probable. When the slow northern sunset begins, long after the children's bedtime, Max and I walk down through the village and around the harbour, over the bridge to the lighthouse island, where we climb steps cut into the hillside and find the hilltop crowded with people in hiking gear speaking German, French, Spanish and Italian and taking photos as the sun drops behind the Westfjords across Breiðafjörður and the lighthouse begins to scythe the sky. People smile at each other, share multi-lingual comments about the wind, stand back to let other people up or down the stairs. An un-Icelandic crowd.

It's raining again in the morning. We go to the pool and laze in a jacuzzi watching the clouds eddy around the mountains and Max running up the stairs, goose-pimpled in the wind, and swooping down the slide, and running up and swooping down, until he's hungry and we're hot. It's still raining. We saunter through the village. Unusually for Iceland, there are few houses built in the last twenty years, and a core of late nineteenth and early twentieth-century buildings, most of which have been meticulously restored, mostly by people who live in Reykjavík and summer here. There are several craft shops and cafés, and three small museums, but the town itself feels like a museum, like some of the villages near my parents' house in the Peak District that have sold themselves until they turn into self-parodies, where it's easier to buy a hand-carved wooden Christmas tree ornament in July than a pint of milk. Most of the houses, even around the edges of the village, look like summer houses; Pétur says that in winter, there are days when the entire peninsula is cut off by snow. I think I might prefer it then.

Guy, who is joining us for the rest of the trip, arrives from the airport with a hire car. It's still raining. We go round the museums, slowly, making the most of each one. Max likes the Volcano Museum, I linger in the Norwegian House, the restored home of a nineteenth-century merchant and scholar who both managed royal Danish estates in the region and campaigned for Icelandic independence. The wooden house is large even by modern Icelandic standards, and must have seemed like a cathedral when surrounded by one-room turf huts. William Morris would have felt at home; there is wood-block wallpaper in shades of duck-egg and storm-grey, polished wooden floorboards and some ornately carved furniture. There are walls of books, including Danish translations of Dickens and Walter Scott, and a music room with a piano. The family lost six of their eleven children in infancy; culture was no protection against the pain of mid-nineteenth-century Icelandic life.

We go up the hill towards the paddle-steamer building, which turns out to be the Library of Water. So many people have told me I *must* see this that I'm predisposed not to like it. It's some kind of avant-garde art installation, I gather, with a writing residency attached.

The entrance reminds me of some of the 1960s library buildings I've used. There are concrete steps, a glass door, and then a rubber-floored atrium where visitors are asked to remove their shoes and put on white towelling slippers. An American couple are protesting about the slippers, which have been worn by other people, and Tobias shoots past them in his socks and begins to run around. Don't worry, the curator tells me, children love it here. I step forwards and am silenced. The building has been hollowed out and filled with glass columns containing water from each of Iceland's glaciers. Even in the rain, light spills not so much across the floor as through the air, as if the building is only a frame for water, glass and air. There are two tables with chessboards in the curved window, and I stand there for a while, looking out at the ordinariness of fishing boats and wet roads and tourists, getting ready to approach the columns again. There is a ping, like someone tapping a glass with a fork to silence wedding guests. Tobias has discovered that the columns make xylophone noises when touched. He runs, weaving between the columns, dodging his own reflection so that a running boy flickers through the room, the kind of visual stereo you get in front of a shop window full of televisions. I grab him as he makes for another one. Could we possibly come back later, I ask the curator? Without the children, when things are quieter? Of course, she says. I can stay open late for you if you have some special reason. I'm not sure I do, really, but Guy wants to take photos and I would like to try to write about this space, and in Iceland that's enough. We return at closing time. When Ragnheiður hears that we know Pétur, are staying in his house, she lets us have the keys and leaves us to play there for as long we like.

I wander between the columns. They look like giant test tubes, reaching from the floor to a white ceiling more than twice an adult height. The floor is rubber in shades of parched earth, terracotta, sand, the red of volcanic soil. Light comes through the glass and the water making lenses of each container, so you see columns of sea, rock and sky with a white bird falling through the water, a red roof and rocks refracted from one column to the next. I can't decide if the columns are actually lit from below or if it's just the alchemic relationship between sky, water and glass producing a kind of fission. I expected to find it peaceful here out-of-hours, but it's not. The columns have things to say to each other, are in a conversation that develops with the changing light. They feel like a forest, like a thicket, with a forest's sense of unseen eyes. Ragnheiður joked when she discovered we knew Pétur that we could spend the night here if we wanted, but I wouldn't. It would be like spending the night in a cathedral or in the Black Forest, a place that belongs to other presences after hours.

I sit on the floor, at the columns' feet. A fly in one of the windows buzzes like a plane taking off. The islands held in the columns in front of me are a mirage. The sea reflected there has the texture of velvet, the rocks are cut from lichen-dyed felt and stuck on. A seagull falls upwards on the other side, but the sea isn't moving there. The glass tubes gather like people at the kind of party where you stand up with a drink, reflecting each other's reflections. On the other side of the room, Guy sits on the floor, his camera peering, appearing in four or five places at the same time. I remember travelling with Kathy, the way we could find a place and pace it, sit in it, be in it, until we were ready to go.

We set off early the next morning. We're going all the way along the peninsula today, creeping around the glacier's feet. We pass farms in the glacial plain behind the town, and then turn west, across a lava field called Berserkjahraun. Berserkers were Vikings who went into trance-states of indiscriminate and uncontrollable violence, usually in battle, and this lava field is named for two berserkers in Eyrbyggjasaga who were killed here by being boiled in a bath-house built over a geothermal spring. Behind Berserkjahraun is a mountain of dark rock, a black cone reaching from the shore far into the sky, where it seems to close in on another dark mountain to the south. The road runs over a causeway between the two. We go over another causeway, and there is a scattering of farms with green in-fields along the bottom of more of those black mountains. The day passes through landscapes that simply don't make sense, mountains the mind can't read. It's like watching God in the act of creation, passing through fells of bare naked lava and rock, like seeing the world before it was finished. We're on day four of Creation, moving back towards day three, a world made of sky, fire, earth and water with none of the complications that came later. The mountains are red, as if the cinders haven't yet cooled, or the black of embers, carved by valleys where it seems that if you watched long enough, you'd see that the rock is still flowing. The elements are translated here: what is solid looks liquid, rock like water, earth like fire.

We stop in a fishing village called Ólafsvík for lunch. There is a local museum, on the first floor of the building that used to house the town's bar, where we look at old toys, butter churns and agricultural equipment. There are mincers with handles to wind and cast-iron balance scales of the kind still in use in my mother's kitchen. We go down the wooden ladder to what is now a craft shop and café on the ground floor, where I wander around stroking the knitwear, and the others stand in the doorway, watching a large fishing boat come in. All the garments, jumpers in heavy wool and hats, scarves and mittens in lacy *einband lopi*, have labels with a woman's first name and an Icelandic phone number in biro. I look up to where a group of women sits around a table in the café, knitting. There are two girls of about ten and twelve behind the counter, setting out coffee on a tray. I wander over, carrying a sweater I like, and one of the knitters catches my eye. I made that one, she says. I look inside and admire her thoroughness in catching down the yarn she was carrying over. It's like a knitters' secret handshake — she smiles and we start to discuss Icelandic increase technique and lacework. I try on the sweater, and Ragga, its maker, tells me that she and her neighbours have established a crafting co-operative. They knit at home, and together in the café, and in summer the visitors come and buy. Ragga takes me over to the table while her daughter wraps my sweater. None of the women is using a pattern, and most of them are doing intricate work, with lace stitches and cabling and multiple colours. I think of the weekly Knit Club I've joined in Cornwall, where we don't distract the person doing a cable row and all watch when Jo's knitting a particularly complicated bit of lace, and soggy photocopied patterns jostle the glasses on the table. Novices. Amateurs. In Ólafsvík they can set the thumbs on lace mittens while recounting what Halla says Jón did after she broke the news. . . It's just traditional piecework, I remind myself, glossed a little for the tourists, but even so I linger a little as Tobias tugs my hand in the doorway.

We go on to the end of the road, and then get out and walk to the lighthouse at the end of the peninsula. There's a different geology here, a glacier of older, black lava calving onto a beach populated by purple-grey pebbles, each round and sensual as an egg, shiny as marble. I steal one. Waves scribble the length of the shore, and Arctic terns scold overhead. The lighthouse speaks of harder weather, its windows arrow-slits doubly barricaded, the door tunnelled like the entrance to an iglu. Today the sun warms our backs and midges cloud the reeds.

We turn back, across the plains between the mountains and the sea, down the other side of the peninsula. Farms are scattered here, on a blanket of flat green fields spread at the feet of the volcanoes. I begin to see how the sagas might make a new kind of sense here. You would end locked in feuds with your neighbours in a place where you can always see them, always know what they are doing, and never see anyone else, where impassable mountains surround a glacier behind you and the Arctic sea laps your fields in front of you. One berserker would go a long way.

*

We leave Stykkishólmur for Akureyri, Iceland's 'second city' with a population of 17,000, 5,000 less than our Cornish 'small town'. Kathy and I were in Akureyri for her nineteenth birthday, sixteen years ago. We blew some money that could have been spent on food on swimming pool entry, and spent most of the afternoon in a jacuzzi, looking at patches of snow on sunbathing mountains and watching fishing boats going up and down the fjord. It was our favourite town, with a high street of early twentieth-century wooden shops and cafés, and gardens foaming with flowers and trees that don't grow anywhere else in the country.

To drive from Stykkishólmur to Akureyri feels like passing through geological time. We take a gravel road around the coast, bumping and leaping through an exaggerated Alpine landscape with a few Norwegian fjords cut-and-pasted around the foothills. There is no other traffic, no people, but grass and blueberry bushes and low birches massing on the hillsides. Streams glitter across the valley in the sun. The fjord is full of swans, and sometimes sheep wander into the road. Birds call. We go on, and up, and up, and down, Guy driving and the rest of us watching the land as if it's some kind of new technology we've never seen before. At last, an hour and a half from the last settlement, there's a farmhouse between the road and the sea, with net curtains in the window and a swing set and trampoline on the grass. How do you think they get their post, I ask, thinking about internet book shopping. How do the kids get to school, asks Anthony. What if you run out of milk? Max looks up from his book and says 'cows'. The Alps end, and with them the summer. Now we're in the Scottish Lowlands, among rolling grey hills. There are herds of cows and low, white farmsteads, and it's early spring, bright and cold, and then the gravel ends and we see ahead the junction that the Sat Nav has been promising for the last twenty-five miles. We find ourselves leaving the coast and climbing into North Yorkshire, where it seems to be November. Fog swirls around the car, and visibility drops until Guy is following the reflective marker-posts along the side of the road. They're twice the height of the ones in North Yorkshire, tall enough to reach up through winter's snow. When the fog clears we have left Earth altogether. The road is winding down a long, broad valley, and on both sides there are battlements, walls, of black rock, too near the vertical to be mountains but higher than the most ambitious skyscraper. These sky-closing fells doodle gargoyles and curlicues of what must be lava along the skyline, such fantasies of wrought iron that they can't possibly stay up. Guy pulls off the road and goes to lie in the middle of Route 1, taking photos.

And so we go down the hills to Akureyri. The town has spread in sixteen years, eating up a couple of outlying villages, and there's the familiar growth of half-built apartment blocks and housing estates spilling up the valley. The apartment I've booked turns out to be in one of these unfinished suburbs. It reminds me of the Big Flat in Garðabær, the same show-home ambitions surrounded by the same unfinished shells. Nonetheless, after ten days of living in quaint, provisional spaces designed for fewer people to spend less time than we are doing, soullessness is fine. While the children dash out to play on the grass, all three grown-ups wander around opening cupboard doors and marvelling at the washing machine, which says 'hello' when you open its door, and the dishwasher, which has a light inside and shines a red beam onto the floor when you switch it on because it's so quiet that otherwise you wouldn't know it was running. There is underfloor heating, granite counters, new IKEA furniture and bedding, candle-holders that still have their price-labels. I remember Matthew saying that he felt implicated in the *kreppa* because he rejoiced in the fruits of commerce when they came to Iceland, and stop playing with the white goods. Pétur doesn't have a dishwasher. His summer house doesn't even have a washing machine.

I look out at the children, who are rolling down the grass bank that screens the ground-floor flats from the road. Between and behind the new buildings, the windows are filled by mountains patched with snow not far above the town's roofs, mountains whose peaks are high enough to shape the clouds. Below the town, there's a fjord that glimmers black under the grey hills as night draws on. By the time the children are asleep – after ten, because timings are slipping and because even to our British parenting it seems wrong to send them to bed when there's sun slanting across the grass and Icelandic children running and laughing around the gardens – darkness is falling. It's August. Night is back. The brightest days are already over, and there's a breath of autumn on the night air.

Akureyri is as pleasing as I remember. The town was built by the Danes at the beginning of the twentieth century, and within the New-Jersey-style periphery there's an old, European town centre. Red and blue clapboard houses crowd the harbour, and there's a pedestrianised main street lined with shops and cafés. Cruise ships call; Max identifies one that visited Falmouth just before we left. I remember that when I discussed a possible trip with some of my students last year, they were ambivalent about Akureyri's colonial architecture, seeing the newer, mall-centred urban sprawl as the face of modern Iceland and refusing to be nostalgic for an era of cold, hunger and social inequality. Middle age looms; I like the painted shop-fronts.

We go to the pool I remember from Kathy's birthday. It's been developed into a complex of pools, built to recognise that babies need to bobble in peace while toddlers splash, that children old enough to want to dive are not old enough to see the point of lane-swimming. A group of people in their eighties sit under an artificial waterfall with hot water playing on their necks and shoulders. It's the seven ages of man in aquatic form. Taking myself off for some proper swimming in the lanes, I notice that there's a similarly lavish playground, offering a trampoline and electric cars for the children to drive, beside the unfenced water. I remember reading last year that the number of child drownings in public swimming pools was falling.

The days are blue and bright, the air so clean that distances are hard to judge. Looking across a valley is like looking down through clear water and not knowing if the rocks are pebbles within reach or boulders ten metres down. Sun and shadow play across the hillsides, and there are mountain tracks leading up to the sky. I know we are not equipped. I know four-year-olds don't climb real mountains. I know that Guy has city shoes and a suede jacket, that this is a family trip with picnics and swimming and time to play with toy cars before supper. I haven't done any real climbing for years, not since I moved to the south of England and started having babies, but those paths call me. Vaðlaheiði, Fjósatungufjall, Stórihnjúkur. Sunrise and sunset happen behind the mountains and we see them reflected in the sky. There are valleys in Iceland where winter is extended by weeks because the horizon is so far up the sky, villages in the shade for all but a few weeks of summer, and mountains named for the day the sun falls behind them.

I pore over the map, looking for family walks that might sate some of my longing for altitude. On the other side of the fjord, there's a track that runs along the hillside, past deserted farms to the beacon on the northern tip of the peninsula. We set off, driving over the causeway in Akureyri that almost bisects the airport's runway and has, Guy notes, a petrol station positioned exactly where an over-shooting plane would crash into Route 1. Then we follow the road along the peninsula until it ends at the fish-processing plant in the village of Grenivík (population 300). Large wooden houses are scattered along the seafront in Grenivík, and the grid of roads takes us past the school, nursery school, swimming pool, church and museum. There is one shop, which is also the petrol station and the café. I go in to buy chocolate to use as an inducement to co-operation on the walk. Sixteen years ago, these village shops had a range of American snacks, Icelandic dairy produce and sliced bread. The only fruit Kathy and I ate was blueberries we picked from the hills. In Grenivík there is olive oil, salami, artisanal cheese and a whole cabinet of fruit and vegetables, including aubergines, kiwis and grapes. Now, I think, approaching the till, here and now in Grenivík I'm going to speak Icelandic, actually say the words, but before I open my mouth the cashier greets me in English. How did you know I was foreign, I ask her, a question I asked myself all of last year and never dared to voice. She smiles, looks from my hiking boots to my dark hair. Well, I don't know you so you're not from round here, she explains, so I speak English.

We park in front of the fish-processing plant, and try to allay Guy's Londoners' anxiety about parking regulations and traffic wardens, the nearest one of whom may be an hour's drive away in Akureyri and is almost certainly not working a Saturday afternoon in August, because Icelanders really don't care that much about parking. We set off along the track. The fjord, full of the deep blue from the top of the sky, sparkles below us, and the hill rises steeply to the east. Cotton grass, buttercups and miniature gentians bow with the grasses and reeds along the path. There are patches of shade, dark as water spilt on cloth, on the mountainside across the fjord, but we are flooded with sunshine. The smell of wild thyme and summer rises like incense from the warm turf. There is a house between the path and the water, a concrete cube mostly covered with peeling pink paint. It has 1960s steel-framed double glazing and a warped wooden front door with an inset glass sunburst. An approximate garden spreads to the north. It looks deserted, and I begin to fantasise about buying it, coming here alone to wander the hills and write, and *en famille* in summer for the children to run wild and mess about in boats, but as we approach we see curtains in the windows and a table in the garden. Someone else's life, and Anthony is muttering about what it would be like in winter. (Fabulous, I think. An unparalleled view of the Northern Lights, and no expectation that anyone should do anything other than stay inside reading and eating and watching the sky.)

After the pink house, the track narrows, and soon the only habitation we can see is across the fjord. Broad streams cross the path; Tobias wants to do the stepping-stones on his own.

We go northwards across the bright day, Max far ahead, making his own relationship with the place, Tobias lagging to pick buttercups and drop stones into pools. The path leads on, out of sight around the headland, and I want to follow it so much that it feels as if my feet can't break the rhythm of walking and stones, but the sun is high, south of the zenith because the solstice was weeks ago and here on the Arctic Circle we can already feel the planet's tilt. Soon people will want lunch and lunch is in the car. We stop. Anthony and the children pick blueberries, Guy stalks us with his camera, and I sit on a high rock, circled by ravens. I can see to the end of Akureyri's long fjord from here, out to the Arctic sea, and back to where the town is a sprinkle of glitter at the foot of mountains dusty in the sunlight. The hills over Eyjafjörður, above the fishing town of Dalvík where one of last year's students remembered her father taking the milk to market on a horse-drawn sledge, are mottled like batik fabric with snow. The water ruffles no more than crêpe paper, currents marked on its surface like lines drawn with a finger on misted glass. I can hear the questioning note of a plover moving across the hillside above me, whinnies from the herd of Icelandic ponies browsing the grass on the headland below, the putter of a fishing boat moving down the fjord towards the sea.

I have made everyone excited about going to Mývatn. I remember a landscape so strange that Kathy and I spent days trying to find a vocabulary to talk about it, where impossible lava formations congregated around boiling mud and unnaturally coloured steaming pools. As we drive, I worry that maybe it's not as startling as I remember, maybe I've exaggerated the effect on a teenager seeing her first volcanic landscape. We pass through a bit of the Peak District and down through the Alpine foothills. The horizon opens around us as we enter the plain, and there's what looks like a stationary tornado on the horizon. Steam. Then there are more plumes of steam, blossoming out of the rock in the distance, and mountains like giant slag-heaps of cinnamon and turmeric, and in the foreground a lake bluer than the sky, which appears to have piles of fresh grass-cuttings floating around on it. Islands, some just big enough for geese to nest. We're starting with the Dimmuborgir, lava formations that I remember as vaguely reminiscent of Mount Rushmore, towering rock presences rising out of the ground. The smell of sulphur seeps into the car. There are signs to the Dimmuborgir, which I'm sure weren't there sixteen years ago, and then a car park and a visitors' centre, which also wasn't there. There are marked, roped trails through the lava, where Kathy and I wandered around sketching and pointing things out to each other, getting pleasurably disoriented as we couldn't tell one clump of birch scrub, one stone giant, from another. But the children have no tolerance for wandering and getting lost, and the loos at the visitors' centre are a good thing, and the groups of Spanish and German tourists, I remind myself, have as much right to be here as we do.

The Dimmuborgir are still strange. The furrows and caves of lava fields are familiar now, seem to me like the Icelandic version of the crazy-paving of fields and hedges that lighten the shoulders of expatriate Brits in holding patterns over Heathrow, the hallmark of home ground. But the Dimmuborgir are vertical, like melting sculptures and buildings, growing tall as houses out of ashy ground and birch scrub. They are black as tarmac, gravity-defying as Gothic

347

stonework, shaped in a way that reminds me of edifices, of dinosaur skeletons, but remains abstract. One, Anthony points out, has a Norman arch. Another is a bit like a giant cactus. Trails wind around them, through low birch bushes filtering the sun. We have been collecting silences on this trip, and stand still to listen. Bees, midges. Birds. Other birds. Birch leaves, sensitive to the breeze. Laughter from the Spanish group who passed us earlier. Can we add it to the collection of silences? No. There is an underlying rumble, the same noise you hear on Saddleworth Moor from the M62 and high in Heiðmörk from Route 41 and on Bodmin Moor from the A30 It's not, I know, reasonable to drive to a place and then resent the sound of traffic.

On, and up to Krafla. There's more steam, some of it coming from the chimneys of a geothermal power station that bestrides the road like a medieval city gateway. Higher and higher, up a valley of desert sand and red mud, part-filled with a frozen river of black lava, and then it looks as if a giant has poured golf-course-green grass down the hillside, and there are sheep grazing, and then another lava spillage. Steam churns from every pore in the ground. The car park at the top is almost full, and there's a queue at the coffee booth and another at the loos, and when we get out we hear the roar again, louder and lower because we're closer to it than we were in the Dimmuborgir. It's not traffic but the ground, the rumble of the planet's rumination.

We set off, across a meadow of crowberries, over turf a brighter green than elsewhere and studded with harebells and gentians, towards the steam and sand. From up here, more mountains come up, and more, rising out of a fjord that is filled with black lava, not blue sea. My brain reads the landscape as water and mountains, with islands in the fjord, very much like what we saw in Eyjafjörður, but it's not water. We cross the lava flow, like walking across a runway or a motorway between the meadow and the boiling mud, and then take the path around the volcano's cone, towards a smaller crater. The wind is sharp up here and Tobias and I have cold hands. We hold them in the steam, happy to find that, unlike at Hveragerði in winter, it's hot enough to help, and then Tobias discovers that the rock is warm to the touch. He lies down on it, pleased. The stone feels like unglazed stoneware, and has the warmth and roughness of hefty pots waiting to be glazed. I put my hand into a crack in the rock, a few inches wide, and steam condenses on it immediately. It's toaster rock, says Tobias, and starts trying to put other things down it. A piece of paper comes out wet. He drops a piece of lava down the crack and becomes convinced that he's made it steam more, and then we all start playing with the toaster rocks, warming our hands, wondering what we could cook, poking it with stones. Tobias suggests that if he takes some back to Cornwall and drops it down a hole, steam will start to come out there too, and begins to imagine his friends' pleasure at this discovery in the school playground. The crater above us looks like pictures of the mouth of hell, a gaping hole with human figures obscured by billowing steam. We follow the path to the top, where there is a for-mation of rocks in something like sandstone, vaguely reminiscent of a Barbara Hepworth and bearing no apparent relation to the lava or the sand. It's like standing on the moun-tain's prow, overhanging the inland sea of black lava, the fertile plains around the lake and the sulphurous steam still rising from the crater, which erupted about the same time as the birth of Christ.

On the last day, we go as far north as possible, to the edge of the island. Akureyri is at the foot of the Tröllaskagi peninsula, and a new tarmac road runs all the way around the edge, to the towns of Dalvík, Ólafsfjörður and Siglufjörður. Ólafs-fjörður and Siglufjörður, separated by two headlands with multiple peaks almost a kilometre high, are linked by two tunnels that were finished last year. Before that, I guess, poring over the map, the quickest way in and out was probably by boat. Weather permitting. There was no road at all into Siglufjörður until 1967, only a mountain pass open for a few weeks most summers. Guy, who's enjoying the madness of Icelandic roads, is eager to go through the tunnels. I, mindful that so far all the fears about Icelandic health and safety that I tried to dismiss as paranoia have been justified by research, would rather trust Guy's driving over the mountain pass than Icelandic engineering through a seven kilometre tunnel. I am outvoted.

The road climbs out of Dalvík, and up and up, clinging to the side of the cliff. There's no safety barrier. There's Grímsey, I say, pointing out to sea where the grey lump on the horizon must be Iceland's northernmost island, forty kilometres off-shore, inside the Arctic Circle and home to ninety people. Don't look, I add to Guy. I'm not, he says. You look, here's the tunnel.

There's an orange flashing light at the entrance. Guy stops. We see no road signs or instructions. Guy inches forward. The tunnel is single track and barely lit at all. What if something

comes the other way? It will come slowly, I suppose, says Guy,
going up to second gear. Anthony wants to back up. Guy
refuses to reverse out of a tunnel onto the edge of a cliff. We
go on. There are headlights coming towards us, not slowly, and
a bay hacked out of the rock on our right. Guy pulls into it,
and a cement truck roars past with a few inches to spare. I
swear. Max bounces with delight in the back. I get it, says
Guy. The orange light meant that oncoming traffic has priority, so when we see headlights we run for the next passing
place and get out of the way. He pulls in again and we wait
while a large jeep comes the other way. Another jeep comes
up behind. Guy edges forward. Another car comes behind
and our passing place is full, but there's a fourth vehicle trying
to get in. The oncoming jeep passes and Guy, watching in the
mirror, gasps as it grazes the car that couldn't fit into the passing place. I close my eyes until the pale sunlight of
Ólafsfjörður shines on my face.

The buildings of Ólafsfjörður have trickled in between the
mountains. There's a spacious graveyard in the middle of the
village, between the harbour and the houses, and behind it the
school, campsite and swimming pool. The houses are large and
detached, most with mid-century dates set in concrete over
the front doors. It's the first time I've seen dates from the
mid-1940s so emblazoned, but the war years brought sudden
prosperity to Iceland's fishing villages and it's not surprising
that there was a building boom. We drive on a gravel road up
the valley, where farms hang on the hillsides, and park beside
a white, red-roofed church, sheltered by a crowd of rowan
trees. A track winds up from the church, past a farm and over
the lip of a higher valley slung between two mountains. We set

off. The farm's wheelie-bins are strapped with broad webbing to wooden stakes set in concrete. It's calm today, but remembering the winter storms in Reykjavík I think that there must be many days on which collecting the bins at all out here is an act of heroism. The farmhouse is the usual white concrete bungalow, but attached to it, reaching the full height of the roof and doubling the house's footprint, is a glass room in which trees brush the walls and roof. An indoor garden? The hothouse smell of growing plants and coddled flowers would be like the breath of God on this hillside in the middle of winter. Above the farmhouse, there's a cluster of summer houses, each with a hot tub on its wooden verandah. A woman sits in the sun knitting outside one of them, chatting to a man who is simmering in the tub, leaning his head back with the sun on his face and the blue sky over him. What about one of those, I ask Anthony, and to my surprise he says yes. But only once the children have grown up, he adds, and only in summer. We're up above the roofs of the farm now, and into the higher valley. The map confirms that there are no dwellings up here, but the track is broad and well-graded. There would once have been higher farms, and feet that walked this path week after week. A river rushes through a gorge. Birds call. We stop and listen to the valley, and then turn back to the car for lunch.

I sit in the back for the long tunnel to Siglufjörður. People who live here must have no nerves at all, and when the tunnel ends I understand why. Siglufjörður has been piped into the valley bottom. The buildings balance on a few hundred metres of steeply sloping ground, with the fjord in front of them and sheer cliffs blocking half the sky behind. The mountain's slopes are fenced and propped above the town, presumably to hold back landslides when the snow melts in spring. There are docks built out into the dark water, and corrugated iron houses on a grid pattern up the lower slope. We park in front of the Herring Era Museum and walk into the town. The big thermometer on the harbour says it's nine degrees, but there's a wind coming straight from the Arctic ice sheets and it feels much colder. Siglufjörður doesn't feel entirely Icelandic to me. There's something provisional about the relationship between the wooden and corrugated iron buildings and the cliffs, as if the geological time of the mountains and sea hasn't meshed with the town's history. Some of the houses are newly painted in shades of duck-egg and lavender-grey, with olive trees on the window-sills framed by Marimekko curtains. Summer houses. Others have sagging grey net curtains and warped wooden doors. Several are empty, with hand-written notices in the windows saying *Til sölu* and giving a phone number. There is a shoal of fishing boats in the harbour, bigger and higher specification than the ones we see in Cornwall, but only a few tourists wandering the streets. We come to the main street which reminds me of Gold Rush towns in Colorado. Most of the buildings have steps up to wooden verandahs in front of plate-glass windows. A few of the shops are still in business – a baker; a fishmonger, with signs in English and German because it's unlikely that the locals need to *buy* fish; a menswear shop with grubby plastic mannequins in the window, and at the top of the street a small supermarket. In between, there are shops converted into houses or standing empty. At the harbour end of the street, washing secured to a line across the street between upstairs windows snaps in the wind like the sails of a disordered ship. The top of the street ends in a flight of broad steps leading to a white wooden church that seems too big for the town. There's a music school – every Icelandic town has a music school – and a Folk Music Centre and a primary school on two storeys that looks big enough to house all the inhabitants of Siglufjörður and Ólafsfjörður and probably Dalvík as well. There's a swimming pool, and a campsite positioned where the village green would be in England, tenanted only by a Belgian couple shivering over a Primus stove. We're all cold, and head for a café in a converted fish shed, the size of several barns, on the harbour-front. Icelanders are sitting outside, drinking beer and soup. Inside we find a huge, dim wooden space like an inflated chalet. When we ask for coffee the waitress starts grinding beans, and the bathrooms have beaten copper basins and soap scented with green tea and orange blossom, as if we were in an expensive part of London or New York. The tunnels aren't big enough for lorries; the marble counters and swan's-neck taps must have come by boat.

The Herring Era Museum (Iceland's largest maritime museum, winner of a Luigi Micheletti award for the most innovative museums in Europe) explains Siglufjörður's Wild West air. At the beginning of the twentieth century, Norwegian fishing fleets, which were bigger and better equipped than those of colonial Iceland, began to appear in Iceland's northern coastal waters. They were following the herring, and needed local labour to clean and salt the catch on shore before it could be sold internationally, mostly to the poor of northern Europe for whom the cheap protein was a godsend. The herring sheds were built for salting and pressing the fish, and people needing work began to move to

Siglufjörður, which has a deep and sheltered natural harbour with immediate access to the open sea. (I begin to recognise parts of this story; fishing towns in the westernmost parts of Cornwall also grew during a late nineteenth-century herring boom, and we sometimes have coffee and cake in converted fish-processing sheds in St Ives and Penzance too.) Icelandic speculators started to buy the new boats and equipment for themselves, and during the First World War, when international fishing was disrupted and Europe's need for imported foods urgent, Icelandic herring production in Iceland overtook that of the Norwegians. Some people say that the herring boom was the economic foundation of Icelandic independence. It lasted almost a century, with the highest ever catches in the mid-1960s generating half of Iceland's annual export income. The population of Siglufjörður rose to about 10,000. Herring are migratory, appearing in the North Atlantic in summer, and in 1969, after years of over-fishing, they didn't come. That was it, the end of the Herring Era. The people and the money left Siglufjörður. Fishing continues, on a much reduced scale, and the harbour is deep enough for cruise ships. The decision to build the tunnel last year was a decision to do whatever was necessary to sustain these remote villages, and it is typically Icelandic that a remote community of barely 1,000 people has an internationally renowned museum and a café where they grind coffee beans. I hope it's enough.

I want to go on round the headland, partly so we can come back over the mountain pass and avoid the tunnels, but it's getting late and the children are tired. Just to the tip of the peninsula, says Guy, leaning over to see the map. Look, where that lighthouse is. We pile back in the car and drive along another unfenced ledge until the cliffs bend back to the south. A gravel track leads down to a farmhouse, improbably positioned on a patch of grass below the cliff-top, and to an orange lighthouse. The car bleeps about loss of traction as Guy pilots it down the slope and positions it behind a concrete signalling shed so it can't slide into the sea. The children, feeling the wind when Guy opens his door, sensibly refuse to leave their seats, so the three of us scurry along the track, laughing in the wind, and stand under the lighthouse at the edge of the north coast, looking back towards Akureyri, Reykyavík and home. I'm still not ready to leave Iceland.

Acknowledgements

Almost everyone we encountered in Iceland has contributed to this book in some way, and I give thanks for Icelanders' enthusiasm and support for writers and writing.

I am especially grateful to those who gave me their time and their stories:

Brynja Brynjarsdóttir

Guy Griffin

Hulda Kristín Jónsdóttir

Katharine MacDonald and Alec Badenoch

Mads Holm and Mæja Garðarsdóttir

Matthew Whelpton

Mark Andrew Zimmer and Sigrún María Kristinsdóttir

Pétur Knútsson and Messíana Tómasdóttir

Þórunn Kristín Emilsdóttir

Ragnheiður Eiríksdóttir

Theódór Áldar Tómasson

Theódór Ólafsson and Margrét Eirikka Sigurbjörnsdóttir

Tómas Gabríel Benjamin

Vilborg Dagbjartsdóttir

The students in the School of English at Háskóli Íslands taught me at least as much as I taught them, and my colleagues in the academic staff and in the administration there supported me throughout the year. I am especially grateful to Pétur Knútsson, Messíana Tómasdóttir and their family; to Matthew Whelpton; and to Mads Holm and Mæja Garðarsdóttir, who gave their friendship as well as their various expertise. I thank everyone who read drafts of this book and took time to correct my errors; Pétur Knútsson in particular read several drafts and met my mistakes with characteristically deep reserves of patience and good humour. I have tried to make sure that all factual statements are correct, but part of being a foreigner is to be wrong. Remaining mistakes are entirely my responsibility.

In England, I thank the University of Kent for allowing me to go to Iceland, and the University of Exeter for receiving me when I came back. I am, as always, grateful to Anna Webber at United Agents. I thank everyone at Granta for being delightful to work with, and especially my editor Sara Holloway, who sees what I mean and makes it better.

U.S. $17.95   TRAVEL/MEMOI

SARAH MOSS HAD A CHILDHOOD DREAM OF MOVING TO ICELAND

sustained by a wild summer there when she was nineteen. In 2009, she saw an advertise ment for a job at the University of Iceland and applied on a whim, despite having tw young children and a comfortable life in Kent. The resulting adventure was shaped b Iceland's economic collapse, which halved the value of her salary, by the eruption Eyjafjallajokull, and by a collection of new friends, including a poet who saw the on bombs fall on Iceland in 1943, a woman who speaks to elves, and a chef who guide Sarah's family around the intricacies of Icelandic cuisine.

Moss explored hillsides of boiling mud and volcanic craters and learned to drive lik an Icelander on the unsurfaced roads that link remote farms and fishing villages in the fa north. She watched the northern lights and the comings and goings of migratory bird and as the weeks and months went by, she and her family learned new ways to live.

Names for the Sea is her compelling, beautiful and very funny account of living in country poised on the edge of Europe, where modernization clashes with living folklor

ADVANCE PRAISE FOR
NAMES FOR THE SEA

"It's then that you realize this isn't the usual hack piece about the foreigner's pratfalls with no speaking da lingo etc. This is a work of humor, for sure, and I loved her puncturing of Icelander tales of derring-do, the obsession with pride and shame. More than that, it's a work of strange intelligence that jars like poetry . . . it has beauty enough to feel fictional." —*The Times* UK

"Honest, funny, frank, and insightful . . . an enviable experience beautifully described."
—**Gavin Francis, author of *True North: Travels in Arctic Europe***

"This tale perfectly evokes the country's natural splendours, but it's the colourful cast of friends and hangers-on that's so touching." —*National Geographic Traveller*

"A beautifully written and acutely observed examination of being an útlendingur—a foreigne A stranger in a strange land, Moss grapples with new foods, customs and landscapes that are both oddly familiar and wildly alien in this absorbing memoir." —*Financial Times*

SARAH MOSS was educated at Oxford University and is Associate Professor of Creative Writing at Warwick University. She is the author of two critically acclaimed novels: *Cold Earth* and *Night Waking*, which was selected for the Fiction Uncovered Award in 2011, and the co-author of *Chocolate: A Global History*. She spent 2009–10 as a visiting lecturer at the University of Iceland and now lives in west Cornwall.

C OUNTERPOINT
www.counterpointpress.com
Distributed by Publishers Group West

COVER PHOTO BY INGÓLFUR BJARGMUNDSSON
COVER DESIGN BY EMMA COFOD